Trust
the
Children

DETROIT PUBLIC LIBRARY

TRUST *the* CHILDREN

A Manual and Activity Guide for

HOMESCHOOLING AND ALTERNATIVE LEARNING

Anna Kealoha

Celestial Arts
Berkeley, California

Celestial Arts
P.O. Box 7327
Berkeley, CA 94707

Cover design by

Book design by Victor Ichioka

Library of Congress Cataloging-in-Publication Data:

Kealoha, Anna
    Trust the children : a manual and activity guide for homeschooling and alternative learning / Anna Kealoha.
        p.   cm.
    Includes bibliographical references and index.
    ISBN 0-89087-748-3
    1. Home schooling—Curricula—Handbooks, manuals, etc. 2. Non-formal education—Curricula—Handbooks, manuals, etc. I. Title.
    LC40.K43   1995   95-15810
    649'.68—dc20   CIP

PRINTED IN CANADA

1 2 3 4 5 99 98 97 96 95

Dedicated
to the
children

Many thanks to the following authors for giving me permission to include their ideas in this book:

John Holt Associates *(Learning all the Time)*

John Taylor Gatto *(Dumbing Us Down)*

Joshua Halpern *(Children of the Dawn)*

Rudy Rucker *(Mind Tools)*

Malcolm Knowles *(Self-Directed Learning)*

Seymour Papert *(Mindstorms: Children, Computers and Powerful Ideas, HarperCollins Publishers, Inc.)*

Stewart Brand *(The Media Lab)*

Ron Gross *(Peak Learning)*

Jay Anderson *(Living History Sourcebook)*

Mona Brooks *(Drawing with Children)*

Peggy Kaye *(Games for Reading, Games for Math, Games for Learning)*

Jean Kerr, Virginia Stenmark, & Ruth Cossey *(Family Math)*

Dover Clip Art *(2001 Decorative Cuts and Ornaments, Vintage Spot Illustrations of Children, Old-Fashioned Illustrations of Books, Reading & Writing, Children and their World)*

California State Department of Education *(History-Social Science Framework for California Public Schools, Handbook for Physical Education, Mathematics Framework)*

Someone told me that 90% of new books that are written are merely regurgitated material from other people's work. At least 10% of the ideas presented in this book are original—if they aren't then what am I doing lying awake at three in the morning? Nevertheless I am indebted to the wealth of materials that I have learned from in preparing this book.

I wrote to many folks for permission to use their material, and for the few I couldn't find or who didn't respond, I apologize. Please write to me and I will correct this situation in future editions. Enjoy.

Anna Kealoha

God waits for man to regain his childhood in wisdom

—Rabindranath Tagore

Acknowledgements

To my children Amarina, Genessa, Joshuwyn, and Oshanna: Thank you for being my most important, exhausting, time-consuming, most rewarding, and definitely most fun job. You are my "give-back" to the universe. I am blessed to be your Mama...even if you eat the last cookie and don't make your beds! To Richard: Thanks for your wisdom and gentle spirit. Thanks for your Daddy-ness.

To Mom & Dad: I am grateful to you for being such darlings. (They dance to the Lawrence Welk Show in their living room—isn't that sweet?) To all my relations—lovers, in-laws, and out-laws too.

To my mentor teachers and dear friends Juanita Ingle and James Mario Inciardi: Thank you for putting the child first and the curriculum second or third. It works!

To all the alternative and homeschooling families of Sonoma County that I have the pleasure of knowing (especially Nonesuch, Harmony, and Sonoma County Homeschoolers Association families): Thanks for trusting your children and helping me with mine, especially Nan, Jubi, Shayna, Sarah, Merryl, Steven, Nancy, Pat, Melissa, Ishi, and Jim...and to Rita for being Rita.

To Pamela Singer: thanks for sharing poetry. To Michael Yezbick & Ka'ala for reminding us to get wet in the waves. To everyone on the Harmony Homeschooling staff (Miriam Shrogin, Joe Wagner, Sybil Rotnicki, & Carol Rogers): for sharing your wisdom with me; I am truly grateful.

To Nan Koehler and Donald Solomon: Thank you for your artwork and child/birth/herbal skills, Nan, and your generous spirit, Donald.

To Robin Williams: Thank you for being a Mac Wizardess and author of funny, sagacious computer books. To all the nice librarians at the Sebastopol Library and Martha Bell at Harmony for their cheerful and expedient helpfulness. To David Hinds: Thank you for turning my book-writing projects into realities. To Laeh Maggie Garfield for helping me get my feet in the doors. To Victor for designing and Veronica for editing this work, and to Barbara Sikora for indexing extraordinaire.

To the reader: Thanks for trusting the children and believing in the sanity of home-schooling and alternative learning.

Most of all to the children and to the wondrous world of the child that always lives within.

To the Great Spirit
for bountiful blessings of family, friends, food, & health.

 Contents

Let me
bring love,
care, and honor
to all earthly creatures and plants.
Let me
sing and speak with a pure spirit,
and think with a wise, clear mind.
Let me
be generous with what I have,
healthy in body and mind,
and work with joy.
Let me
fly with sun-kissed butterfly wings,
surge with the rushing tides,
and soak in the soaring pure mountain air.

Anna Kealoha

Introduction

When my bones lie deep in the earth,
my legacy will not be my wealth nor my job,
only that I was someone special to a child.

Dear Readers,

On a drizzly almost-spring evening in 1978, I gave birth to my first child in the comfort of my own home. Gazing at this tiny bit of flesh cradled in my arms, I was filled with ecstasy and awe; she was the closest experience to perfection I have ever witnessed!

Day one: How, in such a short time, has this newborn girl taught me so much about life's mysteries?? Ironically, she will now need me to teach her about earthly life. How will I teach her everything she needs to know, let alone how to brush her teeth?! My sister Jane was right when she said, "You're never ready!"

Day two: I panic. What about "real" education?? Right now I just need to love, feed, change her, and keep her warm, but at some point I will have to think about letters, numbers, music, art, and . . . and . . . Life as I Know It! How can I teach her when there's so much more I need to learn? All the basic options: public school, private school, or home-schooling seemed flawed. Public schools seemed too much like factories or jails and private schools too elitist. (*Well, most paycheck-to-paycheck families can afford reverse snobbishness on this point.*) I liked the idea of homeschooling. It seemed like a natural extension of home birth and the best way to go. Yet, even though I like staying home, I knew at some point my daughter would need to leave the nest and fly out on her own.

Five years later: We got lucky when the "school" years came (all too quickly) and we couldn't ignore them anymore. In the local public school, we found an alternative teacher who let us send our two older kids to school part-time. We had the best of both worlds: home and school. With a handshake, we sealed our agreement with both the teacher and school superintendent. There was not a speck of paperwork to do. Our kids floated in and out of the classroom whenever they wanted, and flourished! They learned to read and write, do numbers, play with friends, sing and dance. This happy arrangement lasted about five or six years. We then tried full-time homeschooling. This arrangement suited me just fine, but my kids were bored staying home all the time: they wanted to be with their friends, and they wanted to explore life outside the home.

The best way to keep children home is to make the home atmosphere pleasant—and let the air out of the tires.

—Dorothy Parker

Seventeen years later: Now there are four little birds in the nest and they're all flying! (Even the youngest who is only four.) They all want to go places and do things. Sure, they all still need me in different ways, but they also have lives of their own without me. Amarina (17) goes to high school part time and does independent study for Chemistry and Algebra II. She passed her high school equivalency test and might begin attending the local junior college. (Most youths I know say they dislike high school, but go to hang out with their friends.) Ami didn't attend school full-time until she entered fourth grade, and did so then by choice.

Genessa, our twelve-year-old, did home-and-school for three years and homeschooled full time for two years. She is now attending Nonesuch, a small private school modeled somewhat after Summerhill.

Our seven-year-old Joshuwyn attends the Alternative-Homeschool Alliance (AHA!) home-and-school program with a group of seventeen children (ages 5-11) two days a week. Our "curriculum" focuses on experiential learning and group activities such as music, sports, science, and drama. We also do art activities, play games, read, and create books together in various subjects such as Spanish, geometry, geography, and prose. Four-year-old Oshanna is eager to attend soon.

In the past, they all had a chance to attend Rainbow School, a private home-and-school co-op of six to eight families that met two to three days a week.

While I prefer the home-and-school blend, my kids know they have our support in whatever they choose to do. I trust them. After all, the goal of teaching and parenting is to develop independent thinkers and doers, because our success as parents comes when our children can confidently take care of themselves and direct their own life-long course of learning.

Homeschooling

To trust children we must first learn to trust ourselves ... and most of us were taught as children that we could not be trusted.

—John Holt

There are as many reasons why families choose homeschooling as there are families. Some choose to do so for religious reasons, others because they have become disillusioned with the public schools, and some because they live too far away from a school. Some families homeschool for a few years, while others have children that have never set foot inside a classroom. Some families feel that they can do a better job of teaching their children one-on-one. (Most children try hard to learn in a classroom with twenty-five or thirty kids.)

Homeschooling goes against the trend of family disintegration. It keeps the family intact. Most modern families have little opportunity to be together as families because from September to June, going to school dominates the family's life.

Homeschooling styles vary widely and there is no one right way to homeschool. Some families follow the Summerhill approach, pioneered by A. S. Neill. They allow their children total self-direction of the learning experience. Other homeschools mimic regular schools; complete with student style desks, lesson plans, and tests.

Some families choose a home-and-school option, in which the child attends school part-time, from one to four days a week and then homeschools the rest of the time. This is my favorite option, because it gives the child the best of both worlds. However, home-and-school is the most difficult option to initiate because it takes cooperation between the school administrators, teachers, families, and children. The crucial element is a sympathetic teacher who understands and believes in homeschooling. I am thrilled to be able to offer this option to the families with whom I work.

Homeschooling helps keep the joy of learning alive. It also requires enormous patience and flexibility. It is not an option to undertake lightly, nor one to take too seriously. Homeschooling is not a panacea. Children's learning styles and development vary just as widely in homeschooling as they do in traditional schools, yet most homeschooled kids tend to be a grade level or two ahead of their peers.

There are close to a million, (John Taylor Gatto says a million-and-a-half) kids being homeschooled nationwide: no one knows the exact number. In California, the trend began to gain momentum in the mid-80s. At that time, there were about 6,000 families choosing the Independent Study (homeschool) option within the public schools. Today, there are about 100,000 students choosing this option. Even this number does not include all the families that are homeschooling independently of the public schools. Not surprisingly, many homeschooling families are the same ones that pioneered the revival of home births in the 70s and 80s.

Learning is taking place at all times in all circumstances for every person.

—Robert Fulghum

There was an old woman who lived in a shoe
she had so many children she knew what to do.
She gave them some broth without any bread
and whipped them all soundly and put them to bed.

When I read this nursery rhyme to my kids, I always change the line that says "whipped them all soundly..." to "kissed them all soundly...". But, I got to thinking that if I had thirty kids (which most school teachers do for half of a year, I *would* be whipping them (well, at least yelling a lot) and sending them to bed. How many families do you know that have thirty kids in them? This is *not* a normal family ratio! Even if a family were to have five, ten or fifteen kids, (which would be "normal" in a society unplagued by overpopulation and birth control) there would still (hopefully) be two parents involved in raising the kids. Thus, a "natural" ratio is about six, seven or eight to one. What we ask of our thirty students and one teacher to do is unrealistic. Fixing the public schools is so simple, really. Hire four times as many teachers and aides. In the long run, this would save the government billions. There would be more jobs, fewer jails, less drug abuse, less crime, and fewer people needing welfare:

All who have meditated on the art of governing
human beings have been convinced
that the fate of empires depends on the education of youth.
—Aristotle

HOMESCHOOLING FULL-TIME

Here in Northern California, I know lots of folks who homeschool all on their own and do a fantastic job of it. Homeschooling full-time is an enormous commitment, and folks who do so should be respected and praised for their efforts.

I understand and sympathize with people who choose the path of independent homeschooling. However, when these fine people withdraw (or never enter) the public school system, they take their creative energy and talents with them, which is a pity. Every school is worth "saving", because every school is a place for kids! Investigate your local public schools to see if you can help improve them and make them resource centers for all our children.

Home-and-School: The Best of Both

A child educated only at school is an uneducated .child.

—George Santayana

My vision is to create year-round library-style learning centers for everyone using existing school facilities. Public libraries are often world class, as far as public institutions go. They give free loan privileges to everyone in exchange for modest responsibilities. Some offer cozy story times, space for local meetings, and art exhibits. During business hours people are free to come and go as they please. To my knowledge, no one has ever been mass-murdered in a library. I wish I could say the same for the public schools. I wish that schools were run like libraries: I wish schools were year-round resource centers for all our children. There is no reason why homeschoolers cannot create a revolution within the system. There is no reason why we must choose either homeschool or school: we should be able to have both!

There is hope. It's a new and fairly maverick idea. In California, it's called the ISP (Independent Study Program). Under the auspices of the ISP, families who choose to homeschool may also do so in cooperation with their local school districts. I favor quality, service-oriented ISP's for many reasons. To begin with, when you're starting out in homeschooling, it's helpful to employ a teacher as a resource person. Sometimes homeschoolers can even get assistance with educational materials, just as children in the regular classroom receive the same type of services.

California schools are currently broke. Ironically, local school districts are beginning to realize homeschooling is a way to raise revenue. The district can recieve full state funding while the homeschooler places minimal demands on the school infrastructure. Some homeschoolers may benefit enormously from this arrangement with the public schools, while others may find it not to be worth the hassle of bureaucratic regulation and documentation. In the long run, it really doesn't matter what type of educational option you choose for your child: it's the teacher's personality interacting with the child's personality that makes the situation either a good learning experience, or a bad one. For example, even though my oldest daughter and I love each other a lot, when she homeschooled full-time at age seven and eight, she resisted me as her teacher, (of course, it could just be that I wasn't a very good teacher then) so I just gave in and we did *un*schooling. *That* worked out great! (Even though I still wish she was homeschooling, she is now a straight "A" student in high school. Am I a proud parent, even though I don't care for the grading system? You'd better believe it!)

When my next child, Genessa, did full-time homeschooling, we had a blast together, and my now seven-year-old Josh comes to me and insists we do his "schoolwork." Of course, Oshanna, our four-year-old loves to write—on anything and everything!

I work in a public homeschooling program, open to kindergarten through eighth grade students, called Harmony Homestudy. Our five teachers strive to serve the needs of each family. Our homeschool students (for the past eight years from 50-90 students a year and growing), flow in and out of school as they please. They use the school campus as a resource center. Some gather as a group two days a week, some attend workshops of their choice, and some only come to school once or twice a year. During the year, they can choose from a variety of workshops we offer such as arts and crafts, science, math, dance, drama, career development, story writing, music, and creative writing. They can sign up for private tutoring on the homeschool computer. They can use the school library, and can participate in the school's on-campus chorus, drama, sports, or band classes. They can check out educational films from our district's film library. They have access to school texts, materials, and supplies. Finally, they can choose a teacher who will work with them as a resource person and guide.

When families choose the public homeschooling option, the community truly becomes the classroom. I have met with "my" families in parks, libraries, the family home, or at school. Friendships develop between families and teachers, and often continue past the school year.

Of course the state legislature would like to mandate the homeschooling movement into oblivion. (They don't want to pay for homeschoolers.) Yet, many teachers have learned to work creatively within the system and refuse to be stifled by the quagmire of bureaucratic regulations.

Unfortunately, our society now has many single parents and two-income households. Some of these families need to use schools as a baby-sitting service. However, these families can still homeschool by sharing responsibilities with other families. There is no law that says one has to homeschool alone in one's own home!

Homeschoolers are now in a unique and powerful position to create new educational opportunities within the very system that they left or never entered. Most homeschoolers will find their local districts are eager to cooperate with them. I would like to encourage people to initiate homeschooling programs within their local districts and to take advantage of the opportunities available to them through the public schools. It is better to spend public funds on our children than to spend this money on $5,000-screwdrivers for the Pentagon!

The homeschool and alternative education movement embody the qualities of tolerance, freedom, diversity, creativity, and independence. As diverse as we may be, we have already begun to make a significant impact on schools and have helped implement these qualities into the mainstream. After all, parent involvement is the key to educational success, and who is more involved than homeschooling families?

Educators and employers tend to ignore the immense amount of learning that almost everyone does outside of school and college. This is often a personal tragedy, and it prevents our society from benefitting from the "hidden credentials" which Americans could be contributing to business and social life. We are blighting lives and hobbling our progress by failing to find ways to discern, harness, and reward these "hidden credentials."
—Peter Smith

Beginnings:

"The world is our classroom."

❦ HISTORY OF ALTERNATIVE EDUCATION ❦

SOCRATES (469-399 BC) Greek scholar. Believed human nature leads us to act correctly: evil and wrong actions arise from ignorance. Action=Knowledge: virtue is teachable because correct action involves thought. Liked to ask questions rather than just give his students the answer. Socratic Method means inductive reasoning: from facts to general idea or theory.

ROUSSEAU (1712-1778) French. Said he differed from other people only in knowing that he was ignorant. Believed in the natural goodness of humans. Evil comes from corrupt political and social institutions. Wrote *Émile* (1762)—church considered the book dangerous and banned it. Developed new music writing method. Encouraged self-expression. Believed the only good state is completely democratic.

PESTALOZZI (1746-1827) Swiss. Believed children behave better when they are happy and encouraged. Worked with orphans and under-privileged kids in boarding schools. Lived and worked alongside the children. Loved gardening and nature. Believed pupils learn best by using their own senses and discovering things for themselves.

FROEBEL (1782-1852) German. Coined the word "kindergarten" (child garden). Believed in play as form of self-expression. Children learn by doing and "their play can be organized to teach as well as to amuse." Teachers and parents should cooperate with child's innate nature of mystical understanding.

DEWEY (1859-1952) American. Father of progressive education movement. Responsible for initial thrust of integrated curriculum and emphasis on social rather than "academic" skills.

Radical Empiricism: Human experience creates understanding of meaning.

Instrumentalist: Ideas are plans of action; they solve problems.

Experimentalism: Ideas tested by experiments. "No knowledge is ever so certain that it is not subject to new evidence which might result from experiments and experience."

Pragmatism: Judge an idea by how it works. Theory of truth: if an idea does what it intends, it is true, otherwise it is false.

STEINER (1861-1925) German. Founded Waldorf school in Germany. Recognizes that spiritual world creates, nurtures, surrounds, and penetrates visible world, and material world is only a small part of the universe.

Growth Periods: ages 0 to 7 learn through *imitation;* 7 to 14: focus on awakening *feelings;* 14 on: develop powers of *independence.*

Nurtures child's intuition, imagination, and spirit. Instead of texts, children create their own books. Classrooms use natural materials. Usually, parents are not allowed in the classroom, and teachers move up yearly with students. Curriculum balances arts and "basics" equally, and teaches basics later than average because of the belief that premature intellectual

Let the child be a human being, and let the teacher be his friend.

—"Papa" Pestalozzi

Education... is a process of living and not a preparation for future living.

—John Dewey

endeavors destroy children's fantasy life. Some Waldorf schools tend to be fairly rigid about these points, and critics observe that students appear to be isolated from political and social realities.

MONTESSORI (1870-1952) Italian. Psychiatrist and first woman doctor in Italy. Emphasizes child's need to learn by doing. Develops whole being: physical, mental, and emotional.

Offers children maximum of spontaneity. Teachers deal with each child individually in each subject, and children work at their own pace. Encourages self-motivation and discourages the competitive spirit. Some claim that Montessori education is intolerant of individuality, and the Montessori environment can be too austere and regimented.

Fundamental Principles:

1. **Prepared Environment**: Use only materials that logically relate to one another, such as miniature pots and pans, mops and brooms.
2. **Individual Liberty**: Children free to do what they want, but it is not random play because of prepared environment.
3. **Observation**: Teachers refrain from interfering directly with children.

NEILL (1883-1973) Scottish. In 1921, founded Summerhill, an international school in Germany (it later moved to England) which is described as "the most unusual school in the world" and "the world's greatest experiment in bestowing unstinted love and approval on children." The school was the world's first Free School. Neill stated: "I would rather see a school produce a happy street cleaner than a neurotic scholar." Believed children are inherently wise and capable, and develop best without adult interference. Neill's aim of life and education: work joyfully and find happiness. In addition, intellectual development *must* be accompanied by emotional development. Wrote his book *Summerhill* in 1960. Summerhill critics are mortified by the lack of structure and formal curriculum.

HOLT (1923-1985) American. "Trust Children" was his motto. Considered to be the patriarch of the homeschool movement. A grade-school teacher who believed that left alone, children can learn by themselves without adults continually supervising the process. Believes children really want to learn, and will eventually learn what they need to know. Wrote *How Children Fail* in 1964. Wrote ten other books. Whereas Montessori would create a child's environment with miniature replicas of the adult world, Holt would put children into the adult world and let them be. In 1977, began newsletter *Growing Without Schooling* that is still going strong.

KOHL (1937-) American. Champion of public Alternative Education. Has written extensively and currently directs the Coastal Ridge Research in Education Center in Point Arena, California. Most famous books are *The Open Classroom,* (1969), and *36 Children,* (1967). Most fun are *A Book of Puzzlements: Play and Invention with Language,* (1981) and *Mathematical Puzzlements* (1987). Believes education's goal is "to develop informed, thoughtful, and sensitive citizens."

GATTO (1935 -) American. Wrote *The Exhausted School* and *Dumbing Us Down* in 1992. Believes in self-education and the integrity of family. Strong supporter of home education, community, and multi-aged configurations.

"Independent study, community service, adventures and experience, large doses of privacy and solitude, a thousand different apprenticeships, the one-day variety or longer—they are all powerful, cheap, and effective ways to start a real reform of schooling." New York City Teacher of the Year 1991 and 1992, New York State Teacher of the Year in 1991.

❧ FAMILIES LEARNING ❦

Learning All the Time

I love being with my son Joshuwyn. His enthusiasm for life is contagious. A few years ago he wanted to know, "When did the people make the whole world big?" Heavy stuff! What a challenge to explain to him in language that he will understand. Josh is curious about the world, and his curiosity is refreshing and contagious. Unfortunately, the older we get, the less we think about "how the whole world got big." I hope Josh will always retain his curiosity and wonder about life. I hope all of us can!

Learning is a journey, not a destination. Not one among us can ever hear all the music, read all the books, count all the numbers, surf all the waves, paint all the pictures, love all the loves, or smell all the flowers that are part of our beloved world. Considering this, we should treat the knowledge, music, and waves that *do* come to us as the precious gifts that they are.

The foundation of education begins at home. Parents have always been and always will be their children's most important teachers. The more commitment and dedication parents have to their child's education, the more the children will develop to their maximum potentials.

The word educate comes from Latin: *e* means out, and *ducere* means to draw or bring. This definition implies that knowledge is an inherent capacity within each one of us. Becoming educated is an unfolding of both natural and nurtured potentials. Learning is like the carefully tended flower bud that blooms to reveal a multitude of petals: it is gorgeous, delicate, and infinitely varied. Friedrich Froebel, the 19th-century German scholar had the same idea when he coined the word *kindergarten*, which means "child garden." But why on earth should we spend just one year in the garden? Why don't we spend our whole lives in the garden? Can you tell me why learning should be anything but interesting, exciting, fascinating, and fun? If someone presents an idea or concept to others that they dislike or don't understand, then it is the *teacher's* fault, *not* the learners'. Teachers must present ideas to learners in a fashion they can understand and enjoy.

There are many, many roads up the mountain of knowledge. There is no one right way to ascend. Each person has their own unique style of learning, which educators like to call visual, aural, and kinesthetic. (This means people like to learn by either looking, listening, or doing.) Most people learn by doing a combination of all three.

People of all ages have ideas and skills to share with each other. We are all teachers and all learners. Our job as parents and teachers is to put ourselves out of work. By about the age of 13, 14, or 15, kids should have gained the skills they need to become completely autonomous learners. They can continue their studies by utilizing libraries, computers, specific classes at the local junior college, or by finding the appropriate tutor(s). If young people of that age are so motivated, they are perfectly capable of choosing their own course of study. Please refer to *The Teenage Liberation Handbook—how to quit school and get a real life and education* by Grace Llewellyn. She gives plenty of references for learning all sorts of subjects on your own.

Intellectual independence at the earliest possible age should be the object of education.... The initiative should be transferred to the student himself at the earliest practicable stage.

—Arnold Toynbee

Care Begins Before Birth

The responsibility for the well being of our children begins even before they are born. Expectant parents, especially moms, need to create the optimum environment in which to nurture the growing fetus: they need to eat wholesome foods, get plenty of rest, exercise, fresh air, pure water, and eliminate or limit consumption of harmful substances including coffee, cigarettes, sugar, and aspirin. Parents need to develop a peaceful, serene attitude, which is a tremendous challenge in our modern haste-filled world.

Home Birth

The birth of a child is a sacred event. The parents should always be in complete control of the birthing situation. In order to do this, they need to read and learn all they can about pregnancy and natural childbirth. They should not readily give away their birthing power to the medical establishment.

All four of my children were born at home, usually in the presence of family members, close friends, and our dear friend and midwife, Nan Koehler. Homeschooling is a natural continuation of homebirth, and we must reaffirm our right to birth and educate our children in the manner that we feel is best for them.

After the Birth

Stay home with your newborn for the first six weeks. Time passes so quickly. Your newborn has just made an amazing journey from one world to another and everything is new, foreign, and probably a bit scary.

With the exception of our oldest, we kept all our babies home for the first six weeks. We felt this was the most gentle way to introduce these tiny creatures to their new home and family.

Being naïve, I took my oldest to the mall when she was five days old. I felt strangely vulnerable, as if I were walking around stark naked. I was glad she was tucked in a baby carrier fast asleep and hidden from strangers' eyes. Nan, my midwife, encouraged me to stay home, but sometimes even the advice of a sagacious teacher is no substitute for direct experience. It's natural to be proud of the new baby and eager to show her off to the world, but, if you tune into subtler things that are happening to the baby, you'll realize a newborn is very vulnerable, very special, and very holy.

For the optimum development of the growing child, the basic tenets of well being established by the parents during pregnancy must continue. Hold your babies all the time. Strap them to your body in a baby carrier so that they can have skin-to-skin contact with you and they can breastfeed freely. (The traditional Japanese or Chinese carriers are the best ones available.) Modern women from industrialized countries should strive to be more like peasant women: work in the fields (or home or office) 'till the baby comes, then after the baby comes, strap them on and continue working. Nan says, *"Strap them on, and only take them out to change them."*

Children are capable of learning only inasmuch as they feel nurtured and sustained. The ideal nurturing environment is one in which the child feels loved, secure, valued, and confident.

Supplies for the Homeschool

Lots of **books**: storybooks, fairy tales and myths, poetry books and novels, and books about real stuff. Seek out books with beautiful illustrations. Even tiny babies can "read" pictures. Don't forget to use the library as a resource. Build up your personal library by buying inexpensive books at flea markets, garage sales, or thrift shops.

Buy **games** that encourage cooperation, decision making, and other noble truths besides greed and winning.

Stockpile tons of **art supplies**, including an ample supply of blank white paper (round out square corners by trimming) and a variety of **writing implements** from pens, felt-tip markers, paints, crayons (beeswax smells delicious), and pencils.

Collect things that make **music**: from harmonicas and Steinway grands to blades of grass and drums.

Create a **work space**: at least one or two card-table sized surfaces, preferably child-proportioned. Try to keep the work surface free from clutter, or at least allow just one clutter to happen at a time. If your space is limited, buy a 3- or 4-foot-square piece of plywood, sand and varnish it, and use it as a work surface. Lay it on the floor or on bricks. Store it out of the way when not in use. If you are more ambitious, design and build a lap desk.

Collect **plants**, **pictures**, and **natural objects** (such as rocks, crystals, wood, shells, and handmade items of clay, metal, straw, fiber, or wood) to create a peaceful and soothing environment.

Create an **altar**. Arrange some natural items on top of a small wooden box. Cover it with a special cloth. Spend time here. Light candles, burn incense and focus the mind on higher realities. Pray, chant, meditate, or just give thanks.

Nothing in education is so astonishing as the amount of ignorance it accumulates in the form of inert facts.

—Henry Brooks Adams

Imagining the Ideal Learning Place

This makes a special writing or drawing project for the beginning of a new school year.

1. Describe **where** and **how big** your ideal learning place would be.
2. What kinds of **sounds**, if any, would you have in your learning place?
3. What **colors** would enhance your space?
4. What kind of **lighting** and **furniture** would you have?
5. What **decorations** such as pictures, mottoes, or mementos would adorn the walls?
6. What kind of **equipment** would you need: easels, computers, pencils...?

Learning Theories

The old-style mechanistic theories of Pavlov and B. F. Skinner are out (thank goodness!), the organic learning theories of Maslow and Rogers are in. Organic learning promotes the idea that learning should revolve around the student, and that no one is really taught directly. Organic learning recognizes that teachers are only facilitators to learning, that significant learning happens only when we feel the learning will benefit us personally, and that the best learning takes place when we do not feel threatened.

In his book *Peak Learning*, Ronald Gross contrasts these two styles. Amazingly enough, the traditional learning list sounds like a regular classroom, and the alternative learning list sounds like a homeschooler's bible. See for yourself:

TRADITIONAL LEARNING EMPHASIZES:

+ memorization and repetition
+ linear and concrete intellectual development
+ conformity
+ individual/competitive efforts
+ static and rigid processes
+ content learning
+ teachers as information-providers
+ departmentalized learning
+ cultural uniformity
+ isolated teaching environments
+ technology as an isolated tool
+ restricted use of facilities
+ autonomy of the community
+ the industrial age

ALTERNATIVE LEARNING EMPHASIZES:

+ excitement and love of learning
+ total human capacity in ethical, intellectual, and physical development
+ diversity and personal esteem
+ cooperative/collaborative efforts
+ thinking, creativity, and intuition
+ teachers as learning facilitators
+ interdisciplinary learning
+ cultural differences and commonalities

Homeschooling isn't:

The same kids in the same room doing the same thing at the same rate in the same way to achieve the same results because they're the same age.

—Stephen Moitozo

Learning without thought is labor lost; thought without learning is perilous.

—Confucius 551-479 BC

- ✦ technology as an integral tool
- ✦ flexible use of facilities
- ✦ extensive parental partnerships
- ✦ community partnerships
- ✦ an information/learning society

Learning Invocations

Many believe the ancient Greek muses are an artist's inspiration. The spirit of the muse reminds us that creativity comes from a place of receptivity. Learning invocations are calls for help. The following invocations have been inspired by the book *Peak Learning*. Author Ron Gross claims these invocations "work to improve motivation, energy, concentration, understanding, retention, and even inspiration." Invocations work best if they are said or chanted in a somewhat serious vein and repeated many times. Make up some of your own.

I love learning: Use this invocation to develop a love of learning. Socrates insisted that learning begins with Eros (love). At this stage, learners explore new material at random and delight in the treasures of knowledge discovered. They feel free to skip, scan, and read at random, covering only as much as they enjoy. At this stage, don't try to remember facts because the primary goal is to enjoy and have fun. You will create an attitude of eagerness and passion for the chosen field of study. Mr. Gross says:

Keep in mind that every subject, no matter how cut-and-dried it may seem now, was once the passionate preoccupation of some fierce genius who created it out of his or her lifeblood. Discover one of those people, learn about his or her life, and you will find that your subject comes alive.

I feel inspired: Remind yourself that your brain has an enormous untapped potential. Mr. Gross recommends reading a page or two of classic literature a day such as: *Notebooks* by Leonardo da Vinci, *Dialogues* by Plato, *Metaphysics* by Aristotle, or something from the Great Books series by Mortimer Adler.

I can use this new information: Take the new information and connect it to things that you already know: if you can see how the new data fits in somewhere, then you have anchored it in your mind's own cross-referencing system—that, by the way, is more complicated than any library catalogue or computer—so it can be jogged back into awareness.

My brain feels energized: Make whatever adjustments you need to feel relaxed, not too warm nor too cold, nor hungry or thirsty. Notice when your body tenses up when you are learning, and become aware of what message that sends your brain.

Other people inspire me: Even a self-directed auto didactic can and should be inspired by great teachers. Unfortunately, in my experience, perhaps 10% of teachers are truly inspiring. Seek out the inspiring ones and avoid the rest. Seek out teachers who share similar interests. If your children are in a regular school, they will spend half a year with this teacher. Most teachers are okay, but if or when my kids choose to go to school, I want them to spend half a year with a great teacher, not an okay one.

Women make us poets, children make us philosophers.

—Malcolm DeChazal

The object of teaching a child is to enable him to get along without his teacher.

—Elbert Hubbard

Parents as Teachers

Whatever educational method a family adopts—homeschool, public, or private school— the degree of parental involvement will determine the degree of success. The parents or guardians must create a warm and nurturing environment that encourages mutual respect. We are not so much teachers as tool givers, inspirations for creativity, and models to our blossoming children.

It's perfectly all right and even desirable to work on projects with your child. They even call this cooperative learning. Don't feel as if you are "doing" your child's work for her, instead, you are modeling something for her and co-operatively learning with her.

Teaching Styles

In oneself lies the whole world, and if you know how to look and learn, then the door is there and the key is in your hand. Nobody on earth can give you either the key or the door to open, except yourself.

—J. Krishnamurti

A good teacher should learn to use a variety of methods, adapting the methodology to fit the learning situation and not the other way around. No matter what style of teaching you use, remember never, ever bore your children! If you are successful as a parent/teacher, you should eventually put yourself out of a job, as your children become autonomous learners.

Let's look at several styles of teaching and learning. The first five or six are my favorite teaching/learning styles:

1) One-on-one Learning, Individualized Instruction, or Contract Learning

Homeschoolers excel in this area. It's why most of us believe that home learning is a superior method of education. Individualized instruction means that the teacher adapts subjects to fit the learner's unique needs. Learners progress at their own rate. The child is free to say "I don't understand this" and review material as long as necessary.

Contract learning means the teacher assists the learner in designing an individual contract. This is largely the premise in which the public school/homeschooling movement operates, but I have seen teachers in the classroom use it in subjects such as math to promote individualized learning. Most of the "basic" subjects (the three R's) are personal ones. People (usually) read, write, and solve math problems on their own. Because of this, one-on-one is the best way to learn these subjects.

In one hour, what you can accomplish working one-on-one would take an equivalent of ten, twenty, or thirty hours to accomplish in a regular classroom where the poor teachers usually work with a ratio of thirty students to one teacher or worse. Imagine if you had thirty kids in your family. You'd have a hard time just remembering all their names!

If you have a large family (like I do), it may be difficult to find time for one-on-one contact. Try to set aside an hour or two (or even ten minutes) each week or so to be alone with each child. Use this time for academic pursuits, a special activity, playing a game, swinging, baking cookies, working together on a project, or just talking. Have other siblings play with friends, play in another part of the house, take a nap, or go someplace with Dad. In this time, you will find a deep bonding takes place between the two of you.

Another way of finding time for one-on-one is to "tuck" your children in bed at night. Our younger children usually fall asleep in our bed after we have all read stories together. We then move them into their own beds (which are right next to ours). The older children (sometimes even our fourteen-year-old) get tucked into bed in their own rooms. In our family, "tuckee in" involves a ritual of poking the blankets down around the body of the child and lots of kisses and hugs. Our neighbor rubs his daughter's back. My mom used to have me say my prayers. Whatever ritual you choose, having that one-on-one time is an important way for you and your children to connect.

2) Child-led Learning, Invited Learning, or Unschooling

John Holt coined the phrase "unschooling." The learner leads the way. Your job is to throw all the textbooks in the trash and just be around to answer questions. The best learning takes place when it is child-led, meaning that children will "invite" you to teach them a certain skill, or will initiate a learning project all by themselves. If you use this method, base your introduction of new ideas on your children's interests.

3) Integrated Curriculum or Interdisciplinary Studies

Using this method, the teacher coordinates learning material with other subject areas. This is a great way to learn. This style of learning chooses any subject and then finds ways of using a variety of curricular skills within the given subject. It allows children to explore a specific subject in depth and breadth, using the available resources of the school and community.

For example, when I worked in a K-4 (Kindergarten-4th grade) alternative classroom, we developed an Adopted Grandparents program. We visited seniors living in a local convalescent home and learning took place in various curricular areas in the following ways:

1. **Writing:** The children practiced writing skills and learned how to address envelopes by writing letters to their new friends.

2. **Reading:** If the children received letters from their new friends, they read them or had the letters read to them.

3. **Math:** To figure out how old their new friends were, the children (with help) used the senior's birthdates in math problems. They could have learned more about calendar months and days of the week if we had marked each birthdate on a master calendar.

4. **Geography:** We marked each birthplace of our new friends on a world map.

5. **Art:** We sent pictures and craft items to the grandparents.

6. **Music:** The kids learned new songs (old songs really) such as "You Are My Sunshine," to sing to their friends when we visited them. We also had big charts of the songs we sang, which helped the children learn to read by what educators call the *whole word, language experience,* or *whole language* approach.

7. **History:** Children learned about the "olden days" from their new friends and from class discussions.

My holy of holies is the human body, health, intelligence, talent, inspiration, love, and the most absolute freedom imaginable, freedom from violence and lies, no matter what form the latter two take. Such is the program I would adhere to if I were a major artist.

—Anton Pavlovich Chekhov

8. **Social Skills:** The students broadened their social circles, learned about service to others, and learned what it was like to be elderly, disabled, and living in a convalescent home. They felt good about themselves for bringing a little sunshine into the lives of others.

4) Cross-age Tutoring or Peer Teaching

Students assume responsibility for helping each other learn a skill; an excellent way for learners to reinforce and clarify their own knowledge as well as develop self-esteem. My older girls love to help their little brother and sister learn their letters and numbers.

Education is... hanging around until you've caught on.

—Robert Frost

5) Socratic Method

Teacher repeatedly asks questions and learners search for answers. There is a book, *Juniper*, in which the heroine, Juniper, became an apprentice to an older wise woman, called a doran. The doran based one of her teaching methods on the Socratic method. As they walked through the woods, the teacher continually asked Juniper what she had seen and heard, thus developing the girl's powers of observation, what my yoga teacher Al likes to call "conscious wholeself awareness." It is possible to use the Socratic method by yourself.

6) Role Playing

Teacher stages real-life situations and problems while learners learn to solve problems by acting out various roles through improvisation.

7) Team Teaching

Teachers share teaching responsibility with other adults. This is almost a given. I hope we all recognize that we can't personally teach our children *everything!* In most homeschool families, Mom is the primary teacher, while Dad pitches in when he can. Families can hire a network of specialists to teach subjects that the parents are not comfortable teaching (such as music, Spanish, art, swimming, or computer technology).

What one knows is, in youth, of little moment; they know enough who know how to learn.

—Henry Brooks Adams

8) Competency-based

The teacher designs objectives that students must achieve before advancing. (Such as learning all the multiplication factors before learning division.) A variation of this method is called **Mastery Learning**, which emphasizes students working at their own speed. **Programmed instruction** is also similar to the other two methods: the teacher divides the subject into small steps, each step building on the previous one.

9) Drill

The teacher analyzes and demonstrates the skill, and the students practice the skill. This is a traditional way of teaching in elementary school. This method can be *very* boring for children, and should be used sparingly. On the other hand, as a musician, I know very well the value of the drill method for learning music.

10) Lecture

The teacher verbally presents the material and the student records it. This is a traditional method of teaching in high school and college.

Ideal Alternative Teaching Qualities

Look for these qualities in a teacher if you don't homeschool full time and want another teacher as an ally. My friend Jim Inciardi used to run an alternative K-1-2-3 class that operated just like this. Most children thrived in his classroom using these methods.

- **Oasis.** That's what the home (or classroom) feels like. People (students and parents) are always dropping in and enjoy hanging out. They feel welcome and useful. Class gives thanks (sings grace) before eating.

- **Calm environment.** There is no use of threats, bribes, whistles, anger, or yelling to "control" the kids.

- Teacher **prefers the company of children** (or playful adults) and is willing to give up lunches and recesses to be with them. You will hardly ever see this kind of teacher hanging out in the teacher's lounge.

- **Individualized curriculum.** Children have the opportunity to work at their own pace.

- **Learning centers** (such as math, art, language arts). Children have **choices** in what they learn, how they learn it, and how long they may spend doing it.

- **Everyone is welcome** in the home (or classroom). Toddlers, babies, friends, aunts, uncles, grandparents and parents are welcome too and incorporated into the scene.

- **Multi-ages.** Class covers at least two if not more grade levels. (In a "natural" society, this is the way people live.) Multi-ages is an important concept because age segregation (promoted by single-graded groups) forces peers to be each other's role models. Kids in these groups don't have an opportunity to interact with others of different ages, and children raised for thirteen years (remember, they spend *half* of the year in school) in single-aged classrooms miss important opportunities for learning from a wider range of kids with varying ages and intellectual skills. If this situation persists, we will be the old folks, segregated from our loved ones and spending the last lonely years of our lives in nursing homes. As John Taylor Gatto says, "*...without children and old people mixing in daily life, a community has no future and no past, only a continuous present.*"

- Teacher is a **frequent guest at birthday parties** and spends time with a lot of his families outside the classroom.

- Curriculum designed to develop the **whole child:** all eight basic aspects of education: music, art, letters, numbers, nature (science), body world (movement), outer world (human society), and inner world (spirit).

- **Kids learn by hands**-on exploratory method. Teacher uses few (if any) dittoes or reproducibles.

Where we love is home, home that our feet may leave, but not our hearts.

—*Oliver Wendell Holmes*

Kind words can be short and easy to speak but their echoes are truly endless.

—*Mother Theresa*

Children as Learners

Each child needs both individual one-on-one attention *and* opportunities to work within a group as a team. Teamwork should focus on working cooperatively towards a common goal.

We learn best by doing, thus a child's education should include many hands-on activities. Don't bore them with workbooks, dull work sheets, and uninspired dittoes. A more creative approach to teaching is learning through playing games, going places, and creating things together. This takes time and requires the parent to participate in an active way.

When working with kids remember this self-fulfilling prophecy: Children tend to do as well as you expect them to. "I don't care" *really* means "I don't think I can do it."

Communication

When I was a kid, my family's plans (such as trips or visits to friends) were often a mystery to me, only revealed moments before our departure. I *know* I've done the same thing to my own kids. Make sure you tell your kids what the plans are (this is a good topic for family meetings).

It might be a good idea to spend some time with your kids each week discussing how your learning ideas, plans, and interests are going: ways to improve the learning situation, future plans, and any other ideas or problems related to homeschooling. This encourages the development of oral language, problem solving, and critical thinking skills, if anyone should ask you. Likewise, avoid the "educator's trap" of talking too much. You'll bore your kids. Especially don't lecture. Major boring.

The Nurturing Family

1. A nuturing family expresses **love** and **support** all the time. You can be yourself. There is little or no "formal" behavior or phony politeness.

2. Family members are **affectionate** with each other. They hug and kiss spontaneously and have fun together. They laugh at their own corny jokes.

3. They **talk** about almost anything with almost anybody. Family members listen to each other and share feelings. There aren't many secrets.

4. There's **noise**. People laugh, scream, shout, and chuckle. Yet there's also quiet times, but it's a peaceful quiet, not a hospital or graveyard-like silence.

5. They **do things together**. There's a time for working together (such as making meals or doing yardwork) and playing together (such as going to the beach or playing a game).

❧ WHY CHOOSE HOMESCHOOLING? ❧

This list originated when I participated in a radio talk show that aired on our local listener-sponsored station, KPFA. It's a good list to share with people who don't know much about homeschooling or have mixed feelings about it.

Advantages for Family and Child

The direction in which education starts a man will determine his future life

—Plato

- ✦ promotes family unity—keeps family intact
- ✦ opportunity for development of renaissance (multi-talented) personality (á la Leonardo da Vinci)
- ✦ child-led learning (parents can answer questions as they arise)
- ✦ one-on-one learning—best way to learn
- ✦ kids can work at their own pace
- ✦ opportunity to individualize curriculum
- ✦ promotes self-esteem
- ✦ non-competitive environment
- ✦ adults, not peers, become role models
- ✦ no segregation between home and academic life—education becomes a continuum

Why Parents as Teachers

- ✦ parents are naturally their child's best teachers
- ✦ parents understand children better than anyone else (except the children themselves)
- ✦ promotes continuity of educational/personal values through the child's academic years
- ✦ facilitates communication—no communication loss between parents and teachers as found in classroom

Benefits of Being Home to Learn

- ✦ child learns in a home environment not an institutional one
- ✦ ability to be spontaneous—change focus as the desire or need arises
- ✦ multi-generational (no age-segregation—more accurately reflects the natural world)
- ✦ opportunity to use community as classroom
- ✦ maximize opportunities for field trips—don't need permission slips
- ✦ opportunity for study of personal belief systems
- ✦ can play in the mud, go barefoot
- ✦ can take long lunches
- ✦ long recess or play times, not interrupted by the ring of a bell

- ✦ reduces some of the stresses associated with school:
  - ▾ no standing in lines
  - ▾ no constant tests or grades
  - ▾ no sitting in rows of desks
  - ▾ don't have to get a pass to use the bathroom
  - ▾ no rigid time schedules

The whole art of teaching is only the art of awakening the natural curiosity of young minds for the purpose of satisfying it afterwards.

—Anatole France

Educational Philosophy

- ✦ child's successes are directly linked to parental involvement and support
- ✦ nurturing, loving, functioning families produce nurturing, loving and functioning children
- ✦ children will naturally flourish and learn, just as they automatically learned to walk and talk without being taught

How We Learn and Ways to Learn

- ✦ learning is best when we are self-motivated
- ✦ we learn best by doing
- ✦ using integrated curriculum (one idea is learned through a variety of curricular areas)
- ✦ using individualized (one-on-one) learning
- ✦ using cross-age tutoring (i.e., older kids tutor younger ones)
- ✦ seeking out multi-aged multi-ethnic situations
- ✦ learning in groups or teams
- ✦ studying nature: playing with natural objects

What to Learn

- ✦ **Information**: how to gain, organize, and analyze it
- ✦ **Social democracy**: the highest human ideals of equality of rights, opportunity, and treatment
- ✦ **Personal beliefs**: the love of humanity, and a belief in a greater reality
- ✦ **Self**: learning to be autonomous, self-governing individuals: self-reliant, self-motivated, egalitarian, to be successful in endeavors, be trustworthy, responsible, healthy, adaptable, respectful, intelligent, creative, and joyful in work and play.

Visions of the Future

- ✦ develop home-and-school classroom to allow part-time homeschooling, so homeschooling isn't an either/or choice
- ✦ have schools function like libraries or resource centers that are open year round for the entire community

❧ IDEAS FOR LEARNING ❧

Integrated Curriculum Ideas

✦ **Integrated Curriculum** (A study of mud)

Science: What makes mud? Examine it under the microscope—what happens to mud when it dries?

Language Arts: Write a poem or story about mud.

Math: Measure volume of mud, make estimations, etc.

Art: Make mud sculptures, mud pies, adobe bricks.

Music: Write a song about mud or find and sing songs about mud.

Physical Education: Play in the mud!

Food: Find and make a recipe that ends up looking like mud (for example: chocolate mousse).

✦ **Field Trips** (from our family trip to Mexico in 1987)

Math: metric system (converting kilometers into miles), Mexican money system (pesos), monetary conversions, map reading, telling time, time-zone changes.

Language Arts: Spanish immersion, book reading, journal writing, personal Spanish-English dictionaries, sign reading, postcard writing, map reading, storytelling, treasure maps.

Music: Radio and cassette tape music, mariachi bands, nightclub bands, playing guitar, singing.

Art: Visiting museums, mission ruins, churches. Enjoying local architecture and handicrafts, visiting the Mexican circus.

Social Science: Hanging out in the *plazas* or *zocalos* (community centers) of various towns and cities. Side trip to *Barranca del Cobre* (Copper Canyon), land of the *Tarahumara* (natives who live in caves and use burros to plow their fields). First-hand knowledge of other communities and cultures. Watching Mexican films, looking at Mexican books, magazines.

Science: Studying the desert, ocean, fish, seashells, and weather.

Physical Activities: Swimming, boating, frisbee, bike riding, snorkeling, yoga, and hiking.

✦ **ISP (Independent Study Project):**

In-depth study of a subject that interests the child. (For example: make model of a castle, compile a book of poems, studies of important people like Martin Luther King, Jr., Buddha, or Mother Theresa, collect bones, study birds or squirrels, piano…)

The ideal condition would be, I admit, that we should be right by instinct; but since we are all likely to go astray, the reasonable thing is to learn from those who can teach.

—Sophocles

Numbers (Math)

+ using manipulatives (such as Cuisenaire rods, Legos®, beans, and dominoes)
+ playing store (involves money, decimal system, counting, subtraction, addition)
+ doing puzzles (logic)
+ playing card games (can involve numeral matching, identification, sequencing, counting skill, addition)
+ playing board games (Parcheesi, Monopoly, Multiplication Bingo, Backgammon, Ravensburg games, etc.)
+ go food shopping (involves money, comparisons, addition, estimations)
+ coin collecting (may involve conversions, comparisons)
+ cooking (can involve fractions, ratios, division, multiplication)

Letters (Language Arts)

+ make books (such as recipes, songs, games, poems, and stories)
+ write letters (thank-you notes, invitations, addressing envelopes)
+ visit libraries
+ visit bookstores
+ read environmental print (things like stop signs, store signs, labels, and menus)
+ play games (such as Scrabble, Boggle, and Pictionary)
+ make up stories (written and oral)
+ make lists
+ keep journals, travel logs, diaries
+ play singing and rhyming games, make up songs
+ keep personal spelling dictionaries
+ do dramatic play/role playing
+ use the dictionary

Human History

+ visit museums
+ visit people in the community such as old folks, community professionals, or toddlers in daycare
+ attend or create living history events (put on plays, visit local renaissance faires or other living history events)
+ watch films and videos
+ read novels, newspapers, news magazines
+ travel
+ use maps and globes

Music

- ◆ attend concerts, the opera, the ballet, plays
- ◆ take music lessons
- ◆ listen to the radio, tapes, CD's
- ◆ write music
- ◆ join or start a choir
- ◆ visit recording studios

Art

- ◆ draw, paint, work with clay
- ◆ learn home crafts such as sewing or woodworking
- ◆ take art lessons
- ◆ visit art museums
- ◆ visit local artists
- ◆ attend craft fairs

Body World (Physical Education)

- ◆ play! (do things like swinging, sliding, hanging, running, playing hopscotch, or foursquare)
- ◆ play sports (such as soccer, softball, basketball, tennis, and gymnastics)
- ◆ go hiking or walking
- ◆ go bike riding, roller skating, or skateboarding
- ◆ dance or do yoga
- ◆ do outdoor or farm chores (things like raking, carrying wood, gardening)

Nature (Science)

- ◆ take care of animals
- ◆ garden, compost, sprout seeds
- ◆ recycle
- ◆ explore ocean
- ◆ go on herb walks
- ◆ watch whales and birds
- ◆ observe weather
- ◆ go star gazing
- ◆ watch National Geographic films and videos
- ◆ read science books and magazines

Just as the twig is bent, the tree's inclined.

—Alexander Pope

Every student has something important to teach the teacher.

—Robert Fulghum

Health and Life Skills

✦ do household chores (such as kitchen and laundry tasks)
✦ practice personal hygiene (bathing, dental care)
✦ develop cooking skills and nutrition awareness

Outer World (Social Relations)

✦ have family meetings
✦ go to parties
✦ host holiday gatherings
✦ do role playing
✦ play
✦ visit friends and family
✦ go to museums, concerts, temples or churches

Inner World (Spirit)

✦ say grace and prayers, study holy books, meditate, sing
✦ visit sacred sites in nature and visit places of worship (churches, temples, mosques)
✦ have family meetings (this is in Outer World too)

The best teacher-parent in not the one who fills the student's mind with the largest amount of factual data in a minimum of time, or who develops some manual skill almost to the point of uncanniness, but rather the one who kindles an inner fire, arouses moral enthusiasm, inspires the student with a vision of what s/he may become, and reveals the worth and permanency of moral and spiritual and cultural values.

—Harold Garnet Black

Learning Everything:

A Rainbow-Colored Mind

❧ WHAT IS A RAINBOW-COLORED MIND? ❧

Think of a radiant rainbow, sparkling with a multitude of colors. Take one color away, and the rainbow is not complete. It still shines, it's still pleasing and colorful, but it's not a whole rainbow. A complete education is like a rainbow: all the colors shine. Not *only* do we need to learn our letters and numbers, we also need to learn how to get along with everybody and sing and draw, and learn about the planet and the stars, as well as our bodies and souls. Why can't we all be like Leonardo da Vinci?

A Few Colors

A teacher affects eternity; s/he can never tell where his or her influence stops.

—Henry Brooks Adams

Traditional education usually emphasizes just part of the mind's rainbow: the acquisition of reading, writing, and math skills. In most public schools, music and art are extra curricular subjects. Physical education typically entails 30 kids playing dodge-ball 30 minutes a week. Science usually means reading a text book in class or dissecting a frog. Social graces are not a real subject, and God, goddesses, (except ancient Greek and Roman) and prayer are not even whispered about.

We Westerners divide the world into either those who are literate and those who are not. If you can read and write, who cares if you've lost your soul? If you can read, who cares if you hate your neighbor? If you know your times tables, who cares if you don't think about your spirit?

A true scholar needs a rainbow-colored mind. For this individual, the soul is just as important as the times tables. The "colors" of learning are all part of the same source, just like a rainbow. One color arises from the next, each one a compliment of the whole.

In 1983 Howard Gardner proposed the Theory of Multiple Intelligences in his book *Frames of Mind*. He believes that we learn best when we are allowed to learn in ways most suited to our various temperaments. He calls these intelligences: linguistic, musical, logical-mathematical, spatial, bodily-kinesthetic, interpersonal, and intrapersonal. This is my version of the body/mind/spirit theory.

Which Came First?

I believe it was music and art. Our ancestors drew pictures and sang songs way before they began to write letters and numbers! Thus, it seems natural to assume that art and music came before letters and numbers. In truth, we have to learn to "read" pictures before we learn to read letters. The alphabet of art is simple: there are just five basic shapes. Letters are just complex pictures (especially Chinese!) that take more time to learn. Scribbles (made of simple lines and curves) are easier symbols to draw than letters and numbers (which are made from more complex lines and curves). Pictures come before letters, therefore the language of pictures (art) precedes the alphabet (reading and writing). Even a tiny infant can "read" a picture. Musical rhythms come in cyclic variations of twos and threes. Rhythm is based on mathematical formulas and musicians are mathematicians whether they know it or not. In addition, songs also involve language in a subtle and profound manner. How wonderful it is that the language of the universe is music and numbers and its eyes are colors and shapes.

The Mind's Colors

*To teach is to
learn twice.*

*—Joseph
Joubert*

ART (Vision, Perception, Creativity)

Art is ability to think in pictures and to perceive the visual world accurately and re-create (or alter) it in our minds or on paper. Here, we learn to use our eyes and look carefully around us at the visually awesome world of colors, things, letters, and numbers.

MUSIC (Aural art, Listening, Singing, Playing Instruments, Composing)

Music is the ability to understand, create, and play music. (Or at least to play records, tapes, and CDs.) Here we learn how to use our ears to perceive the aural world of sounds, words, music, and more subtle vibrations. Music is truly the gift of the gods *and* the universal language.

LETTERS (Language, Linguistics, ABC's)

Learning letters is the ability to be sensitive, fluent, and coherent in reading, writing, listening and speaking. In this realm, we also learn how to listen and communicate with each other in a positive way, and how to respect silence.

NUMBERS (Math, Logic, 123's)

Numbers teach us mathematics and logical skills. With numbers, we need to learn about invention and research. We need to know how to gain, organize, and analyze information.

NATURE (Earth, Science)

Nature teaches us about animals, plants, rocks, chemicals, and outer space. We need to learn how to love and respect dear ol' Mother Earth, and all things upon her. Here, we learn how to nurture animals, plants, and rocks and make them our allies.

BODY WORLD (Exercise, Movement)

Body awareness is using our bodies in a skilled way and making them do what we want them to do. We can learn to engage our whole body in graceful movements such as: skipping, swimming, surfing, making love, dancing, yoga, running, gymnastics, and riding on horses or shopping carts. (That's my list of all-time favorites.) Choosing and preparing wholesome foods is part of Body World, because a healthy body means a happy mind. We can also use our hands to create exquisite and lasting things, delicious food, running cars, and to hold each other tenderly.

OUTER WORLD (Human history, social skills, relationships, families, parties)

Social grace is the ability to perceive and understand the moods, desires, and motivations of others. It is the development of social compassion in work or play. Social compassion includes the qualities of self-reliance, initiative, kindness, spontaneity, resourcefulness, courage, trustworthiness, responsibility, adaptableness, respectfulness, creativity, and joy. We must learn to be a WORLD FAMILY, to see how we're both the same and different. It is and always has been true that if we can work out our family problems, we can work out the world's problems. Enlightenment in the outer world means using the great

Socialist/Democratic principles of equal rights, opportunity, and treatment, for betterment of ourselves and society. Here we also study human history: for fun, to learn how and why we are what we are today, and (hopefully) to learn from the mistakes of our ancestors.

INNER WORLD (The Great Mystery, spirit, intuition, dreams, soul, or religion)

The inner world is where we gain the ability to understand our inner emotions, to understand our spirits, our Great Spirits, and our holiness. The most important things we need to know are loving kindness, respect, and patience, the "Golden Rule" found in every major religion. Besides the Golden Rule, two concepts found in all major religions are: Honor all agreements you make; and: Don't mess with other people's stuff. Religion should help us become better people and experience unconditional love.

A scholar with a rainbow-colored mind will have reverence for life. Such a scholar will learn about self-awareness (body and soul), nature (because we live here), social graces, *and* letters and numbers. When all the colors come together, they make white light, which is a symbol of the spirit, the awesome and truly mysterious source of All. With one color missing, there is no white light. As scholars of Life, our earthly goal is the continual creation of minds, souls, and bodies that are "painted" with strong, bright colors from every aspect of the spectrum.

If nobody learns as much as the teacher, then turn students into teachers.

—Robert Fulghum

Art

❧ ART APPRECIATION ❧

The fine arts include music, art, creative writing, and drama. These disciplines are important to us because they allow us to express our inner creative spirits. In the broadest definition, art is the skill of making or doing. This definition applies equally to a gardener, piano tuner, cook, or baseball player.

Creation of Art

There are two reasons for creating art: beauty and significance. We create **beauty** in art (and beauty is entirely a subjective decision) because we humans have a desire to create and design, and because we like to make and enjoy things we consider beautiful. Sometimes we create **significant** art to mark special events. This began in ancient times with planting, harvesting, and hunting rituals and continues today with spiritual or religious observations, graduation ceremonies, and other special events. Works of art can remind us of parts of life that we value.

Life is earnest, art is gay.

—Johann Christoph Friedrich von Schiller

Elements of Art

Elements of visual art include aesthetics, beauty, composition, design, perspective, rhythm, and style. Art has two broad categories. The first is one-dimensional and includes photography, oil painting, water colors, lithographs, etchings, prints, and the like. Three-dimensional art includes sculpture, glass making, architecture, woodwork, pottery, and jewelry.

Power of Art

Fine art has the power to grab us and the artist who creates it may devote many hours bringing an inner vision to life. When creating, artists may experience a profound shift of consciousness because we now know that artists (right handers, that is!) "create" art in the right half of the brain, which is the intuitive half. In this mode, normal states of consciousness are suspended, and artists may enter a dream-like state of reality.

True Art

There is a vast difference, open to subjectivity and taste, between True Art and Entertainment. True Art deepens our eyes. We look into our human family's soul. All our attention is open and given to the beauty of the art. We come away from the experience feeling greatly exalted. Entertainment, while pleasurable, does not reach deeply inside us. It may relieve us of troubles or boredom, but it will not inspire us on deeper levels.

Unfortunately, art is undervalued in the educational curriculum. In fact, visual art is the basis of reading and writing. Give art the attention it deserves. You will greatly enrich your life and the lives of your children.

Kinds of Art

Architecture	Carving	Ceramics
Commercial Art	Dance	Decorative Art
Drama	Drawing	Engraving
Fashion	Film	Graphics
Interior Decorating	Literature	Lithography
Music	Painting	Photography
Poetry	Sculpture	Theater
Textiles	Writing	Video

*A work of art is a corner of creation
seen through a temperament.*

—Emile Zola

❧ ART EDUCATION ❧

Monart

(Monart student)

There are more valid facts and details in works of art than there are in history books.

—Charlie Chaplin

Mona Brooks created the Monart method of art instruction. Her method teaches many styles of drawing and then allows the children to draw in any style they desire. She has written two excellent books about developing children's art: *Drawing with Children,* and *Drawing with Older Children and Teens.* I first learned of her work through a homeschooling mom who raved about her. The mom was quite a talented artist so I figured she must be right. After I studied the Monart method, I found myself suddenly drawing a very respectable hippopotamus! (And I'm one of those people who considers herself artistically ungifted!)

Mona's method helps learners as young as four develop abilities in realistic drawing, which is a type of knowledge that only 1% of us are born with. Realistic drawing helps develop fine motor skills. Some educators believe that forcing artistic realism at an early age can somehow harm a child's fantasy world. With fifteen years of experience to draw upon, Mona knows that encouraging children to learn realistic drawing in no way impairs their ability or desire to draw free-style.

The Elements of Art

Monart uses an "alphabet" of five elements that can be combined to make any shape there is. There are two "families" within this system: one has to do with roundish elements and the other represents lines. These five elements are:

+ *Dots*: any roundish shape that is colored or filled in.

+ *Circles*: any roundish shape that is empty.

+ *Straight lines*: a line with no bends, which can be short, long, thick, or thin.

+ *Curved lines*: any line that bends without becoming a circle, such as the letter *C* or a spiral.

+ *Angle lines*: a line that bends so much it finally makes a point, such as the letter *V*.

One technique she recommends for beginners is learning to draw with black ink. She feels that pencil creates "sloppy eyes" and the ink lends itself to making the eyes perceive more accurately. When the child gains confidence with line and proportions, she then explains how to use many different kinds of media. The results are quite charming and delightfully colored drawings. She also recommends using smaller paper for younger children who are working on a detailed drawing, as a larger one may be overwhelming to them. Many art educators all over the country have noticed that "children who are given the realistic drawing information as well as the freedom to free-draw will have far more creativity and raw creative energy than those who only have a few years of free-draw experience and then quit at age eight or nine, never to draw again."

One way to begin is to have children practice drawing a variety of elements, just as they might practice their letters and numbers...maybe even *before* they practice them. Please refer to her book for a wealth of information.

Conceptual Drawing

This type of drawing is conceived in the artist's mind, rather than derived from the artist's immediate surrounding. It could also probably be called memory drawing.

Drawing by Joey Lasley

> *We need religion for religion's sake, morality for morality's sake, art for art's sake.*
>
> —*Victor Cousin*

Gesture Drawing

This drawing attempts to capture the form of movement. It is made quickly while the hand attempts to follow the movement of the eye.

Drawing by Amarina Stara (age 15)

> *No great artist ever sees things as they really are. If s/he did, s/he would cease to be an artist.*
>
> —*Oscar Wilde*

UPSIDE-DOWN DRAWING

Find a good line-art drawing, turn it upside down, and draw it. Here is an upside-down drawing modeled after a Picasso picture.

Great nations write their autobiographies in three manuscripts— the book of their deeds, the book of their words, and the book of their art.

—John Ruskin

CONTOUR DRAWING

In drawing, a contour means an edge as *you* perceive it. Here is a contour drawing. It was made by my daughter one evening at the kitchen table. She held an orange in her hand and drew what she saw. A variation of this is the *blind contour* drawing in which the artist never looks at the paper. For this technique, it is useful to tape the drawing paper to the table.

Drawings by Genessa Marie (age 9)

❧ ART RECIPES ❧

RUBBERY PLAY DOUGH

2 cups baking soda
1 ½ cups water
1 cup cornstarch

Boil on medium heat till thick

PLAY CLAY

1 cup flour
1 cup salt
1 tablespoon powdered alum
1 cup water
food coloring

Mix dry ingredients, then slowly add water and food coloring.

PAPER MACHE

1. In a large bowl, rip 30 sheets of **newspaper** into 1" squares.
2. Cover with hot water and soak overnight.
3. Squeeze out excess water, add 1 cup **paste** (⅓ cup flour to ¼ cup water) to 3 cups paper.
4. Knead in a plastic bag.

PAINT

½ cup cold water
½ cup laundry starch
4 cups boiling water
1 tablespoon glycerin
powdered tempera paints

Mix starch and cold water. Slowly pour in boiling water and stir. Add glycerin and cool. Pour mixture into small containers and put paint into each container.

FINGER-PAINT

3 tablespoons sugar
½ cup cornstarch
2 cups cold water
2 teaspoons boric acid
1 tablespoon glycerin
food coloring

1. Mix everything but glycerin and boric acid in a saucepan (add water to cornstarch and flour slowly) and cook on low heat until thick.
2. Pour into muffin tin and add different colors.
3. Dampen art paper before beginning to finger-paint.

SPACKLE ART

Mix spackling powder with water until stiff like whip cream, not lumpy. Stir in powdered paint. Pour into styrofoam food tray. Let set until stiff. Make a hand print, press in shells, leaves, twigs, etc.

HOMEMADE PAINT

½ teaspoon vinegar
½ teaspoon cornstarch
½ teaspoon glycerin
food coloring

Shake it up in a jar. Add food coloring.

DRIPLESS PAINT

¾ cup cornstarch
water

Add water to cornstarch to make a smooth, thick paste. Stir in boiling water to make a thick and nearly clear liquid. Divide and add **tempera paint** to the mixtures.

Great art is the expression of a solution of the conflict between the demands of the world without and that within.

—Edith Hamilton

SOAPSUDS CLAY

¾ powdered soap (such as Ivory Snow)
1 tablespoon warm water

Mix ingredients in a bowl and beat with an electric mixer until a clay-like substance is formed. Mold into desired shape. Dries to a hard finish.

GLOOP

Mix two parts white glue to one part liquid starch. Cover and refrigerate overnight. This has the consistency of silly putty, and can be cut with scissors, pulled, and twisted.

NUT INK

With a **hammer**, crush eight **walnut shells** in a piece of **cloth**. Bring them to a boil in a **saucepan** with 1 cup **water,** then let simmer for about an hour. Cool, pour mixture through a **strainer** into a small glass **jar.** Add ½ tsp. each **vinegar** and **salt.** Keep in tightly closed container.

BERRY INK

Fill a **strainer** with ½ cup ripe **berries** (any kind). Hold the strainer over a **bowl** and mash the berries with the back of a **spoon** into the bowl. To the juice in the bowl, add ½ tsp. each vinegar and salt. Store in a tightly sealed jar.

QUILL AND WOOD NIB PENS

Use a **jack knife** to whittle a point on a pencil-sized **twig.** For a quill pen, find a large **feather** and cut off the tip at an angle.

The most beautiful thing we can experience is the mysterious. It is the source of all true art and science.

—Albert Einstein

❧ ARTS AND CRAFTS ❧

MARBLEIZED PAPER

Fill a 9" x 12" **pan** with **water.** Use **scissors** or a **vegetable peeler** to scrape pieces of **colored chalk** into the water. Quickly dip **white construction paper** into the water. Let it dry. Use paper as a background for making fans, hearts, silhouettes or writing poems.

SANDPAPER PICTURES

Glue a sheet of **sandpaper** to the back of a piece of **paper**. Draw with **crayons** on the paper. Use different textures.

FOOT PAINTING

(Do this outside) Spread a large sheet of **butcher paper** on the ground. Pour **liquid starch** into a large, shallow **pan** and add **tempera paint**. Have children step in the paint and make designs on the paper with their feet. Have **towel** and another pan filled with **soapy water** handy for cleanup.

MILKY CHALK DRAWING

Casein, a natural fixative found in milk, has been used by artists for a long time.

Dip **chalk** into **milk** and draw on paper, or use a **paper towel** to spread the milk on the paper. The colors will be brilliant.

MEDICINE DROPPER ART

Buy some **medicine droppers** at a drug store. Mix small amounts of **tempera paint** with water. Dampen a piece of paper with a wet **sponge**. Drop paint onto the paper with droppers.

WATERCOLOR/CRAYON WASH

Draw a picture on regular **paper** with **crayons**. Go over it with a **watercolor** wash.

BLACK CRAYON SCRATCH

Solidly color your whole paper with different color **crayons**. On top of this, cover the whole picture with **black crayon**. Scratch a design into the picture with the end of a **paper clip**.

INSIDE OUT PICTURES

Begin with a small piece of colored **construction paper**. With **scissors**, cut out shapes around the inside of the border. **Paste** the shapes onto a larger piece of paper, so that cutouts fold back from their original position.

You must never tell a thing. You must illustrate it. We learn through the eye and not the noggin.

—*Will Rogers*

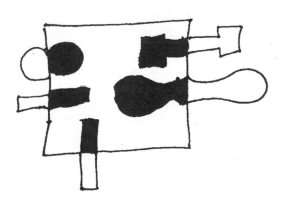

STYROFOAM ETCHINGS

Use a thick **pencil** to etch a design into a **styrofoam** tray. Dip a **paint roller** into a **tray of paint**. Move the roller over the picture and press a sheet of paper on the tray to make a print.

SALT DESIGNS

Use **watercolors** to paint several pieces of paper. Sprinkle **salt** on the paint while it is still wet to create a marbleized effect. Cut paper into shapes such as hearts or eggs.

NATURAL PAINTBRUSHES

Use **pine branches, pine cones, feathers,** or **grasses** as paintbrushes. For pictures that look like fireworks, use **Queen Anne's Lace**.

BUBBLE PAINTING

Mix $\frac{1}{3}$ cup **tempera paint** with $\frac{1}{3}$ cup **dish soap** in a quart **jar**. Add some **water** and let the mixture sit overnight. Pour mixture into a shallow pan and blow bubbles in it using stiff **straws**. Place a **paper** over the bubbles when they reach the top of the pan for beautiful designs. (Use paper for poems and the likes.)

RECORD PLAYER DESIGNS

Put a **paper plate** on an old **record player**. Use **felt-tip pens** to draw a design.

ART VISUALIZATION

Choose a famous piece of art. Don't show it to anyone. Describe it to your children in as much detail as possible while they try to visualize the picture. Have them try to draw the picture from their mind's eye.

ICE CRYSTAL PICTURE

Draw a picture with **crayons** on a dark piece of **construction paper.** Prepare a mix of equal parts **water** and **epsom salts.** Paint this solution over your picture. When it dries, "ice crystals" will form!

STINKY FISH PRINT

Get an old **flounder** from the market. Paint it with different colors of tempera paints. Lay the painted fish on a piece of **white** or light-colored **construction paper** to make a print. (Idea from the Carl family.)

Get a copy of *Don't Move the Muffin Tins* by Bev Bos for more arts and crafts ideas.

There are Six Essentials in painting. The first is called spirit; the second, rhythm; the third, thought; the fourth, scenery; the fifth, the brush; and the last is the ink.

—*Ching Hao*

 *Music*

The word *music* comes from ancient Greece. The Grecians believed that nine muses (goddesses) served as divine guardians to the arts, and a person visited by one of the muses was thought to be divinely inspired. Even today, musicians talk about being visited by the muse; clearly music has always been linked to the divine. Music expresses spiritual *and* emotional feelings that are both personal and universal. Music integrates and harmonizes the body and mind, promotes a sense of well being, and is intellectually pleasing. Music resonates deeply within the fabric of every culture that has ever been on earth.

Rhythm

Rhythm is the essence of music, and rhythmic patterns are the basis of life itself. For the most part, slow rhythms create inward (yin) feelings such as resignation, contemplation, and melancholy, while faster tempos create outward (yang) feelings such as excitement, expansion, and exhilaration. People have a natural tendency to rock, sway, tap their feet, or clap their hands to the rhythmic undulation of the musical beat.

Physical Effects of Music

Physically, music effects everyone who hears it. The power of musical vibrations makes an impact on our whole body: nerves, spinal column, muscles, and even the bones resonate to musical vibrations. In addition, depending on the style of music being played, musical notes can raise or lower the pulse and blood pressure, and increase or decrease respiration. Resonant vibrations also stimulate the medullary mitochondria (lower brain stem) which produces ATP (adenosine triphosphate molecules). This is an important key to energy balance in all living things.

A study by Kathleen McCormick of the Gerontology Research center, National Institute on Aging (in Bethesda, Md.) observed that a group of opera singers (28-65 years old, including some smokers) had stronger than average chest walls and heart pumping capabilities and maintained diaphragmatic breathing with large lung volumes (air-intake capacity). Their hearts worked more efficiently, and they had lower heart rates than a control group of non-singers, all under forty. Ms. McCormick says: *"This kind of (aerobic) singing is a conditioning exercise of the muscles of respiration. It very efficiently tones up the chest in a manner similar to swimming, rowing, and yoga."* Singing helps maintain the resiliency of the heart and lungs. It also stimulates the thyroid gland, and deficiency in this gland can cause mental dullness.

Where the word stops, there starts the song, exultation of the mind bursting forth into the voice.

—*Thomas Aquinas*

Emotional Effects of Music

Changes in voice quality reflect changes in the emotions. Often, words are secondary to vocal inflection. Tone infuses words with a force that gives them a deeper, more penetrating meaning. When listening to music, we heighten our sensory stimulus, thus experiencing different moods more easily. Music is clearly the language of emotions. Music can create a myriad of feelings such as pleasure and displeasure, calm, joy, and peace. Various forms of music can help ease fear, anxiety, and grief. We can use music as an ally to create order and harmony within: music helps us meditate without thought.

Spiritual Effects of Music

Musical training is a more potent instrument than any other, because rhythm and harmony find their way into the inward places of the soul.

—Plato

Who can imagine a worship service without music? Singing sacred songs in a devotional manner helps raise our consciousness and increases our inner peace. Hindus believe that the shortest path to spiritual attainment is through singing, because singing, like meditation and prayer, brings us directly into the ever-present moment. *Spiritus* means breath in Latin, and Hindus call breath *Prana*, which also means the essence of life itself. This underscores the importance of breath to spirituality. Breath is indeed an essential part of singing and the playing of wind instruments. The health benefits of deep, rhythmic breathing have already been mentioned. In addition conscious breathing, as exemplified by the slow rhythmic intake and output that singers use, has other subtle spiritual benefits as well. In fact, *inspire* or *inspiration* literally means to breathe in and to be filled with spirit. For more information please read *Sound Medicine* by Laeh Maggie Garfield.

Singing

Breathing, as I have mentioned, is essential to good singing. Notice the organic rhythms of the respiratory system and observe how the diaphragm supports the breath. Become aware that you can fill all cavities in the body with air. The lungs, throat, mouth, nasal, and sinus cavities can all resonate with musical tones.

Keep in mind that vowel sounds have lower frequencies than consonants. The throat is most open and unobstructed when singing vowels, and when pronouncing or singing vowels, the throat forms the shape of a circle, which is also a symbol for infinity. Hebrew tradition holds vowels so sacred that vowels are written as dots, not letters. Singers naturally sustain this open vowel sound and bring consonants into play only at the beginning and end of words.

Improvisation

Musical improvisation is not just about "doing your own thing," for freedom without structure soon leads to cacophony. Improvisation helps us become spontaneous, exuberant collaborators.

Play games like "Finish the Tune" (one person begins a melody, and the other person finishes it) to start, or sing your way through a comic strip in the newspaper. Sing poems and literary anecdotes in various scales and modes. You might want to experiment with different meters and with different melodic and percussive instruments as accompaniment.

Learning to Play Instruments

Goals and tips for beginning musicians
- ✦ To read music and follow fingerings.
- ✦ To sight-read (you must be exposed to a multitude of music to master this).
- ✦ Remember to sit (or stand) straight and tall and hold hands in correct position (for piano, curve fingers and hold wrists in a natural position, cut fingernails short).
- ✦ Practice slowly!
- ✦ Practice difficult sections alone (for piano, hands alone, if necessary).
- ✦ Attend to phrasing, staccato, and other dynamic markings.
- ✦ Before playing, check piece for tempo, clef, key, and time signature.
- ✦ Memorize a few selections a year.

Suggested practice technique for beginners
- ✦ practice each piece six times:
- ✦ 2 times naming (singing) notes out loud
- ✦ 2 times counting out loud
- ✦ 2 times singing (if there are words)

Indian Music

About twenty years ago, I had the great fortune to attend Ali Akbar School of Music in Marin, California. The one thing I remember Khansahib telling us on the first day of class was, "Play it a hundred times, and then you'll know it."

His father was a master musician. It is said that he used to practice his instrument twenty hours a day. He would sit cross-legged on the floor of the room, long hair tied to a rope that was secured to the ceiling. That way, if he drifted to sleep, the tug on his hair would awaken him and he would continue to play.

The big difference in classical Indian music, is that there is a tacit understanding among the people that the music is used for spiritual enlightenment. In fact, it is a compliment to Indian musicians if you fall asleep at their concerts. It just means their music has transported you into other realms.

Their musical scales (ragas) are meant to reflect the spectrum of emotions and related moods of various times of day. There is a saying, *Ranjayati it Ragah*—"That which colors the mind is a raga." The nine (actually ten) sentiments found in Indian music are:

1. **Shringara:** romantic, erotic sentiment, sometimes longing for an absent lover. It also represents the universal creative force.
2. **Hasya:** cosmic and humorous.
3. **Karuna:** pathetic, tearful, sad, expressing loneliness for a god or lover.

4. **Raudra:** fury or excited anger (thunderstorm)
5. **Veera:** heroism, bravery, majesty, glory, grandeur
6. **Bhayanaka:** frightful or fearful
7. **Vibhatsa:** disgustful
8. **Adbhuta:** wonderment, amazement, exhilaration
9. **Shanta:** peace, tranquility, relaxation
10. **Bhakti:** religious (a combination of *shanta*, *karuna*, and *adbhuta*)

(For more theory information, please refer to my book *Songs of the Earth*.)

*The trouble with music appreciation in
general is that people are taught
to have too much respect for music;
they should be taught to love it instead.*

—Igor Stravinsky

*Music is the gossamer gown and
conversation is the calico apron in the
wardrobe of human expressions.*

—Douglas Meador

❧ FOUR METHODS OF MUSIC EDUCATION ❧

DALCROZE (1865-1950)

Dalcroze founded a private school of music in New York and was a devoted teacher of the self-developed "eurhythmics" approach to music instruction. Eurhythmics strives to develop rhythmic responses to music through physical experience, body movement, and gymnastics.

"Music acts on the whole of the organism like a magic force which supresses the understanding and irresistability takes possession of the entire being. To insist on analyzing this force is to destroy its very essence." —Dalcroze

KODALY (1882-1967)

He lived and composed in Hungary. Kodaly taught music education by use of hand signals to learn the various musical notes and nonsense syllables to learn rhythm. (For example: *ta-ta-ti-ti-ta*; ta=quarter note, ti=eighth note). Popular in Europe, I personally find his method boring. He was an ardent collector of folk songs.

ORFF (1895-1982)

The German Orff-Schulwerk method believes that children can discover musical elements for themselves. Orff observed that children need to participate in music before learning its intellectual jargon. This is comparable to learning to talk before learning how to read and write. He believed that speech and movement are natural ways to teach music. Orff instruction uses chants, nursery rhymes, familiar words, and quotes.

For instrumentation, Orff classes use *gamelan* (xylophone-type) instruments. These are the most famous of the so-called Orff instruments. (These instruments are indigenous to Indonesian culture.) A unique feature of these instruments is their removable notes. This gives great success to beginning players. Orff instruction uses many other instruments such as recorders, triangles, drums, and wood blocks.

Orff employs body movements such as running, skipping, hopping, and jumping as well as speech patterns to reinforce rhythm. Early melodies introduced in instruction are based on what Orff perceives to be the universal children's melody: the falling third. This configuration is found in chants like: *Nanny, nanny, nanny goat*, and is notated thusly:

(falling minor third)

Children go on to learn a five-note (pentatonic) scale. They play solos and join in ensembles. Music is always played from memory, and kids don't learn notation until they are well versed in rhythmic and melodic patterns. In the first lessons, Orff instruction introduces clapping, patschen (slapping the knees), and stamping. The aim is for musical quality: to develop freedom of movement and awareness of tempo changes and dynamics.

Music washes away from the soul the dust of everyday life.

—Keynote

Music alone has the power of restoring us to ourselves.

—James Gibbons Huneker

Orff is most famous for his *Carmina Burana* symphony and operas *Der Mond* and *Die Kluge*, written in the 1930's.

Orff music "*...has an archaic flavor reminding one of trouvères, jongleurs, and Italian dances of the fourteenth century.*" (Arnold Walter)

SUZUKI (1898-   )

This musical training method from Japan has gained much popularity in the last thirty years and is a very successful approach to teaching violin, piano, and other instruments. Instruction now takes place on a variety of instruments. In its pure form, it begins at preschool level and requires the participation of the parent. Ear training is very important to the Suzuki method. Children listen repeatedly to the selections of music they are trying to learn. They gain a high level of technical proficiency through imitation before beginning to read musical notation.

At the time of this writing, Dr. Suzuki is 95 years young. He still arises at 4:30 in the morning. He spends his time listening to tapes of students that are sent to him by Suzuki teachers and lecturing teachers on the Suzuki method of music instruction.

RAVI SHANKAR ON MUSIC

Our tradition teaches us that sound is God—Nada Brahma. That is, musical sound and the musical experience are steps to the realization of the self. We view music as a kind of spiritual discipline that raises one's inner being to divine peacefulness and bliss. We are taught that one of the fundamental goals a Hindu works toward in his lifetime is a knowledge of the true meaning of the universe; its unchanging, eternal essence, and this is realized first by a complete knowledge of one's self and one's own nature. The highest aim of music is to reveal the essence of the universe it reflects, and the ragas are among the means by which this essence can be apprehended. Thus, through music, one can reach God.

Music is to make people happy.

—Willie "Bunk" Johnson

MOZART ON MUSIC

...All this fires my soul, and, provided I am not disturbed, my subject enlarges itself, becomes methodized and defined, and the whole, though it be long, stands almost complete and finished in my mind, so that I can survey, like a fine picture or a beautiful state, at a glance. Nor do I hear in my imagination the parts successively, but I hear them, as it were, all at once. What a delight this is I cannot tell! All this inventing, this producing takes place in a pleasingly lively dream. Still the actual hearing of the finished ensemble is, after all, the best. What has been thus produced, I do not easily forget, and this is perhaps the best gift I have my Divine maker to thank for.

LEONARD BERNSTEIN ON MUSIC

Q: Do you think it is possible that through conscious listening to music, you could reverse the order of the creative stage?

A: (Leonard) And get back to the state the composer was in when he wrote it, through the music you're hearing, is that what you're saying? I guess it's conceivable. That's a very mystical idea. I think that's more mystical than anything I've said.

🌿 MUSICAL GAMES 🌿

I have taught children's chorus off and on for years. Here are some of the best games I've found to teach musical ideas to kids. While some of these games adapt easily to one-on-one use, they are really a lot more fun to do in a group.

Rhythm Games

HAND RHYTHMS

Have children practice moving their hands to various rhythms. I usually start with whole notes (four beats), then dotted half notes (three beats), half note (two beats), quarter (one beat), and eighth note (half a beat). I sing a little song accompanied by guitar that goes like this (with the kids rolling their hands to whole notes.)

Rol-ling, (3-4) Rol-ling, (3-4) Rol-ling, (3-4) Rol-ling (3-4)

We sing three verses:
1. Rolling, 3, 4, rolling, 3, 4, rolling, 3, 4, rolling, 3, 4...
2. Whole note, 3, 4, whole note, 3, 4, whole note, 3, 4, whole note, 3, 4...
3. 1, 2, 3, 4, 1, 2, 3, 4, 1, 2, 3, 4, 1, 2, 3, 4,...

Other hand rhythms include: clapping, holding, snapping, folding, pulling, tying, scratching, pointing, squeezing, swinging, swimming, stretching, drooping, reaching, carrying, resting, sweeping, throwing, waving, and touching.

BEAN BAG RHYTHMS

Sit in a circle. Toss around one to four **bean bags**, depending on the size of the group. Instruct participants to toss the bag only on pre-determined beats (usually 1, 2, 3, or 4).

COPY-CAT RHYTHMS

Everyone sits or stands in a circle. To the beat of a **drum** or recorded music, begin a simple rhythmic movement. Suggestions are: clapping, head or knee patting, palm brushing, hand waving, finger waving, or head nodding. Do the movements all with a wide range of dynamics. Try to let everyone have a chance to lead the group. A similar African dance goes like this: each person dances into the middle of the circle, and everyone repeats the leader's movements as the person in the middle dances back into the circle.

The Chinese word for music is the same as that for "joy," "happiness," or "to rejoice."

—Bertha Ashton Gardner

Of all the cultural forms of entertainment, the most widespread and most spontaneous participation is gained through song.

—Earl Robinson

PATTERN RHYTHMS

Get two different colors of **crêpe paper** and cut them into two- or three-foot lengths. Everyone stands in a circle. Pass out the streamers, alternating colors. (You may add a third and fourth color if you want and make up your own patterns.) The leader in the middle raises alternating streamers, and the dancers respond accordingly.

DRUM MONKEYS

Again, sit in a circle. Give **drums** to two participants. One plays a simple rhythm pattern and the other copies it, then passes the drum on.

RHYTHM PATTERNS

The leader chants and acts out a pattern that the others repeat:

Clap, clap, clap, clap
Pat, pat, pat, pat
Stamp, stamp, stamp, stamp
Snap, snap, snap, snap

Vary the pattern with sequences such as: clap, rest, clap, rest…

LUMMI STICKS

Simple rhythmic sticks may be made from **wooden dowels** (1" diameter, 4' long). These traditional Maori instruments can be used in many ways. Partners sit opposite each other on the floor, and the whole group forms a long chain, holding two sticks at a vertical angle and tapping them on the floor. Variations include: clicking sticks with partner (straight on or cross-wise), tossing them back and forth, and clicking with person next to you. You may wish to chant as you use the sticks.

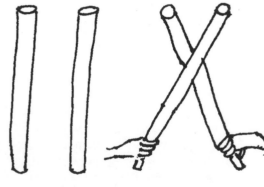

cross click   floor click   partner click

Conducting Games

TV TURN ON AND OFF

This is a good game to practice getting the kids to watch the conductor. Choose any song that everyone knows, and have the leader "turn on" the group. Everyone sings until the leader "turns off" the TV, at which point everyone must stop singing. I tell the kids it is a magic TV, and is like a VCR. When you turn the TV back on, it begins exactly where it left off. If someone isn't listening and the TV doesn't turn off, I bang on the imaginary TV and threaten to take it in to be fixed.

Variation: Everyone keeps singing the melody silently to themselves while the TV is turned off. The song then "turns on" to this new place in the song.

Singing Games

SYMPHONY OF SYLLABLES

Everyone except *It* (who leaves the room) sits in a circle. Choose a three-syllable word, such as *musical.* Then, go around the circle assigning each person, in order, a different syllable from the word *(mu-si-cal)* Then, pick a simple tune, like *Baa Baa Black Sheep*, and when *It* comes back into the room, everyone sings his or her syllable while *It* tries to guess what the word is (i.e., one group sings *"mu-mu-mu,"* the next, *"si-si-si,"* and the last, *"cal-cal-cal").*

OPERA DAY

Have an opera day. On the chosen day, try to sing all of your conversations. Be sure to use your best operatic voice.

MUSICAL TELEPHONE

Sit in a circle. The leader sings a short musical phrase to the person seated next to him. That person repeats it to the next person, and on around the circle until it reaches the leader. Has the melody changed?

LUCY LOCKET

Pick any simple nursery rhyme (*Lucy Locket* works well). The person designated as *It* (more than one person can be *It* if the group is large) leaves the room while another person hides an object. When *It* comes back into the room, she finds the hidden object because the children begin to sing loudly if she comes near the object, or softly if she is not near it. (This is the musical version of "hot and cold.")

MYSTERY SINGER

Choose one person to be *It. It* turns her back to the group, and the leader silently chooses one person to sing a phrase of a song in a disguised voice. *It* must decide who did the singing.

Man made music in the form of rhythms before he developed speech. Rhythm is life itself.

—Arthur Leslie Jacobs

Echo Patterns

The leader plays a simple tune on the piano and kids respond, either as a group or individually by singing back the melody.

La-La Songs

One person hums or sings "la" on a song of her choice. The others try to identify the song she is singing.

Missing-Word Songs

Try singing a familiar song and select important words to leave out. As the group sings, silence takes place for the chosen words.

High Jump Singing

Players race, one at a time to a chosen spot, pause, and sing their lowest and highest notes.

Instrument Games

The artist has no right to waste the time of his listener.

—Erik Satie

Orchestra

Select a piece of pre-recorded music to play for the children. Whisper the name of an instrument found in the selection to each child. Play the music, and when the child hears the instrument, he begins to pantomime the playing of that instrument.

Mystery Instrument Sounds

Gather several **instruments** and play each one for the group. Everyone but the leader closes their eyes, and the leader makes a sound on one of the instruments. The group has to guess which instrument is being played.

Follow the Sound

Again, have several **instruments** displayed. One or two people are *It*. They are blindfolded. Then, another person moves to any spot in the room and plays the instrument. *It* has to locate the sound. A variation of this game may be found as *Sound Detective* (pg. 10) in *Games for Learning* by Peggy Kaye.

Sound Orchestra

Draw or find **pictures** of various objects that make sounds and mount them on **stiff paper** (suggestions include radio, baby, ocean, bird, cat, whistle, bee). Choose one person to conduct. The other people choose a sound card to share. They all stand in a group. (If the group is small, each person can have a card.) When the conductor points to the group (or to the person), they begin making their sound. The conductor can make the group louder or softer, cut them off, or bring them back in.

ORCHESTRA TAG

Give each player a **card** with an **instrument picture** on it. Players sit in a circle, except *It*. *It* calls out an instrument name, and everyone holding that card exchanges places. *It* tries to grab a place in the circle. If she does, the one left becomes the new *It*.

Other Musical Games

PIANO-FORTE

Play or sing a short melody that varies from soft to loud. If the melody is soft, the kids hug themselves. If it is loud, they stretch out their hands.

MUSIC TO FEEL BY

Give the children three **pictures** with contrasting themes, such as a tiger, a river, or a sleeping baby. Play a piece of recorded music and have the children select the picture that seems to express the music.

STORY SOUNDS

Make up a story that has many sounds in it. As you talk about the sounds in the story, everyone makes the appropriate sound. Halloween stories lend themselves well to this format and can include sounds such as moaning ghosts, cackling or giggling witches, howling wind or cats.

SAME SOUNDS

On piano, guitar, or resonator bells, play one note. Then play other notes at random. It is the task of the group to raise their hands when they hear that note again. You may want to try melodies too.

MUSICAL CHAIRS VARIATIONS

> **Statues:** Each person freezes when the music stops.
> **Islands:** Everyone must land on a small mat or newspaper ("island") when the music stops.
> **Gods and Goddesses:** To stately music, try balancing books.

❧ MUSIC RESOURCES ❧

Rhythm Band, Inc.
PO Box 126
Fort Worth, TX 76101

Musical instruments for education include instructional materials, Orff Schulwerk Instruments, records, and games.

Music for Little People
Box 1460
Redway, CA 95560

Musical tapes, instruments, books, and toys.

❧ BOOKS ABOUT MUSIC ❧

PICTURE BOOKS

Max, the Music Maker by Miriam Stecher, 1980.
Miranda by Tricia Macmillan, 1985.
Ty's One-Man Band by Mildred P. Walter, 1980.

STORIES FOR AGES 8-14

Will Call It Georgie's Blues by Suzanne Newton, 1983.
Very Far Away from Anything Else by Ursula Le Guin, 1976.
You Can't Be Timid with a Trumpet by Betty Lou English, 1980.

NON-FICTION

Make Mine Music by Tom Walther, 1981.
Behind the Scenes of a Broadway Musical by Bill Powers, 1982.
Paul Robeson by Eloise Greenfield, 1975.

SONG BOOKS

Songs of the Earth by Anna Kealoha, 1989.
Rise Up Singing Peter Blood-Patterson, ed., 1988.
1,000 Jumbo, the Children's Songbook Carl Anderson, ed., 1975.

Letters

anguage Arts—educationese for sounds and letters—is one of my passions. Books are my sleeping pills, and rare is the night that I don't fall asleep with a book in my arms. We read to our children almost every night that we're home.

Language and math are the most important skills, of course. Yes and no. Reading and writing are only a *part* of life, *only part* of a rainbow-colored mind. An education is indeed narrow if reading and writing are thought to be the bones of knowledge.

Basic literary skills help us open the doors of knowledge more easily. Indeed, reading allows us to commune with the souls of great writers. We readers can read our way around town and order from menus. Marvelous skills! Yet people with vision or hearing challenges learn to adjust.

We can see the same analogy in music. Many famous musicians don't read a note of music, but are sublime musicians. Think about the genius of Ray Charles and Stevie Wonder! Think about famous Indian musicians like Ravi Shankar! (Talk about playing by ear!) Did you know that Indian music has existed for eons without notation? Notation for Indian music was only invented to teach Westerners! Musicians who do read musical notation can probably access more music in less time than musicians who play by ear. Yet in music, the ear is so much more important than the eye: the ear *is* the vehicle for music.

So don't worry if your child is not reading "up to grade-level." Trust them on this one! Children don't all get potty-trained at the same time and they don't all learn to read at the same time either. Parents and teachers seem more anxious about acquiring reading skills than about anything else. Kids can be obnoxious brats who steal, lie, and cheat, but if they read, we call them educated! If kids want to read badly enough, they'll teach themselves to do it eventually. Do trust them...and turn off the TV!

Reading is to the mind what exercise is to the body.

—Sir Richard Steele

❧ BRANCHES OF LANGUAGE ❦

The study of language covers four major areas:

- ✦ Reading
- ✦ Writing
- ✦ Listening
- ✦ Speaking

Of the four, most educators consider reading the most important skill with writing coming right in on its heels. We take listening and speaking skills for granted. However, if we *really* listened to each other and *really* said what we meant we would have world peace! We all need to remember good listening and speaking etiquette, *especially* the politicians!

(You know who you are!) Good listening and speaking skills involve the ear, the voice, the mind, and especially the heart.

English is one of the more difficult languages to learn. It has a more throaty, gutteral consonant sound than the Romance languages such as Spanish and French. However, there are a few tricks to learning how to read it.

My basic philosophy about reading is simple. Read to the kids a lot, and let them use any games or workbooks that spark their enthusiasm towards reading. Educators call this the whole language method, as opposed to the traditional phonics method. Phonics is based on the dissection of the language and whole language is based on the whole word, not letters in the words. (Does my bias show?) I limit most of my phonics instruction to songs. The following games, ideas, and information about Language Arts should be of interest and use to learners of all ages. For more excellent games about letters, please buy a copy of the excellent books by Peggy Kaye *Games for Reading* (NY: Pantheon Books, 1984, and *Games for Learning* (NY: Farrar, Straus, & Giroux, Inc., 1991.)

Not all the games or ideas will interest all kids (or grown-ups). Use only the games and ideas that your child finds interesting. Learning *will* take place if you force your children to do things they don't like, but it probably won't be the learning that you might expect.

Oh for a book and a shady nook, either indoor or out.

With the green leaves whispering overhead,

Or the street cries all about.

Where I may read all at my ease,

Both of the new and the old;

For a jolly good book whereon to look,

Is better to me than gold.

—John Wilson

🦋 LISTENING 🦋

Ear Training

Ears are the second most important sense organ we possess. For musicians, ear training is an essential subject. As a dedicated musician and children's choral director, I know how important it is to learn to listen.

Playing music, especially jamming with other musicians, requires a great deal of listening. Jams are great fun if the musicians are listening to each other and exchanging riffs. However, if all the players are wailing away and not listening to each other, the music can sound like a mass of tangled sounds. Listening to each musician in the group *very* carefully and only then adding your complimentary music to the overall sound is the key to ecstatic jamming. This is also true with listening and speaking: listen, then speak, and when you speak, speak from the heart.

When I'm playing piano, especially my beloved *Prelude in G* by Bach, I will find my mind wandering, creating a mental shopping list or something as equally mundane. It's easy to let my fingers wiggle over the keys and render a mechanical performance. To most people, this would sound just fine. However, to someone with trained ears, it would sound like mud. Listening to what you play (*really* listening) is the subtle nuance that distinguishes a person who performs the mechanical act of playing an instrument from the one who plays as a true artist. Musicians develop their art by constantly listening to what they play and adjusting their body actions in a very subtle way to achieve the desired sound. It sounds so simple, doesn't it?

The biggest problem of communication is the illusion that it has been achieved.

—Anonymous

Listening

Just as we *speak* more than we *write*, we *listen* more than we *read*. Intelligent listening requires a will to hear and to understand. Good listeners listen with their full attention. They look at the people that are speaking to them. They turn their whole bodies to the source of the sound. This helps them listen better, because sound waves travel outward like a ripple on a pond, and to "catch" a sound wave more clearly, you must face it. Thus, facing the source of the sound will enable you to hear it more clearly. Sound travels relatively slowly, a bit under 2,000 miles per hour. Light reaches us much more quickly than sound. (Interesting…is that what makes vision a more important sense than hearing?) However, hearing is also the last sense to shut down when we sleep and also when we die. (Hey, who figured *that* out?) It is also the first sense that we develop in utero.

When we make a conscious effort to hear the sounds around us, we give heed to the ever-present now. That is the secret of good listening: attending closely to what is happening now. This is the main point of the famous book *Be Here Now* by Ram Das.

When I was a child, I could always tell when my mom hadn't heard a word that I had said. She'd stand at the sink washing dishes or something. I'd tell her something and she'd mutter, "Mm hm." I *knew* she hadn't been listening to me. It was one of the things I

Go right on and listen as thou goest.

—Dante

vowed I wouldn't *ever* do to my own kids. Guess who stands at the sink washing dishes saying "Mm hm"? Face the music, momma!

Good Listeners

People who are excellent listeners have:
1. A **genuine interest** in other people.
2. **Patience** in hearing the viewpoints of others (no interrupting).
3. **Respect** for the opinions of others.
4. **Interest** in other points of view.
5. Interest in **broadening a viewpoint** rather than defending a position.

Listening Games

For more listening games, please see the section on Musical Games, page 46.

SIMON SAYS

This classic game involves close listening. The leader makes statements such as: "Simon says 'touch your toes,' " "Simon says 'pat your head.' " Players follow the leader's instructions. She eventually gives a direction omitting "Simon says." Then, players must *not* follow the directions.

TELEPHONE

This is another classic listening game.

Players form a circle. The first player whispers a sentence to her neighbor, such as *"I love to eat tamales with hot sauce and avocadoes."* The neighbor then whispers what he heard to the next player and so on. If the neighbor doesn't understand the sentence, he may say, "Telephone." and the player repeats the sentence again. The final player repeats the sentence out loud. It's fun to re-trace the sentence, getting each person's version of what they *thought* they heard.

Variation: Use Telephone to learn math equations, history facts, or other information. Use math equations such as: $4 \times 3 = 10 + 2$.

RED LIGHT, GREEN LIGHT

Yet another classic game. Did you know you were learning good listening skills when you played it?

The person who is *It* stands about 20 feet away from the rest of the players, who stand in a line. When *It* calls out, *"Green Light!"*, he turns his back to the group and players move towards him. However, when he calls out, *"Red Light!"*, and turns to face the group, any player that is caught moving must go back to the starting line. First player to reach *It* and tag him, becomes the next *It*.

❧ SPEAKING ❦

What Is Speaking?

The act of speaking includes communication, conversation, reading out loud, storytelling, acting, public speaking, debating, and forum discussion. Children learn to speak automatically by imitating the people around them. They will pick up the dialect and speech habits of their role models (usually Mom and Dad). Mom and Dad won't even teach them to speak: they'll just learn how by listening. Amazing.

Communication means sharing information. Sometimes it's difficult to say what we mean, and we find that people misunderstand us or that we are unable to communicate clearly. Disasters have arisen from poor communication. There are four steps in all communication (which includes speech, letters, radio, TV, and computers):

1. A speaker must **deliver** the message.
2. The listener must **receive** the message.
3. The listener must **interpret** the message.
4. Finally, the listener must **accept** the message and act upon it.

Speech difficulties include lisping, stuttering, and shyness. Children with these challenges can possibly be helped by working with speech therapists. Even people with no sense of hearing can learn how to talk.

Witty Conversation

The ability to be an interesting and engaging conversationalist is an important skill to develop. The following qualities help make a good speaker:

✦ A good speaker has a **variety of interests**. The person who has absorbed ideas from other people, books, and keen observation has a solid foundation for interesting conversations.

✦ **Naturalness** in speaking originates from organizing thoughts in the mind *before* they come out of the mouth. In my family I am famous for saying things like, *"Get the thing-a-ma-jig off the what-cha ma call it."* Great conversationalist, huh? Listen to your mind before you speak it.

✦ Also important in good conversation is **sincerity** and **warmth.** Being sincere, *truly* sincere, not the "read my lips" sincerity of politicians, will help many a speaker when words falter. Intention is more important than content.

✦ Be sure to **acknowledge** your listeners when you talk. Look them in the eye, or at least nod in their direction. By looking someone in the eyes, you can be 90% sure you have your listener's attention. The eyes, as you know, are the mirror of the soul. This is why good actors and public speakers look out at their audiences, even if they're not looking at individuals in the crowd, they are seeking to engage the audience's attention by looking in their direction.

> *Do not be arrogant because of your knowledge, but confer with the ignorant man as with the learned...Good speech is more hidden than malachite, yet it is found in the possession of women slaves at the millstones.*
>
> *—Ptahhotpe (24th century B.C.)*

> *Silence seldom doth harm.*
>
> *—Anonymous*

✦ Another quality that is an asset to speakers is **humor**. We all like to be amused or entertained as well as informed. Humor helps lighten awkward situations. A witty conversationalist is a sparkling gem among dull stones.

✦ A person's **voice quality** will also enhance conversation. A pleasant speaking voice is a powerful tool. *You can get more flies from honey than vinegar* is a wonderful maxim to remember and apply next time you want your kids to mop the floor. (However, I've always wondered why people would want to attract flies to them anyhow...) A pleasant voice is especially important in phone conversations.

✦ Voice **inflection** is also important. It is a quality that is so pronounced and so easy to understand, yet so paradoxically subtle. For example, when someone in my family is talking on the phone, I can usually tell the sex and status of the person they are talking to (sometimes down to pin-pointing the exact person) based solely on voice inflections. Once my friend Merryl was visiting. Her then-mate Steve called on the phone, and when I answered, because of the way I said *hello,* he thought I was Merryl, and because of the way he talked to me, *I* thought he was my mate Richard. We talked quite a while before realizing our mistake.

✦ The invisible code of **body language**, including gestures of face (eyes, eyebrows, and mouth), hands, arms and other body parts, adds emphasis to what we say.

✦ **Semantics** is the study of the meaning of words. Communication is often blocked because different people give different meanings to the same messages based on semantical interpretation. It is the job of a good speaker to adjust his language to fit the background of the person or group to whom he is talking.

✦ Clear **articulation, enunciation,** and **pronunciation** are other areas of importance. Unfortunately for us, the English language is a hard language to speak correctly. Sadly, English has no fixed rules of pronunciation like other languages. However, English is eloquent and we have a large selection of words to vary our expressions.

✦ Good speakers have **large, colorful vocabularies**. Reading (especially the dictionary) is one of the best ways to build a strong vocabulary. (I once got as far as *Au* in an unabridged dictionary. Someday I'll get to *B*... What I learned from this dictionary study is that 75 to 85% of words in the dictionary are scientific or other technical terms.)

Vocabulary is always changing and growing. In the ancient Anglo-Saxon language, which is the root of English, there are approximately 50,000 words. No one knows the exact number of words there are in modern English, but it is probably safe to say there are at least 600,000 words. In addition, our *active* (speaking) vocabularies (on the average of 10,000 words) are often smaller than our *passive* (reading and listening) vocabularies, which is three to four times the size of our active vocabulary. Vocabulary range displays culture, education, and general intelligence. A five-year-old has a vocabulary of 3,000 to 4,000 words, while a college graduate's vocabulary may include 10,000 to 30,000 words.

✦ Finally, a good speaker is always a **good listener** and **respectful** towards his audience. My dad is one of the smartest people I know. He's not really *all* that quiet, but if you ask him why he doesn't talk much, he'll tell you that by listening, he knows what he knows *and* what the other person knows.

Public Speaking

Let thy speech be short, comprehending much in few words.

—Ecclesiaticus 32:8

I usually think of public speaking in terms of formally prepared speeches given in front of large audiences, but the *real* definition of public speaking is any time you speak in a group of three or more. The people who can speak effectively often become leaders of the group. These people present information clearly. They are effective in getting groups to agree upon or change their opinions about issues and ideas.

According to ancient Greek traditions, an orator is a skillful speaker who uses a definite set of rules. The father of oratory is the Greek scholar Corax, who lived in 460 BC. His rules of speech are still valuable to modern speakers. According to Corax, the five parts of a good speech consist of:

1) *proem* (introduction)
2) narrative
3) arguments
4) subsidiary remarks
5) summary

Modern speakers should consider these four main points:

1. **Subject**: Sources include direct and indirect experience. Direct experiences will usually provide the speaker with a more effective speech, and, as you know, there is no substitute for direct experience. The three types of speech subjects are: *information, persuasion* (the only type of speech a politician gives), and *entertainment*.

2. **Audience**: Speakers need to gear their speeches to their audiences. People only listen to speakers if they think her ideas will benefit them in some way, so it is up to the speaker to capture the attention of the audience.

The limits of my language stand for the limits of my world.

—Ludwig Wittgenstein

3. **Personality of the speaker:** This is probably the most important factor in influencing audiences. Speakers should strive to walk gracefully, stand erect, and make eye contact with the audience. They should talk directly to the members of the audience and speak in a firm, clear voice. To avoid monotonous speeches, they should vary the pitch and volume of their voices.

4. The **occasion**: Be sensitive to the situation, for example cracking jokes at a memorial service is probably inappropriate.

Preparing a Speech

1. Pick your **purpose** and type of speech (informative, persuasive, or entertaining).
2. The **Introduction** of the speech usually has two parts: the **opening**, which captures the attention and interest of the audience, and the **statement of purpose** that tells the audience exactly what the speaker intends to do in his speech.
3. The **body** of the speech consists of the **main idea** and **supporting materials**. In informative speeches, the main idea should answer the questions *who?, what?, where?, when?, why?,* and *how?* In a persuasive speech, the main ideas will be the reasons for your beliefs or ideas. For supporting materials choose *descriptions, comparisons, examples, narrations, testimonies, statistics,* and *visual aids* such as charts, graphs, demonstrations, slides, maps, videos, samples, or working models that help illustrate your main idea.
4. The **conclusion** of the speech varies with the type of speech being presented. In *informative* speeches, the conclusion should include a summary of the main ideas and purpose. *Persuasive* speeches should combine a summary with a final appeal, and *entertaining* speeches can end any way they please, usually with a joke.
5. An **outline** of the speech may be prepared by the speaker and used when the speech is given, or the speaker may use the outline as a basis to write a complete speech. It is usually easier for a beginning speaker to work from a written speech, while veteran speakers may prefer the freedom of an outline. A speech delivered from an outline is thought of as *extempore*, not to be confused with *impromptu* speeches that are made on the fly (the kind most of us give).

Choral Speaking

In ancient Greek drama, passages of poetry or prose were often recited by a group of speakers. These speaking parts were orchestrated like a piece of music. The practice has made a comeback in rap music.

Storytelling

Storytelling speaks to us of ancient days, crackling fires and star-lit nights. All of ancient history comes to us in the form of stories. Storytelling offers us priceless experiences: glimpses of ancient, fantasy, and new worlds. TV and movies don't even come close! Besides, storytelling is fun. It helps people gain confidence in public speaking. To make things interesting for other people is an important part of being socially accepted, and storytelling can help us become interesting people in a very real way. Storytelling also demands good listening, so storytelling can help improve listening skills. Organize a **Storytelling Day** and let kids (and adults) prepare stories to tell.

TIPS FOR STORYTELLERS:

- ✦ Read several stories before you select one to tell.
- ✦ Read your story through several times.
- ✦ Without looking at the book, try to visualize the main incidents of the story.
- ✦ Use a tape recorder to tape your story two or three times in a row and listen to the tape several times.
- ✦ Step into your characters' lives, empathize, and feel as if you are them.
- ✦ Make a pictorial outline of your story. (Stick figures are fine.) Include dialogue in balloons above the character's heads.
- ✦ Define the beginning, middle, and end of the story.
- ✦ Use your own words to tell the story, but consider memorizing the first and last lines of the story so that you can begin and end with confidence.
- ✦ Look for places in the story to invite audience participation.
- ✦ Practice your story in front of a mirror, or tell your story to an imaginary audience: pets, trees, or stuffed animals.
- ✦ When telling your story, if a certain part escapes you *improvise!* Don't let your audience feel as if you are at a loss for words. Fool them!

Voice

- ✦ The voice is the storyteller's most important tool. Below are ideas on how to improve your storytelling techniques. Storytelling, public speaking, acting, and musical performance will all benefit from practicing the techniques below.

Expression

- ✦ Practice saying, "I lost my candy bar" ten times, changing your voice to reflect: sadness, gladness, frustration, fury, pomposity, nervousness, sleepiness, rudeness, belligerence, and laziness.
- ✦ Count to 10 as: 1) a parent telling your kid to do chores before the count of 10; 2) a toddler just learning to count; 3) a referee for a boxing match; 4) from ten-to-one announcing the blast-off of a rocket ship; 5) a kid counting cars on the road.

Feeling and Mood

- ✦ Say the following words, using the feeling or mood of the word as you say it: *blast-off, sleep, splash, gurgle, roar, splatter, bang, crackle, buzz, clap, grunt, bubble, sniffle, sneeze, coo,* or *bang.*

Pitch

- ✦ Pitch in the voice (highness and lowness) can indicate different emotions and can portray different characters in the story. Practice with *The Three Bears* (Papa, Mama, and Baby). Say "Someone has been eating my porridge" in each character's voice.

The speech of man is like embroidered tapestries, since like them this too has to be extended in order to display its patterns, but when it is rolled up it conceals and distorts them.

—*Themistocles*

Mend your speech a little, lest you may mar your fortunes.

—*Shakespeare*

Volume

+ Focus on the back row of listeners. Speak to the corner of the back wall and the ceiling.
+ Breathe from the diaphragm. (**Exercise:** Lie on the floor on your back. Place a book on your diaphragm, just above your waistline. Watch the book slowly rise and fall.)

Tempo and Rate

+ Say "I just found a million dollars." 1) quickly to show excitement; 2) normally to show indifference; 3) slowly to show disappointment.
+ Pause at appropriate places. ("There was a small knock at the door. He opened it, and there stood (pause) a tiny elf.")

Word Emphasis

+ Completely change the meaning of the following sentence by emphasizing a new word each time: *Will* Michael give Rachel the ring? Will *Michael* give Rachel the ring?

Facial Expressions

+ Try to say "I'd love to come to your party" in a pleasant voice with a sad expression on your face. Then reverse it. Walk across the room with a happy look on your face and a sad body. Reverse it.

Gestures and Movements

+ Get everyone to stand in a circle. "Throw" an invisible object to one person (such as a tarantula, china cup, feather, elephant, or balloon). Players must throw and catch the objects using appropriate body and facial movements.
+ Everyone walks in a circle in the following manner: 1) you are coming in from play and have to do all your chores; 2) walking through four feet of snow; 3) barefoot through molasses; 4) with your left foot in a cast; 5) on hot sand.

Poise and Presence

+ Face your audience, smile, and make eye contact with them. Speak up! Enunciate your words.

Introduction

+ Think about your introduction. You may wish to say your name, the title of the story, country of the story's origin, or the author's name.

Performance

+ Everyone feels nervous when performing. When you feel nervous, remember that it's a good sign: it means that you care about what you're doing. Nervousness (adrenaline) is the body's way of dealing with new and exciting situations. Use this energy to become more dynamic and infuse life into your story. The confidence of knowing your material well will help override feelings of nervousness. Remember: replace self-consciousness with self-confidence.

Stories for Storytelling

Use the whole story or chapters from a story for storytelling purposes.

MYTHS

Myths fall into three major categories:

1) MYTHS take place in a timeless past and attempt to explain the mysteries of life. Myths are found in all societies, the most famous in western societies coming from Greek, Roman, and Norse cultures.

2) FOLKTALES are narratives set in time, usually concerned with more social than religious ideas. Good folktales include: *Brer Rabbit* folktales, *The Wind in the Willows, Dr. Doolittle, How the Ox Star Fell from Heaven, The Woodcutter's Mitten, Such a Noise!, Strega Nona*, and *One Fine Day*.

3) LEGENDS recount and embellish the sagas of heroes, real or imaginary. Fine storytelling legends include: *Paul Bunyan, The Legend of the Bluebonnet: An Old Tale of Texas, The Legend of the Indian Paintbrush, The Mud Pony: A Traditional Skidi Pawnee Tale, John Henry*, or *The King's Bride*.

> *Speech is civilization itself.*
> *The words, even the most contradictory word, preserves contact—it is silence which isolates.*
>
> *—Thomas Mann*

FAIRY TALES

Fairy tales are all about the land of make-believe. Some stories that are good for storytelling include: *The Crane Maiden, The Fool and the Fish, The Little Match Girl, Puss in Boots,* and *The Snow Child*. (All of Hans Christian Anderson's fairy tales are excellent material.)

CONTEMPORARY CHILDREN'S LITERATURE

The Journey Home, Lily and the Bears, Little Beaver and the Echo, The True Story of the Three Little Pigs, Wilfrid Gordon McDonald Partridge, Jumanji.

Speaking Games

ONE MINUTE

Choose a topic: anything from "Why men wear ties" to "How many kinds of fairies live in your garden?" to "What in the World is going on now?" Each person speaks for one minute, and can make up anything, as long as she sticks to the subject, doesn't repeat herself, or pause too long.

TONGUE TWISTERS

Take turns repeating tongue twisters. Try making some up, too.

❦ READING ❧

Children and Reading

Reading specialists have their own little world of semantics, syntax, and phonographemics. Kids have their own little worlds too, and it does *not* have these words in it! Kids learn to read from worlds that are print-rich: environments that are full of books, magazines, trips to the library, story times, and such. Leave your phonographemes at home, o ye of little faith! All children learn to talk and walk without formal instruction, right? I have seen a kindergarten child read at a 4th grade level, and 7th graders who read at 4th grade levels. (Our oldest read at three-and-a-half and the next one read at seven.) Just because children read early doesn't mean they do it better! Some children begin to read at three, some at ten. I also know a person who didn't learn to read until age 30! Woodrow Wilson didn't read until age eleven.

For some, becoming a reader will take two or three years, while others will seemingly "get it" overnight. Don't worry! Leave the kids alone, give them lots of books to look at, turn off the TV, and kids will eventually learn how to read all on their own. Be patient. Help, however well intended, that comes too fast or with impatience can cause a child to become anxious about reading. Don't forget to remind kids that reading is its own reward.

A bit of phonics is okay, but too much emphasis on phonics confuses kids. What are "hard" and "soft" sounds or "short" and "long" sounds to kids? The most kids need to know about phonics is first, that the vowels are special, second, that each of the vowels, and some of the consonants have more than one sound, and third, that some consonants come together in blends to make unique sounds too. (Well, at least 70 or so sounds and 26 letters is less than Chinese!)

Remember, reading is about communicating through writing, and just because a child can read doesn't mean he understands what he reads. Getting the *meaning* from the print is what reading is all about.

Raising Readers

+ Have **lots of books** in the home. Make sure kids can reach the books by themselves. Five hundred books is not too many. You can find great deals on used books at flea markets, garage sales, and thrift shops.

+ Get **library cards** for everyone in the family and use them. I used to think I checked out a lot of books, but one family I know has been known to check out up to 90 books at a time! They have a special place to keep their books (you can use baskets, boxes, or cloth bags). They also get a computer print-out of their transactions to help them return books on time. Now they're thinking of getting a card for their two-year-old so they can check out even more books!

Books to the ceiling, books to the sky.
My piles of books are a mile high.
How I love them!
How I need them! I'll have a long beard by the time I read them.

—Arnold Lobel

I cannot live without books.

—Thomas Jefferson

✦ Read **environmental print** wherever you go. Read street signs, store signs, and cereal boxes. *Stop* and *Exit* are two examples of environmental print that kids can learn to read very early. Language is everywhere—make the most of it where you find it! One game our son made up when he was four is **road-sign reading**. He asks his dad to read the signs on one side of the road, and I read the signs on the other side, even the numbers on mailboxes!

✦ Make **bedtime stories** a regular routine. Make sure to honor requests for familiar stories, even if you have to read the same one twenty times. Children love the familiar and feel confident with routine.

✦ While reading, **trace under words** with your finger as you read so the children can follow along. Most of us learn to read by this "bouncing ball" method.

✦ Remember to **read poetry**, especially nursery rhymes, to the very young.

✦ **Be a reader yourself.** Talk about what you are reading.

✦ **Give books as gifts.** They'll last a lifetime.

✦ **Keep books in the car** and bring them with you when you travel.

✦ **Treasure books.** They're wonderful allies, better than gold or candy.

✦ Put a **frieze of alphabet card-letters** (I like the *Flower Fairies* series by Cicely M. Barker) on the wall. Better yet, make your own friezes, and illustrate them with pictures that begin with each letter.

✦ Get **magnetic alphabet letters** for your fridge.

✦ Make **squiggle art** out of letters, both upper and lower case, cursive and printed. Take any letter, squint your eyes, and turn each letter into a picture. For example, capital A could be a hat or a tipi. (That's 104 symbols we need to learn, almost as many as in Chinese!)

Reading Out Loud

✦ **Be expressive.** Pretend you're acting. Change your voice (pitch and quality) when reading different characters' voices in the story. Read with accents. Raise and lower the pitch of your voice.

✦ **Create a mood for reading.** We like to read at night, just before bedtime, all snuggled in bed when everyone is freshly bathed and in pajamas.

✦ **Be patient and answer questions**. Remember questions mean that you've gotten your child's curiosity aroused.

✦ **Read slowly.** Don't rush, or it will be hard for your listeners to follow.

✦ **Read a variety of books.** If the text is boring or too advanced for your children, just look at the pictures in the books. We "read" quite a few books this way.

✦ **Enjoy yourself.** It's not just reading to kids that makes the difference, it's enjoying the books with them and reflecting on their form and content.

Reading Games

WORD SAUSAGES

Draw eleven (or so) linked circles as shown. Write a word in the first circle. Next, have your child write (or you do it for her) the first word that comes to mind in the next circle. When you complete the links, have your child read the words back to you. (Adapted from Word Link from *Games for Learning* by Peggy Kaye, ©1991.)

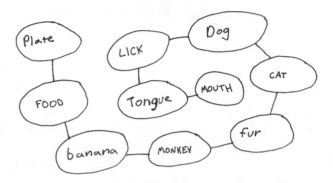

Variation: (from John Holt *What Do I Do Monday,* Holt Associates 1994.) Make up a list of 10-20 words and read a word every five seconds. Have the other people write down the first word that comes to mind.

FEEL THE WORDS

This game helps children to read out loud with expression.

Ask your child to say "I'm so sad" in a happy voice. Can you say "Is that a dangerous banana?" in a scared voice? A thrilled voice? A snobbish voice? Make up your own sentences and feelings to go with them. Also repeat this sentence: "I don't care what you say." emphasizing a different word in the sentence each time you say it. (Adapted from Feel the Words in *Games for Learning* by Peggy Kaye, ©1991.)

ALPHABET CHAIN

Cut twenty-six 3"x 5" index cards in half to make fifty-two cards. Write all the letters of the alphabet on the cards two times. (That is, each letter should be written twice.) Shuffle the cards and deal six to each player. The rest go in a pile in the middle, facing down, top card being turned over and placed next to the pile. Play like rummy: the object is to get three letters in a row. (Younger children might want to have an alphabet sequence in front of them.) When it is your turn, you may either pick the turned up card or one from the top of the pile. You must discard after each turn. Play until everyone wins.

SPECIAL WORDS

1. Ask your child to pick a special word.
2. Write it down on an **index card**. As you write, sound out the letters of the word.

3. Ask the child to read the word.

4. Decorate the card with **crayons** or **felt tip markers**. (You may or may not want to draw a picture on the card. I personally feel it is okay to use visual picture cues to learn to read.)

5. The child may trace the word on the bottom half of the card.

6. Make a special envelope out of construction paper and keep the cards in the envelope.

7. Add one or two words to the envelope each day.

8. After you have several cards, begin reviewing them.

9. Have your child dictate a short story to you using the special word at least twice. See if he can pick out the special word in the story.

This game I first found in Sylvia Ashton-Warner's *Teacher* and is also a combination of two of Peggy Kaye's games in *Games for Reading*: Gift Words, and Word Collection Box.

All that mankind has done, thought, gained or been: it is lying as in magic preservation in the pages of books.

—Thomas Carlyle

READING HOPSCOTCH

On a large piece of **cardboard** or outside on the sidewalk, draw a playing field like the one shown. Have your child jump to the various letters, using the following types of dialogue:

> *Jump to the letter that makes the* ah *sound.*
> *Jump to the first letter in dog.*
> *Jump to the last letter in dog.*

Later, you can add blends:

> *Jump to the last sound in lump.*
> *Jump to the beginning sound in three.*
> *Jump to the beginning sound in pretty.*

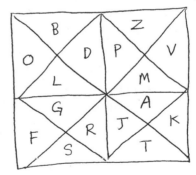

(Adapted from Rabbit Sounds from *Games for Reading* by Peggy Kaye, © 1984.)

SOUNDS AND TREATS

Put out three small **cups** and give your child some **raisins** or **peanuts**. Her job is to put the raisins or nuts in the cups that are labeled *beginning, middle,* and *end*. Ask questions such as:

> *Where is the* l *sound in jelly?*
> *Where is the* m *sound in mother?*

Where is the s sound in stop?
Where is the p sound in surprise?

At the end of the game, the child gets to eat the raisins or peanuts.

(Adapted from Where's the Sound in *Games for Reading* by Peggy Kaye, ©1984, and First Sound, Last Sound in *Games for Learning* by Peggy Kaye, ©1991.)

Jigsaw Sentences

While studying in England, my friend Jim Inciardi learned this game, which he attributes to the Bradley (language experience) Method. Peggy Kaye introduces her own version of this game in her book *Games for Reading*.

Use **paper, pen**, and **scissors** to cut up sentences that you and your child create. Have the child reconstruct the sentences. Sentences don't have to be alliterative, (words beginning with the same sound) but it can be fun if they are.

The girl ate six eggs at breakfast.
The alligator saw a whale on a bicycle.
My mother likes trains.
Ten vultures came to lunch.
The powerful people piling peas.
My mommy makes magic muffins.
The wild, wailing wind blows around the willow tree.
My son Josh jumps for joy.
Sarah sat in the sunlight.
Kelly keeps kangaroos in the kitchen.
Manzanitas make marvelous mugs.
Riya reaches for raisins.

ECHOIC READING

Read a section of print out loud and have your child read it back to you. Using this method, you provide proper word attack, fluency, and expression for your child to repeat.

READER'S THEATER

Dramatize your favorite stories. Activities may include:

- ✦ Creating a **script**, making up **dialogue.**
- ✦ **Character** selection (focusing on the feelings and expressions of the characters).
- ✦ **Narrator** selection (can describe setting, present the scene, or introduce the background of the story).
- ✦ Selecting simple **props** for the dramatization.
- ✦ **Performance** of piece for family and friends, at the local retirement home…

CHORAL READING

Choral reading is like choral singing. Instead of singing a song together, read the same words together at the same time. This is a good activity for readers who need to build sight-word vocabulary and reading confidence.

READING POETRY

Children love poetry, and most children can recite a few nursery rhymes out loud at an early age. Shel Silverstein's *Where the Sidewalk Ends* is a contemporary book of poetry that is fun to read out loud. For those inclined, maybe even improvise a melody too. Reading out loud, as I have mentioned, is a very important part of the reading process.

NAMES

Family names are good beginning reading material. On one half of an **index card**, write the names of important family members, neighbors, pets, and (if you are so inclined) cars. Our best car name has to be *Shirley Rutabaga Duck Motor Mini Bus Maxi Van.*

> *There is no accident in our choice of reading. All our sources are related.*
>
> *—François Mauriac*

Music, Sounds, and Letters

Vowels are letters that make sounds that are "open." When making the sounds of *a, e, i, o,* and *u,* the throat remains open in the shape of a circle. Music can be a great help in understanding those pesky vowel sounds.

Try this: right now say, *"A-e-i-o-u."* Notice that you barely even move your lips. Singers recognize that the *open* throat used in making vowel sounds makes a more "pure" sound than the *closed* throat that we use when making consonant sounds. When we sing, the only sounds we hold on to are vowel sounds. Try singing your name using long, sustained notes. You held the sound of the vowels, right? Now try singing your name holding consonant sounds. Try the dog's name. Sounds interesting, huh? In fact, Sanskrit, Hebrew and Arabic are written without vowels: diacritical marks take their place. Think of vowels as the singing letters.

Consonants are made using the lips, teeth, and tongue. Say a few *b*'s, *p*'s, *k*'s or *t*'s (the noisiest letters), your mouth explodes with movement and air. Consonants are the bread of words, and vowels are the peanut butter: the bread shapes the sandwich, but the peanut butter holds the bread together. All consonant sounds, except *h* (wouldn't you know there'd be one exception?) use the lips, teeth, tongue, and roof of the mouth to make their sounds.

Almost everybody learns the letters of the alphabet by memorizing and singing the alphabet song. This is one of the first introductions children have to the alphabet, and it is done with music.

Repetition is essential in learning new concepts. By using the natural hypnotic effect of music as a learning vehicle, the tedium that is associated with repetition is eliminated. Children tend to learn to read words more quickly and easily when those words are related to large muscle activity, aesthetic experience, and rhymes.

Music can also provide practice in decoding skills, *(darn, that educationese just slipped in there!)* it can help build sight and oral vocabulary, and improve the rate of comprehension:

> *"When (the child's) beginning reading vocabulary is introduced through music, the child's psychological involvement in the experience is intensified. When the child sings words, the rhythm and phrasing of the text emerge with greater clarity than when the words are spoken."* (M. Kuhmarker)

Singing enhances reading skills because language is a key element of singing. Melodies are composed to complement the meaning of the words, *and* to complement the natural rhythms and accents of language.

Some Music and Letter-Learning Ideas

✦ Make a **songbook** of your families' favorite songs and sing along with them. Pick songs that the kids already know. These familiar tunes will best enhance reading skills.

✦ **Pantomime** your favorite songs by singing the words while acting out the meaning.

✦ Start or join a **children's chorus** or a **family chorus.** Sing together at least two times a month.

✦ Make a **giant (2' x 3') songbook.** Put in easy-to-sing songs with simple repetitive word and sounds. Two of my favorites are the Indigenous songs *Yana Wana Yana* and *Hey Hungawa.* (You will find these songs and many others in my book *Songs of the Earth.*)

✦ **Make up musical jingles** or songs to help children remember basic phonic and grammar rules. If a melody is attached to these concepts it will increase the likelihood that children will remember these concepts.

Learning to Read with Music

The following songs teach reading through both vowel and consonant awareness (phonics) as well as through the whole language (whole word) method. **Sargham** (the words that are used in the second part of the song below) are the names of musical notes in India, which corresponds to *solfège* (do-re-mi) in Western music. The names of the notes in the Indian scale are: SA, RE, GA, MA, PA, DHA, NI, and SA.

Be sure to trace underneath the words of the song as you sing it with your child. Feel free to make up your own melodies, get out the pots and pans, and march or dance around the room.

SARGHAM-VOWEL SONG

A - E - I - E - I - E, A - E - I - O - U.
A - E - I - E - I - E, A - E - I - O - U.
SA - PA - MA - PA - MA - PA,
SA - PA - MA - GA - SA.
SA - PA - MA - PA - MA - PA,
SA - PA - MA - GA - SA.

APPLES AND BANANAS

For each verse, substitute new vowel sound in the words *ate, apples* and *bananas.*

1. I like to eat, eat, eat, apples and bananas
   I like to eat, eat, eat, apples and bananas.
2. ate   3. eat   4. ite   5. ote   6. ute (i.e., *upples and bununus.*)

Letters That Never Change

Great literature, past or present, is the expression of great knowledge of the human heart.
—Edith Hamilton

English actually has nineteen letters whose sounds are constant *if* they are followed by a vowel. (Ah, well, we're stuck with this exceptions-to-the-rule language for right now!) But never fear, there's actually only about 26 "regular" blends, six "special" sounds, and six "odd" sounds, making a total of (including the fearsome long-and-short vowel sounds) around 70 or so sounds!

The following letters always have the same sound when followed by a vowel:

✦ *b, d, k, p, t* (the most explosive sounds)
✦ *j, s, v, z* (next loudest)
✦ *f, h, r, w, x, y* (next)
✦ *l, m, & n* (the "softest" consonants)

Here are examples of songs you can make up about these sounds. There is one song from each category: Make up your own melodies or use the ones from my tape and booklet, *The Beetle Bug Band Sings Letter Loving Songs.*

BOOM-BOOM SONG

1. The Beetle Bug bangs on bongos.
   The Beetle Bug bangs on bells.
   The Beetle Bug bangs on bagpipes.

(Chorus)
   But the big baboon goes, "Boom-boom-boom-boom!"
   But the big baboon goes, "Boom-boom-boom-boom!"
   ...at the beach.

2. The Beetle Bug bangs on banjos.
   The Beetle Bug bangs on bark.
   The Beetle Bug bangs on buckets.

(Chorus)
   But the big baboon goes, "Boom, boom, boom boom!"
   But the big baboon goes, "Boom, boom, boom boom!"
   ...at the beach.

SIX SEALS ON THE SEA

1. Six seals on the sea, singing on saxophones.
   Six seals on the sea, singing on saxophones.

(Chorus)
   Silly seals, s - s - s - s - s,
   Silly seals, s - s - s - s - s.
   Silly seals!

2. Six seals on the sea, sewing silk socks.
   Six seals on the sea, sewing silk socks.

3. Six seals on the sea, serving soup and sandwich.
   Six seals on the sea, serving soup and sandwich.

THE HIPPOPOTAMUS

1. The hippopotamus has a house,
   The hippopotamus has a house,
   The hippopotamus has a house,
   The hen has a hold on a hammer.

2. The hippopotamus has a house,
   The hippopotamus has a house,
   The hippopotamus has a house,
   The horse has a hold on a horn.

3. The hippopotamus has a house,
   The hippopotamus has a house,
   The hippopotamus has a house,
   The hamster has a hold on a hat.

LAKE LIZARDS LIKE LEAPFROG

1. Lake lizards like leapfrog in the library,
Lake lizards like leapfrog in the lagoon,
Lake lizards like leapfrog on the leafy logs,
Lake lizards like to lick.

(Chorus)
La, la, la, la, la, la,
La, la, la, la, la, la…
La, la, la, la, la, la,
La, la, la, la, la, la!

2. Leprechauns lick lollipops in the library,
Leprechauns lick lollipops in the lagoon,
Leprechauns lick lollipops on the leafy logs.
Lake lizards like to lick.

Two Letters: Each Has Two Sounds

Wouldn't you know there are two letters (*c* and *g*) that can't make up their mind what to sound like? And one of them, letter *c* takes its sound from two other letters: *k* and *s!* Usually letter *g* is good and makes its own sound, but sometimes it likes to sound like letter *j*.

Here is a song that uses the letter *g*'s "*j*" (juh) sound.

GENTLE GENESSA

Gentle Genessa, the genuine gypsy is such a gem.
Gentle Genessa, the genuine gypsy is such a gem.
She gallops…on a giant giraffe, she gallops…on a giant giraffe.
Gentle Genessa, the genuine gypsy is such a gem.
Gentle Genessa, the genuine gypsy is such a gem.
She's a gymnast…with genious feet, she's a gymnast…with genius feet!

Letters That Make Blends

Some words begin with two or three consonants and are called **blends**.

✦ Ten of the blends consist of blending *b, c, f, g*, and *p* with either *l* or *r*. (*Bl, br, cl, cr, fl, fr, gl, gr, pl*, and *pr*.)

✦ *D* only blends with *r* (*dr*), and

✦ *T* blends with *r and w* (*tr* and *tw*.)

✦ *S* is another question! *S* has nine blends with one other letter, (*sc, sk, sl, sn, sm, sp, sq, st*, and *sw*) and four triple-letter blends (*spl, spr, str*, and *scr*).

In a blend, each letter stands for its own sound, but the sounds are blended (smooshed) together to make a unique sound.

The following songs are examples of songs you can make up using consonant blends:

The more you read, the more you know. The more you know, the smarter you grow. The smarter you grow, the stronger your voice, when speaking your mind or making your choice.

—Anonymous

FLYING FLAMINGOS

1. Flying flamingos flop on de flowers,
Flapping an' floating for hours an' hours.
Flying flamingos flop on de floor,
Flapping an' floating for hours an' hours.

(Chorus)
(oh, oh, oh)
Fleas flatten de flutes
(Lemme tell ya)
Fleas flatten de flutes
(oh, oh, oh)
Fleas flatten de flutes
(lemme tell ya)
Fleas flatten de flutes.

2. Flashing flags flip on de floor,
Flipping an' flying for hours an' hours.
Flashing flags flip on de floor,
Flipping an' flying for hours an' hours.

TWELVE TWIRLING TWINS

1. Twelve twirling twins upon a twilight twirl,
Take two twanging twigs, to twiddle, tweak, and twist.

(Chorus)
Twenty twinkling stars, twine about the twins,
Twenty twinkling stars, twine about the twins.

2. Tweet, tweet, tweet, tweet, tweet,
Twitter, twitter, twitter, twitter, twitter,
Tweet, tweet, tweet, tweet, tweet,
Twitter, twitter, twitter, twitter, twitter,
(twice more).

THE SPLENDID SPLISH-SPLASH SPIDER

1. The splendid splish-splash spider,
sprawling on the spout
The splendid splish-splash spider,
strolling with a strut.

(Chorus)
Splitter, splatter, splitter, splitter, splatter,
Sprinkle, sprang, sprinkle, sprinkle, sprang.
Splitter, splatter, splitter, splitter, splatter,
Straddle, straggle, stroll, stroll, strut!

2. The splendid splish-splash spider,
scratching with a screech,
The splendid splish-splash spider,
struggles with the straw.

Letters With Special Sounds

Luckily, there are only six "special" sounds to learn: *ch, sh, th, wh, thr,* and *shr.* These six sounds have no letters of their very own (how sad!), so they must share two letters together to make one sound. Notice that *t* and *s* are the only letters that make three-letter blends (*thr* and *shr*). (Also notice in the following song, the word *choir* breaks the rules!)

CHILDREN CHIME FOR CHOCOLATE CHUNKS

    1. **Ch**ildren **ch**ime for **ch**ocolate **ch**unks,
    Children **ch**ant for **ch**eese,
    Children **ch**eer for **ch**ewy **ch**erries,
    Chipmunks **ch**ew the **ch**air.

    (**Ch**orus)
    The **ch**oir of **ch**arming **ch**ildren,
    chant the **ch**orus with **ch**eers.
    The **ch**oir of **ch**arming **ch**ildren,
    chase the **ch**ipmunk with **ch**ins.

    2. **Ch**ildren **ch**ime for **ch**eckers and **ch**ess,
    Children **ch**ant for **ch**uckles,
    Children **ch**eer for **ch**ickens with **ch**eeks.
    Chipmunks **ch**ew the **ch**air.

Letters With Oddball Sounds

The six oddball sounds are: *kn, gn, wr, gh, ph,* and *rh.* Oddballs may look weird, but they always make the same sounds together. Be nice to them—they're odd!

THE KNIGHT KNOWS

    The **kn**ight **kn**ows how to **kn**ock,
    The **kn**ight **kn**ows how to **kn**eel,
    The **kn**ight **kn**ows there's a **kn**ife in his **kn**apsack,
    The **kn**ight **kn**ows how to **kn**it.

    (Chorus)
    Oh!
    No one **kn**ows the **kn**ight's **kn**itting's in **kn**ots,
    No one **kn**ows the **kn**ight's **kn**itting is new.
    No one **kn**ows but the **kn**uckle-headed **kn**ight,
    No one **kn**ows it's true.

You may have tangible wealth untold caskets of jewels and coffers of gold, richer than I you can never be— I had a mother who read to me.

—Strickland Gillilan

Reading opens the world to me and keeps me open to the world.

—Barbara Bush

Book Reports

Try to avoid them. Seriously! They are usually very boring for kids. Many, many children are turned off to reading by being forced to do book reports. If you feel the need for book reports in your life, do try to make them interesting.

IDEAS FOR OLDER READERS

Reading Reactions

Use this method while the book is being read, and have kids react to one of the following items:

1. Find a new **vocabulary word** and guess what it means.
2. **Ask a question** that will help you understand the story.
3. **Describe your feelings** for a character in the story.
4. **Pick a passage** in the book that you feel is important and **reflect on its meaning.**
5. **Make a prediction** about what you think will happen next in the book.
6. **Describe a difficult situation** that the character is in. How would you behave in such a situation?
7. Comment on the **author's writing style**, especially a style you enjoyed.
8. **Do the character's actions parallel anything in your own life?**
9. **Copy a favorite passage** and comment on it.
10. **Give your opinion on a problem** or how the problem can be resolved.

Other Unusual Book Report Ideas

+ Make a **time line** to illustrate a book you've read.
+ Do **author research** for a writer whose books you admire.
+ Design a **miniature newspaper** that could have been written during the period in which the book's story is set.
+ Write a **new original adventure** that stars the characters found in the book you have just read. Try to write in the style of the author.
+ Make a **diorama** of a scene from the book. (A *diorama* is a 3-D scene of the book, usually constructed in an old shoe box.)

IDEAS FOR YOUNGER READERS

+ **Story maps.** The child creates a map that shows, with a combination of drawings and explanations, how one event leads to another. Character, setting, and situations can be shown along the way.

HANSEL AND GRETEL

✦ **Story Mountains** help children understand how action happens in a story. Write each event of the story on a separate strip of paper and then place them in order. Place the most exciting part on a higher level than the others creating a "peak" or "mountain."

✦ **Sketch-to-Stretch.** Do this by folding a legal-sized (8 ½ x 14) paper into thirds. The child can then make three pictures (beginning, middle, and end) to summarize the story.

It is chiefly through books that we enjoy intercourse with superior minds…God be thanked for books. They are the voices of the distant and the dead, and make us heirs of the spiritual life of past ages. Books are true levelers. They give to all who will faithfully use them, the society, the spiritual presence, of the best and greatest of our race.

—William Ellery Channing

❧ LIBRARIES ❧

Visit your local library on a regular basis, at least once a month. Make field trips to visit all the libraries within an hour or so of your home. You'll find treasures like books, magazines, periodicals, maps, records, and tapes: all for free at libraries.

In college, I was once "caught" by one of my professors wandering around among the stacks at the library. (Actually, the only reason he caught me is that he was doing the same thing!) Some of us just like to start at one end of a library and wander through as far as we can before we have to leave.

Classification Systems

The love of learning, the sequestered nooks, and all the sweet serenity of books.

—Henry Wadsworth Longfellow

Most libraries use the Dewey Decimal System, but many universities favor another system called Library of Congress. The Library of Congress system, as you will see, has more classifications than the Dewey system, and a slightly different order of presentation. Most libraries have free copies of their classification system. Our library even has a special one just for children.

DEWEY DECIMAL SYSTEM

000-099 **General Works** (Computers, UFO's, libraries, encyclopedias, almanacs)

110-190 **Philosophy** (Human mind and thought)

210-296 **Religion & Mythology**

310-390 **Sociology** (Holidays, fairy tales, customs, careers, government, humanhood, transportation, festival, legends)

420-490 **Language** (Words, dictionaries, foreign language)

507-590 **Science** (Insects, animals, flowers, shells, birds, rocks, stars, physics, math)

609-697 **Technology** (Applied Science: ships, cars, airplanes, pets, food, medicine, inventions, engineering, manufacturing, farming, cooking)

704-799 **Fine Arts and Recreation** (Riddles, sports, dance, painting, music, hobbies, parties, theater)

808-890 **Literature** (Poetry, plays, humor, short stories)

901-970 **Geography and History**

Biography: B + name of person

Library of Congress System

A	General Works	J	Political Science
B	Philosophy, Religion	K	Law
C	History (Biography)	L	Education
D	History (Topography)	LB	Special Days
E	America (general)	M	Music
F	Americas	N	Fine Arts
G	Geography/Anthropology	P	Language and Literature
GT	Manners and Customs	Q	Science
H	Social Sciences, Economics	R	Medicine
HF	Advertising, Business	S	Agriculture, Plants, and Animals
HG	Finance	T	Technology
HJ	Public Finance	U	Military Science
HM	Sociology	V	Naval Science
HQ	Family, Marriage, Home	Z	Bibliography and Library Science
HS	Associations		

Library Games

Book Exploration

Each player discovers something interesting in encyclopedias, dictionaries, atlases, or other reference books. Share what you find.

Book Classification

Gather several books from home or the library and then classify them in alphabetical order, using either the title or the author's last name.

Information Scavenger Hunt #1 (older children)

For each player or group, list a few questions like the ones suggested below. Have players consult various books to search for the information:

+ The winning team of the 1969 World Series.
+ The distance between Earth and Venus.
+ Author and publication date of the novel, *Love in the Time of Cholera.*
+ The location of Bali (longitude and latitude).
+ The title of a Robin William's movie.

For I bless God in the libraries of the learned and for all the booksellers in the world.

—Christopher Smart

INFORMATION SCAVENGER HUNT #2

- ✦ Name two magazines that tell about either nature, current events, or sports.
- ✦ If you want to learn how to fly, fish, or build a house (choose one) where would you look?
- ✦ Find a recent article about either a Washington politician, an astronaut, or the environment. Give the name of the article as well as the name and date of the magazine it is in.
- ✦ Give the title of another book by the author who wrote either *The Voyage of the Dawn Treader*, *Kidnapped*, or *Wilma*.
- ✦ Give the call number for either the *Guinness' Book of Records*, *Famous First Facts*, or *Encyclopedia of Comics*.
- ✦ How many books in your library are by one of the following authors: Judy Blume, John Steinbeck, or C. S. Lewis?
- ✦ What are the numbers under which you could find a book on either travel, education, or weather?
- ✦ Find the latest book written about either medicine, art, or nature. Give the publisher and the publication date.
- ✦ Who is the illustrator of a book by either Elizabeth Yates, Jules Verne, or Laura Ingalls Wilder? (Note: sometimes different editions have different illustrators.)
- ✦ Give the name of a reference book about either ancient civilizations, sports, or a foreign country.
- ✦ When and where did either physician James Derham, singer Judy Garland, or architect Frank Lloyd Wright live?

Excerpted from COBBLESTONE'S November 1983 issue: Checking Out Libraries, © *1983, Cobblestone Publishing, Inc. 7 School St., Peterborough, NH 03458. Reprinted by gracious permission of the publisher.*

> *To be a well-favored man is the gift of fortune; but to write and read comes by nature.*
>
> *—Shakespeare*

FIND A BOOK GAME (FOR YOUNGER CHILDREN)

- ✦ Find a book that has a picture of a tree on the cover.
- ✦ Find a book that has a red jacket or cover.
- ✦ Find a book that is divided into chapters.
- ✦ Find a book by an author whose last name begins with *P*.
- ✦ Find a book about science.
- ✦ Find a book about someone's life (biography).
- ✦ Find a book by your favorite author.
- ✦ Find a book that is very small.

LIBRARY TREASURE HUNT (FOR OLDER CHILDREN)

- ✦ Find book with the call letters 704 -750.
- ✦ Find a book about poetry.
- ✦ Find a book about maps.
- ✦ Find a book by an author that has written more than five books.
- ✦ Find a book with the call letters 880-890.
- ✦ Find a record that teaches Spanish.

- Find a book in a foreign language.
- Find a book that is a biography.
- Find a book that is non-fiction.
- Find a book by your favorite author.

NEWSPAPER SCAVENGER HUNT

While technically not a library activity, this game is included here because it's about gathering information. Each person (or team) needs a newspaper, scissors, glue, and a piece of large paper. Have each player find then glue on their papers (make a time limit if you wish) the following items:

- Newspaper masthead
- Index
- Classified ad
- Two letters to the editor; one angry, one complimentary
- A story about, or reference to children
- A story about a city within 100 miles of your hometown
- A sports headline with photo

PERSONAL INTEREST LISTS

Obtain a copy of the Dewey Decimal or Library of Congress System from your librarian. (They should be more detailed than the ones found in this book.) Go down the list and read every category. On a piece of paper, write down each subject that interests you, including the call letters. You will now have a list of all the subjects that interest you, as well as where to find out about your interests.

*The one thing I regret is that
I will never have time to read all
the books I want to read.*

—Françoise Sagan

❦ Writing ❦

Art and Writing Letters

Art comes *before* writing letters. All systems of writing originated from cave paintings. After many centuries passed, pictures gradually began to represent ideas. For example, a sun would represent heat or light. In this way, our modern alphabet was formed. However, it is easier to draw and scribble than to learn how to write letters. Sometimes it's physically hard for little kids to hold a pencil for a long time. When children don't want to write, let them draw instead. You can always write for them. Even when they dictate what to write, you are still modeling the writing process for them. Always ask children how they want to pursue a writing project. There are several different ways to assist beginning writers:

✦ You write everything for them (dictation).

✦ You write in yellow crayon or pencil and let them trace over it.

✦ You write the words on a separate piece of paper and they copy them.

✦ You spell each letter in the word for them.

✦ You dot-to-dot the words for them and they fill in the words.

Writing is a code. When we read, we *decode* language (break the code) and when writing, we *encode* – put language into code. The main point of writing is the message, not the code itself. Yet to communicate well, one must learn to master the code.

Writing is the slowest form of communication and can be a frustrating process because our thoughts come so much faster than our hands and tongues can process them.

The Inner Voice and Creative Writing

Creative writing is an important vehicle for self-expression and can be used as a tool to gain insights into the workings of our minds. Styles of writing include poetry, short stories, journals, diaries, novels, and letters.

Not everything that people write needs to be shared. Most of Emily Dickinson's poems were published after she died. I wonder if she hadn't wanted it that way. Good writers have a strong, comfortable relationship with their inner voices. The following suggestions will help develop awareness of the inner voice:

✦ Think about how you think. Do you think in words, pictures, feelings, or a combination of these?

✦ Talk silently to yourself. Do you talk to yourself in an "I" (first person) or in a "you" (second person) voice? Do you talk to yourself or another person? Is the voice loud, soft, humorous, angry...?

✦ Talk silently to yourself in someone else's voice (mother, father, teacher, friend.) What did this voice say? Can you describe it?

✦ Talk silently to yourself for 15 seconds. Can you remember one word of what you said? Repeat the exercise and try to write down verbatim (word for word)

> *Too often, I think, children are required to write before they have anything to say. Teach them to think and read and talk without self-repression, and they will write because they cannot help it.*
>
> —Anne Sullivan

what you said to yourself. Can you write the whole thought?

✦ Picture a room in your house or a familiar piece of furniture. Close your eyes and try to see it. Write down what you see in your mind.

General Writing Standards

Writing combines the ability to talk, think, spell, and punctuate. Writing can be a passionate and fulfilling occupation or avocation. Learn the standard rules, then claim artistic license to break them!

✦ Use the **active voice:** (Josh ate a banana.) rather than the passive voice (The banana was eaten by Josh.)

✦ Make writing **colorful** (consult a thesaurus): (instead of *eaten* substitute *devoured* or *demolished*)

✦ Be **specific:** (banana, *not* fruit)

✦ Be **concise:** omit unnecessary words: ('He ate hungrily,' *not* 'he ate in a hungry way.')

✦ Use the **same verb tenses** within a sentence: (*Not* 'Josh devours the banana and was drinking milk.')

✦ Mix writing with **descriptions, explanations, facts, reasons, comparisons,** and **statistics.**

✦ Write events in their **natural order of sequence.**

✦ **Stick to the subject.**

✦ Use **humor, quotations, questions, and examples** to develop ideas.

✦ Use a **variety of sentences**: simple, compound, and complex.

✦ Link paragraphs with **transitional sentences**.

✦ Link ideas by using **conjunctions** or repeating words.

✦ **Keep related words together.** ('He ate the sweet banana,' *not* 'He ate the banana that was sweet.')

✦ Culminate writing on a **decisive note.**

Prewriting

Prewriting = thinkwriting. It includes any experience or activity that inspires the writer to write, any experience that creates ideas and materials for writing, or any experience that focuses a writer's feelings and attentions on a particular subject. Below is a list of some of my favorite prewriting strategies:

✦ **Dictation:** Not what we grew up with. This is the opposite. Older kids write down the thoughts and ideas of the younger kids. This is a great deal of fun with the little ones.

✦ **Brainstorming:** (Listing ideas and thoughts about a central idea for the writing project.) Brainstorming involves making a list that sticks to the theme. Brainstorms and clustering are sometimes used interchangeably.

All good books are alike in that they are truer than if they had really happened, and after you are finished reading one you will feel that all that happened to you, and afterwards it all belongs to you: the good and the bad, the ecstasy, the remorse and sorrow, the people, and the places and how the weather was. If you can get so that you can give that to people, then you are a writer.

—Ernest Hemingway

Corn

cornhusk dolls	mideast states	corn-on-the-cob
corn meal	silos	creamed corn
corn bread	corn silk	corn silk
corn field	popcorn	harvest
	carmel corn	popcorn balls

✦ **Clustering or Webbing:** An open-ended brainstorm. It is based on associations, and gives the writer the possibility of going off on tangents. Can you guess which word began this cluster? A **web** (as far as I can tell) is a **cluster** that sticks to a theme.

> *In the world of words, the imagination is one of the forces of nature.*
>
> *—Wallace Stevens*

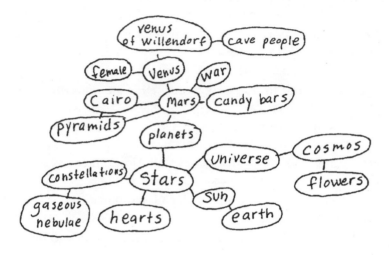

✦ **Facts:** If you are a detective, these are your famous five W's.

WHO ?	WHAT ?	WHERE ?	WHEN ?	WHY ?
Josh Oshanna Oro the dog	Went for a walk and picked flowers.	In the woods to Dani's house.	Sunday morning	To play spaceships with Dani.

✦ **Sensory Detail:** A good way to make kids aware of the five senses.

SEE	HEAR	TASTE	SMELL	FEEL
trees flowers sun rise birds deer	birds voices wind in the trees	wild straw-berries wild onions black berries	violets pine trees earth	sun earth

✦ **Bubbling:** For younger kids, pick a theme for the sensory detail, such as a piece of fruit, a flower, or other object.

popcorn

see	hear	taste	smell	feel
white fluffy puppy	popping humming	crunchy buttery yeasty	yummy "like the movies"	light airy

✦ **Outlining:** Use the "detective" model when thinking about outlines. Outlines help us view our random thoughts from various experiences in an organized fashion. Here is a sample outline:

GROWING FLOWERS
    I. Seed and Bulb Selection
        A. Early bloomers
            1. Tulips
                a. Dutch Tulips
                b. Royal Tulip
            2. Daffodils
        B. Late bloomers
            1. Daisy
            2. Black-eyed Susan
    II. Cultivation
        A. Hoe garden
            1. Remove rocks
        B. Rake
        C. Fertilize
            1. Clean goat pen
        D. Plant seeds
        E. Water seedlings
   III. Flower Arrangement
        A. Select container
        B. Arrange colors

✦ **Mapping:** This is an easier way of outlining. It consists of a main idea, supported with specific examples:

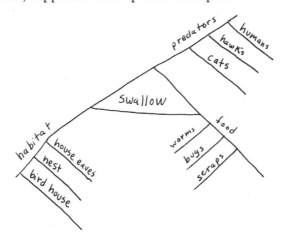

Take away the art of writing from this world, and you will probably take away its glory.

—F. Chateaubriand

Poetry begins in childhood, and the poet who can remember his or her childhood exactly has an obligation to write for children.

—William Jay Smith

Kinds of Writing and Writing Reactions

Use these categories to think about what you are writing

Transactions: Instructions, lists, messages, reports, bank notes.

Expressive: Journals, diaries, letters, stories.

Poetic: Poems and songs.

Use these four categories to determine what style of writing you will use when reacting to what you have read or heard.

Factual: Write only about the **facts** you have read.

Descriptive: Describe the **events** that you read.

Opinion: Write about your **reactions** or **feelings** of what you have read.

Summary: Write a **summary** of what you read.

❧ POETRY ❧

There are two classes of poets— the poets by education and practice, these we respect; and poets by nature, these we love.

—Ralph Waldo Emerson

People create poems for many reasons: they want to express their feelings, thoughts, ideas, and passions. To me, poetry is the music of words. I enjoy poems in which the words seem to sing to me. Poetry is ancient. In olden times, before the written word, oral history was passed on from generation to generation with the help of poetry.

The most important ingredient in poetry is *content*. Many well-meaning teachers share only poetry *forms* with their students, thus depriving them of the prime element of poetry: as a vehicle for expressing deep inner feelings.

I am lucky to know a good poet, Pamela Singer, who for many years has taught in the Poet-in-the-Schools program. She has taught hundreds of youngsters how to write poetry, how to dig past superficial feelings and convey deep emotions through poetry. She has written a computer program for kids about learning poetry, which has been used by thousands of children.

Pamela emphasizes over and over to children that there is no right or wrong in the world of poetry. Whatever you feel and want to write about is valid. She also encourages children who are beginning to write poetry not to worry about spelling, grammar, or punctuation. That stuff comes much later.

Illustrating poems is usually fun for kids. You might even want to get rice paper and India ink for writing and illustrating poems. Pictures help poems come to life, especially for younger children.

So, bearing in mind that *content* is the most important ingredient to poetry, I have chosen several poetry *forms* to share with you.

Remember that the *structure* of a poem should be secondary to the *content*. You can also use poems to teach various literary techniques such as alliteration and personification.

Inner-Self Poetry

This is one of my favorites. It can be used successfully with all ages.

On a piece of paper, write a vertical list containing all of the following categories:

1. Element (choose either earth, air, fire, or water)
2. Animal
3. Color
4. Flower
5. Food
6. Gem
7. Place
8. Sound
9. Tree
10. Weather

From this list, write down one object from each category that describes you or that perhaps you feel drawn to. You may wish to draw pictures of the objects you have chosen. Next, write a poem using the images you have picked. Use them all, or just use a few.

Two-Word Poems

In a two-word poem, you may only have two words per line and as many lines as you wish:

My children

loving them

day, night

laughing, crying

cooing screaming

sticky fingers

deep love

shines bright.

Window Poem

One of the easiest ways to begin poetry writing is to look out the window and describe what you see:

Sparkling leaves sway lazily

heavy with summer sun

Mammoth redwood

with craggy bark

guards the door.

Poetry teaches the enormous force of a few words, and, in proportion to the inspiration, checks loquacity.

—Ralph Waldo Emerson

Detective Poem

A detective poem answers the following questions: *Who, What, When, Where,* and *Why.* Each line of the poem answers a different question:

The fairies (who)
flutter about (what)
in the twilight (when)
through the silent meadow (where)
to Midsummer's Ball. (why)

Color Poem

Pick a color, any color. Now, from where you sit look around and find that color. Instant poem!

Green
Green plants soften the room
Green pictures make me smile.
Green posters
of green rain forests
on great green earth.

Sensory Poem

On a piece of paper, list the following categories. Take a walk, look out the window, or take a walk in your mind, and list two or three items for each category:

SEE	HEAR	FEEL	TASTE	SMELL
flowers	birds	grass	peach	flowers
birds	hammering	tree bark	water	dog
trees	voices	water	bread	cat

Now write a poem using some of these sensory images.

I see the fairy flowers, flitting birds,
and swaying trees.
I hear the chirping birds and feel the grass
scrunch between my toes.
The ambrosial peach juice dribbles down my chin,
the dog and the cat smell.

Another way to write sensory poems is to use a more structured format. Pick a subject, then begin to write:

Line 1: Write the word *this*.

Line 2: Two words that describe the **sound** of your subject.

Line 3: Two words that describe its **looks**.

Line 4: Two words that describe how it **feels**.

Line 5: Two words that tell how it **tastes**. (You might have to imagine this)

Line 6: Two words that tell how it **smells**.

Line 7: Write the word *as*, and what your subject **reminds** you of.

Line 8: Write the word you just described.

> This
>
> humming buzzing
>
> gray plastic
>
> wizard brain
>
> cold metallic
>
> factory office
>
> brain.
>
> Computer.

Haiku

This is a classic Japanese style of poetry. It can be very beautiful, and is a good way for kids to learn about syllables. The Haiku is only three lines long. Each line has a fixed number of syllables. Line #1: five, Line #2: seven, and Line #3 five. Lines aren't expected to rhyme. Traditional Haiku focus on one season of the year, and this is usually a good place to start. You might want to make a list of words associated with each season:

SPRING	SUMMER	AUTUMN	WINTER
daffodils	beach	apples	snow
showers	hot	pumpkins	ice
clouds	relaxed	colors	bare

> Ocean waves break cool
>
> Deep blue dive in rolling surf:
>
> I am washed and new.

Cinquain

A five-line poem. Each line carries a special meaning and form:

1) two syllables: title

2) four syllables: describe the title

3) six syllables: action

I wish our clever young poets would remember by homely definitions of prose and poetry; that is, prose = words in their best order; poetry = the best words in their best order.

—Samuel Taylor Coleridge

4) eight syllables: feeling
5) two syllables: synonym for title

Tall trees.

Big, leafy-green

rustling in the cool breeze.

Their leafy arms embrace my soul.

Redwood.

Diamante: Diamond Poem

This poem takes the shape of a diamond and, like the Cinquain, each line has a special meaning and form:

1) one word: poem's subject
2) two words: adjectives describing subject
3) three words: participles (*ing* words) about subject
4) four words: nouns about first and last line
5) three words: participles about last line
6) two words: adjectives about last line
7) one word: opposite of poem's subject

You can see that it is important to know where you are going when you pick your subject for this poem.

Summer

spicy hot

swimming, camping, playing

beaches, fairs, fires, snowballs

freezing, raining, shivering

icy cold

Winter.

Couplet: Two-Line Poem

A couplet is the easiest way to introduce rhymes in poetry. First, make up one sentence for your poem:

I want to go flying to far-off lands.

Next, list all the words you can think of that rhyme with the last word in the line (I usually just go through the alphabet):

...and, bland, canned, clan, gland, hand, sand...

Now you are ready to write the second line:

I want to go flying to far-off lands,

I want to sleep all night in gentle sands.

> *The poet, described in ideal perfection, brings the whole soul of man into activity, with the subordination of its faculties to each other, according to their relative worth and dignity. He diffuses a tone and spirit of unity that blends and (as it were) fuses each into each, by that synthetic and magical power... imagination.*
>
> —Samuel Taylor Coleridge

Triplet: Three-Line Poem

A triplet, as you might expect, has three lines that rhyme. It's probably a good idea to pick out your rhyming words before you begin the poem. Try rhyming words with these suffixes:

-ip, -am, -ight, -are, -ox, -ug, -ump, -am, -all, -ear, -ell, -unk.

Onomatopoeia: Echo Poem

These words imitate natural sounds such as: *bow-wow, meow, buzz, fizz, hiss, moo, sizzle, splat,* and *gurgle.* They are fun to use in poetry:

"Buzz, buzz, buzz," sang the bee.
"Swish, swish, swish," cried the flea.
"Ha, ha, ha," he laughed at me.

Comparison Poem: Similes and Metaphors

No discussion of poetry or writing would be complete without discussing similes and metaphors. These ways of comparing things to each other is what gives poetry (and writing) "color." When writers use the words *like* or *as* in their work, they are using *similes,* comparing one thing to another:

Your eyes sparkle like jewels,
your hair is as gold as the sun.

When a poet or writer compares two things by *equating one with the other,* or implying one is the other, then a *metaphor* is being used:

He is a young wild stallion racing the wind.

(or)

The moon is a gleaming pearl in the sky.

Alliteration: Same Sound Poem

Alliteration is fun. It is the repetition of a *sound* within a word, line, or phrase. Limericks rely heavily on alliteration. It makes writing more lyrical. Pick a letter of the alphabet and try making a sentence or two using only that letter:

My mother makes muffins Monday morning.
Mr. Muffet marvels madly at mommy's muffins.

Whatever a poet writes with enthusiasm and a divine inspiration is very fine.

—Democritus
c. 460-400 BC

Painting is silent poetry, and poetry painting that speaks.

—Simonides
556-468 BC

Poetry is the mother tongue of mankind.

—Johann Georg Hamann

Another way to use alliteration is to make up alliterative animals for each letter of the alphabet, such as Big Beautiful Bear, Slimy Sam Snake.

Personification:
Things-as-People Poem

Who or what are personifications? Mickey Mouse, the Cheshire Cat, Brer Rabbit, Mr. Toad, Mr. Ed, and the North Wind are! These characters are our old friends. We use personification to make non-human animals and things seem human. Use your poetic voice to write a poem and make all the non-human objects in your poem come alive.

Hey Mr. Wind,
stop 'wind-ing' my hair!
The dancing flowers are very tired
and the tree's hair is falling out!

Sound Poem

This poetry lesson excerpt comes from Pamela Singer, used by gracious permission.

Three Native American words help express the essence of poetry: *Leip-pya*, which means "messenger of the imagination," *Qaartsiluni*, which means "to wait in silence and stillness for creativity," and *nierrka*, which expresses the idea of "a passageway between two worlds." There is an imaginary doorway in everybody's mind that opens many different worlds. When we are still, then we are able to express some of the worlds that we are in touch with.

What do these words have to do with writing poetry? Poems come from a place deep inside each of us. Poems give expression to our feelings. We write what we are feeling by listening to our imaginations. Poetry trains you to be more sensitive to your own feelings and to the outer world.

Thoughts come and we don't always know where they come from. When you write poetry it is important to just let your mind wander. Since you are expressing your feelings, it is impossible to be wrong. There is no good or bad or right or wrong poem.

In poetry writing it is important to use fewer words than in other types of writing. In a story you might write, "In the dark night, the moon rose over the ocean." The poetic way of saying this might be: "Dark night—moon over ocean." The reason for this is that in a poem each word must count. All unnecessary words must be omitted. Since poems are comprised of words, it is essential that you use strong, descriptive words.

Poems are made of words, so let's look at where words come from. Before you speak, you are silent, so words come from silence. So where do words come from? Vowels and consonants. A vowel like *a, e, i o,* or *u* makes a word fluid. Or, a vowel opens the word while the consonant sound closes the word.

To write a sound poem, choose a vowel sound and that will be your first line. Write it three times, leaving lots of space between the letters. For the second line, add another vowel sound. Your third line will be two vowel sounds and one consonant sound. Continue combining vowel and consonant sounds for six lines. Then look at your work and see if you have a word or perhaps more than one word included in your sounds. Let this word or words be your final line or lines.

o	o	o
oa	oa	oa
oab	oab	oab
oabt	oabt	oabt
oaebt	oaebt	oaebt
oaebtk	oaebtk	oaebtk
oat	oat	oat
oak	oak	oak

Family Journals

WHY KEEP JOURNALS?

+ Books are **treasures**: we keep and re-read things that are bound together.
+ Journals are outlets for our **creative spirit.**
+ They are a meaningful way to **reflect** upon our speeding lives.
+ Journals create **time capsules** of yearly events.
+ You may **write whatever you want**, in whatever form you want.
+ They are a safe place to express **feelings.**

Note: the word *diary* and *journal* both come from the Latin word for *daily*.

THINGS TO PUT IN JOURNALS

+ pressed flowers
+ poems
+ feelings
+ dreams
+ artwork
+ photos
+ conversations
+ newspaper articles
+ birthday cards
+ ticket stubs
+ song lyrics
+ letters
+ postcards
+ stories kids dictate to adults
+ pictures from magazines

> *Poetry is the breath and finer spirit of all knowledge; it is the impassioned expression which is in the countenance of all Science.*
>
> —*William Wordsworth*

> *Poets are the unacknowledged legislators of the world.*
>
> —*Percy Bysshe Shelley*

- biology sketches
- records of special events such as trips, birthdays, and holidays
- records of events such as films, programs, musical experiences, and books
- lists, brainstormed ideas (parents may jot down ideas for kids.)
- free writing

WHO, WHAT, WHERE, WHEN, WHY, AND HOW

- Keep individual journals, or the family can keep one together.
- Spend about 5-20 minutes a day, two to four times a week with journals.
- Parents can write in kid's journals (or vice-versa), do the gluing, or whatever is mutually acceptable.
- Share your journals with each other and with friends (unless you're shy).
- Even three-year-olds can scribble in journals. Give them beautiful pictures to color, or let them make their own pictures.
- Vary writing instruments (and colors) from colored pencils to felt-tip pens to regular pens to pencils.

FAMOUS JOURNAL KEEPERS

- **Thomas Edison** (who was a homeschooler) has journals that fill up a warehouse.
- **Leonardo da Vinci** kept journals that are now world-famous.
- **Buckminster Fuller** created perhaps the most profound journals of the 20th century.
- **Benjamin Franklin** has journals that are still widely read.
- **Anaïs Nin's** published diary gives important insights into her mind and her era.

❧ WRITING GAMES AND IDEAS ❧

Bookmaking

Writing, like life itself, is a voyage of discovery.

—Henry Miller

Anything that is bound, whether it be stapled together with covers of construction paper or elaborately stitched-and-glued creations, becomes more precious. The best home-made books have blank pages in them that give the writer more freedom and room to do artwork.

Mini Book

1. Take a regular piece of paper and fold it in half lengthwise.
2. Open it, and fold it in half crosswise.

3. Fold it crosswise again.

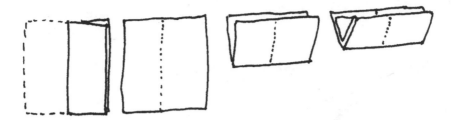

4. Unfold paper and re-fold it so that the paper is folded as in step 2 above (half crosswise) and cut a slit halfway up the middle as shown:

5. Open the paper and fold it lengthwise as folded in step 1. The slit is on the top.

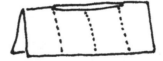

6. Hold it at opposite ends and push the ends of the slit together like this:

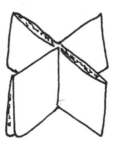

Fold it at one edge to make a book.
Punch two holes along the folded edge.
Tie **yarn** or **string** through the holes to bind the book's pages together.

You learn as much by writing as you do by reading.

—Eric Hoffer

Bound Book

1. Use five to eight pieces of 8½" x 11" **paper** folded along the width to make 8½" x 5½" pages. Make sure there is one extra sheet to use for the end papers.
2. With an **awl** or **compass** point, poke holes in the crevice of the folded pages about 1" apart.
3. **Measure** and cut a piece of **thread** that is four times the length of your book. Double it over, thread it through a **needle** and knot the end.
4. Starting from the outside, sew in and out of the pages to one end, then turn and come back through the same holes.
5. Cut two pieces of **mat board** slightly bigger than your pages. With insides facing you, place them on the table ½" apart.
6. Use **masking tape** to tape them together.
7. Turn the covers to the outside and tape them together with **cloth tape**, wrapping the extra tape around to the inside of the cover.
8. **Glue** the end papers to the inside of the cover.
9. Decorate the cover and write your story!

The difference between the right word and the almost right word is the difference between the lightning and the lightning bug.

—Mark Twain

Post Office

Everyone loves to get mail. Make each person in the family a mailbox out of two **paper plates**. **Cut** one in half and **staple** the whole and half-plates together. You may want to put each person's picture on the mailbox or just his name. Supply postage stamps, ink pad, envelopes, stickers, other stamps, paper, pencils, and pens for letter making.

Synonyms

Make a list of ten or so words and give a copy to each player or team. In about a minute, each player or team tries to think of a synonym (similar meaning) for each word.

ADDRESSES OF PUBLIC OFFICIALS

Write to these guys and let them know what you think about education, ecology, energy, national or international affairs. Officials tend to believe that one measly letter represents the opinions of 500 people! Don't forget to write letters to the editor of your local newspaper too! When you write be sure to:

- ✦ Use your own words.
- ✦ Ask for a reply (include your return address).
- ✦ Keep your letter short.
- ✦ Discuss only one issue per letter and identify your subject clearly.
- ✦ Ask for some specific action (like introducing a bill to outlaw compulsory schooling).
- ✦ Explain why the issue is important to you.
- ✦ Be polite. Avoid being antagonistic, threatening, or insulting.

The President
The White House
Washington, DC 20500

The Honorable (Governor's name)
Governor of (State)
State Capitol Building
(City, State, ZIP)

The Honorable (Senator's name)
United States Senate
Washington, DC 20510

The Honorable (Representative's
    name)
House of Representatives
Washington, DC 20515

Greetings for Letters

Dear_____,
Dearest_____,
Dear People,
Hello,
Howdy!
Hi!
Greetings!
To Whom it May Concern,
¿Qué pasa?

Closings

Always,
Best Wishes,
As Ever,
Love,
Love & Kisses,
Sincerely,
Yours Truly,
Your Friend,
C-ya!
Yours till the …butter flies, Niagara Falls, door
    stops, ocean waves …

Messages to the Letter Carrier

This oughta get there right away
So get a wiggle on today.

Postman, postman skinny or fat
Take this letter to a real cool cat.

D-liver D-letter D-sooner D-better.

Postie, postie, don't be slow
Go like Elvis, Go man go!

Good Letter Form

Date → April 16, 1993

Greeting → Dear Josh,

Body → I sure had fun at your
birthday party! It was
exciting to build a cardboard
spaceship. The mud pie was
delicious!

Closure → Love,
       Mom

Rebus Words

> *Clear thinking becomes clear writing: one can't exist without the other.*
>
> —*William Zinsser*

For younger kids, make simple rebus (a picture that stands for a word) cards such as:

I *(draw an eye)*
love or heart *(heart)*
you, *(letter u)*
be *(bee)*
a *(letter a)*
dear *(deer)*
can *(tin can)*
see *(letter c)*
are *(letter r)*
ate *(number 8)*
saw *(carpentry saw)*
tea *(letter t)*
would *(wood)*
knows *(nose)*
for *(letter 4)*
why *(letter y)*

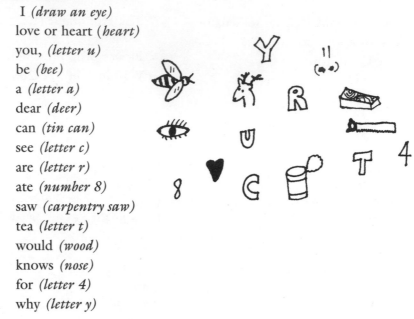

Outcomes

Sit in a circle. Each player, on the top of a long paper, writes the name of a female, then folds the paper and passes it to the left. (For two players, pass it back and forth.) The next player writes, *"met _____ (name of male)."* The next person writes, *"at, beside, (or) in _____ (where)."* The next writes, *"He said, "————————."* The next person, *"She said, "————————————."* The next, *"The outcome was_____."* Then finally, *"And the world said,_____."*

Lots of Things to Write

Ads, advice column, anecdotes, announcements, autobiographies, awards, ballads, bedtime stories, biographies, brochures, bumper stickers, cartoons, commercials, conversations, diaries, dictionaries, dreams, editorials, epitaphs, essays, exaggerations, fables, fairy tales, fantasies, folklore, fortunes, game rules, graffiti, greeting cards, grocery lists, horoscopes, invitations, jokes, journals, jump rope rhymes, labels, legends, letters, lists, love notes, magazines, memories, metaphors, movie reviews, movie scripts, mysteries, myths, newspapers, nonsense, notebooks, nursery rhymes, odes, palindromes, parodies, plays, poems, post cards, posters, prayers, predictions, proposals, proverbs, puppet shows, puns, quips, questionnaires, quotations, reactions, recipes, resumes, riddles, satires, schedules, slogans, songs, telegrams, thank-you notes, tributes, want ads, wills, wishes, yarns.

Words to Use Instead of "Said" (Synonyms)

Use these words when writing stories. Add adverbs or phrases to elaborate on what your characters say instead of *said:*

Chatted happily, chatted like a squirrel, pleaded calmly, pleaded with passion...

Happy: chat, cheer, chuckle, crow, greet, jest, laugh, praise, rejoice, smile, snicker...

Unhappy: argue, bawl, berate, croak, cry, glare, gulp, jeer, lament, leer, mock, needle, quibble, rant, renounce, retort, roar, sass, scowl, simper, smirk, snap, sob, storm, wail, weep, yell...

Question: ask, inquire, plead, pray, question, quiz, request, suggest, wonder...

Loud: babble, blurt, brag, call, declare, demand, exclaim, fret, gasp, order, rant...

Soft: mumble, murmur, mutter, nod, nudge, sigh, stammer, stutter, whisper...

Answers: answer, reply, retort...

Truth: acknowledge, admit, confess, reveal...

Other: add, advise, begin, caution, claim, coax, correct, dare, decide, deny, end, hint, inform, insist, lie, observe, name, nod, nudge, offer, order, pant, promise, quote, remind, state, tell, tempt, warn...

Less common: admonish, assent, atone, banter, bemoan, broach, cajole, carp, challenge, cite, concede, demure, denounce, disclose, drawl, drone, enjoin, enumerate, espouse, estimate, evince, indicate, opine, outline, present, proffer, project, rebuke, speculate, sputter, squelch, stipulate, theorize, vocalize, volunteer...

People get better at using language when they use it to say things they really want to say to people they really want to say them to, in a context in which they can express themselves freely and honestly.

—John Holt

Words to Use Instead of "Wonderful"

Giving pleasure or **joy:** pleasant, delightful, enjoyable.
Beyond believing: astonishing, marvelous, fabulous.
Unusually fine or **excellent:** splendid, superb, spectacular, great.

Composition Derby

To encourage "shy" writers, divide into teams and declare the winner the one who writes the most in about five minutes. Spelling doesn't count, but you can write something, *not* just "dog dog dog." When John Holt used this idea with his students, he found their average output increased from ten words a minute to over twenty in a few short months.

Variation: Non-stop paper. Increase the time. If you run out of ideas, copy the last sentence you wrote until you get more ideas. (John Holt says he was inspired by S.I. Hayakawa in *Language in Thought and Action.*)

Sensory Words

Sensory detail is so important to writing! The more writers learn to paint pictures with words, the more readers can step into the story and can create their own pictures in their mind's eye. Use the following lists in conjunction with the sensory detail pre-writing ideas:

> *Reading maketh a full man, conference a ready man, and writing an exact man.*
>
> *—Francis Bacon*

SOUND WORDS

Birds: squawk, chatter, flutter, chirp, cheep, cackle, gobble, peck, scold, trill, warble, scratch, whistle, coo, caw, twitter, cuckoo, screech, honk, quack, crow, call, peep...

Animals: howl, scratch, cough, roar, squeal, lick, buzz, thump, pant, yawn, squeak, bellow, caterwaul, squeak, moo, low, bay, bleat, grunt, purr, snore, whinny, growl, rattle...

People: murmur, kiss, puff, coo, cry, yell, scream, clap, whoop, sing, slurp, rave, sip, smack, chew, wail, giggle, laugh, cry, sneeze, cough, chuckle, gargle, sing, talk, moan, grunt, groan, shuffle, warble, yodel, sigh, whisper, snore, whimper...

Things: whistle, crash, crack, rattle, vibrate, buzz, zoom, rumble, hammer, roar, tick, bong, ring, explode, blow, howl (as in howling wind), scream, bump, clank, toot, boom, bang, thud, crackle, blast, hum, drip, chug, thunder, muffle, drum, thump, thud, pop, splash, twang, scrunch, tinkle, patter, any musical sound...

Reactions to sounds: melodic, anxious, shrill, raspy, flowing, recurrent, discordant, clear, mournful, quavering, weird, flat, faint, plaintive, liquid, soft, characteristic, loud, resonant, vibrating, monotonous, throaty, sonorous, rhythmic, stealthy, frightened...

Personal reaction: superb, appalling, jarring, agreeable, maddening, horrid, hideous, meaningless, soothing, sweet, blissful, pleasing, pleasant, beautiful, breathtaking, unbelievable, painful, harmonious, ear-splitting, obnoxious, lovely, magnificent, exasperating, joyful, glorious, shocking...

TASTE WORDS

Good: delicious, refreshing, cool, tasty, yummy, mouth-watering, earthy, aromatic, flavorful, savory, fresh, raw, moist...

Sweet: sweet, creamy, bittersweet, minty, sugary, saccharine, candied, juicy, flavored (vanilla, chocolate, strawberry, etc.), nutty, sugared, syrupy...

Sharp or salty: fizzy, tart, sticky, hot, peppery, salty, vinegary, winey, tangy, cheesy, garlicky, sharp, gingery, oniony, pungent, smoky...

Bitter or bland: gritty, sandy, fermented, boiled, green or unripe, sickening, greasy, lukewarm, bitter, rotten, tinny, poisonous, nauseous, burnt, insipid, racy, rancid, tasteless, rank, stale, mushy, dry, undercooked, tasteless, doughy, overripe, overcooked...

TOUCH WORDS

Touch includes texture, movement, temperature, and degree of dryness or wetness.

Texture: scratchy, furry, scaly, sharp, rough, dull, silky, bony, satiny, paper-smooth, velvety, knotty, spongy, grainy, mossy, springy, crumbly, porous, granular, holey, sandy, slippery, muddy, crinkled, sticky, hard, fragile, soft, peach-like, powdery, dusty, netlike, cobweb-like, papery, doughy, mucky, saw-toothed, shocking (electrical)...

Movement: convulsive, flowing, rushing, wiggly, slithering, slow, frantic, steady, intermittent, sudden, in circles, spinning, stirring, creeping, rolling, rhythmic, hopping, jiggling, twitching, fidgety, restless, flopping, shaky...

Temperature: chilly, freezing cold, frigid, cool, cold, wintry, benumbing, warm, tepid, lukewarm, scorching, burning hot, toasty, boiling, searing, fiery, steamy, stifling, balmy, humid, windy...

Degree of dryness or wetness: dewy, slimy, moist, soggy, bone-dry, wringing wet, dry as dust, thick and sticky, half-melted, steamy, foamy, bubbly, soapy, sudsy, misty, frothy, drizzling, foggy, pouring, driving rain, pelting hail, clear, hurricane, changeable, blustery, cloudy, stormy, sunny, rainy, sultry, snowy...

Reaction to touch: snug, cozy, painful, feverish, satisfying, frightening, exciting, desperate, refreshing, sensuous, strange, distressing, uncomfortable, unpleasant, curious, thrilling, startling, bizarre, agreeable, indescribable...

Smell words

Good: enticing, fragrant, mouth-watering, savory...

Sweet: flowery, freshly laundered, fruity, lavender, perfumed...

Sharp: herby, incense, minty, musky, cheesy, fishy, garlicky, gingery, oniony, new lumber, freshly painted, pine, pungent, sawdust, sharp, smoky, spicy, tangy, vinegary, yeasty...

Bitter: acrid, antiseptic, beery, bitter, burnt, chlorinated, dank, disgusting, dusty, fermented, fetid, foul, gaseous, medicinal, moldy, musty, nauseous, offensive, oily, putrid, rancid, rank, repulsive, rotten, sickening, singed, skunky, sour...

Sight Words

The world of sight encompasses everything you can see. Look around to get some ideas. The basic structure of sight is shapes and colors:

Shape: round, square, cube, oval, ellipse, egg-like, stringy, cylindrical, rope-like, flat, wavy, bead-like, triangle, rectangular, kidney, pentagon, hexagon, octagon, irregular quadrilateral, parallelogram, rhombus or diamond, cube, trapezoid...

Colors: Besides the basic rainbow colors (red, orange, yellow, green, blue, purple, violet) think of Crayola crayons:

"Hot" colors: red-orange, yellow-orange, carnation pink, tan, raw sienna, mulberry, maroon, magenta, peach, burnt orange, melon, red violet, mahogany, copper, gold, brown, rose, cocoa, lemon yellow...

"Cool" colors: teal, midnight-blue, jungle-green, lavender, spring-green, olive, pine, aquamarine, blue-green, sea-green, orchid, cornflower, forest-green, turquoise, silver...

Good writing, writing that is a true extension and expression of ourselves, helps us to know ourselves, to make ourselves known to others, and to know them.

—John Holt

DESCRIBE THESE WORDS USING ALL FIVE SENSES

thunderstorm, elephant, snowstorm, birthday cake, new clothes, special toy, campfire, bird, home, popcorn, soap, milk, chocolate, zoo, party, ocean, guitar, gym, summer day, fire, bread, rose, watermelon, computer, airplane, Halloween, Chanukah, Christmas, apple, cat, dog, money, garbage can, car...

Flip-Flop Words

Use flip-flop words in poems, songs, and stories.

abba-dabba, bibble-babble, boo-hoo, boogie-woogie, bow-wow, chiller-diller, chit-chat, click-clack, clickety-clackety, clip-clop, dilly-dally, ding-a-ling, ding-dong, dribble-drabble, ducky-wucky, even-Steven, flim-flam, flip-flop, fuddy-duddy, fuzzy-wuzzy, giggle-gaggle, hanky-panky, harum-scarum, heebie-jeebies, helter-skelter, hippety-hoppety, hocus-pocus, hoity-toity, hokey-pokey, hootchie-cootchie, hully-gully, humpty-dumpty, hurdy-gurdy, hurly-burly, itsy-bitsy, jibber-jabber, jingle-jangle, lovey-dovey, mish-mash, mumbo-jumbo, namby-pamby, okey-dokey, palsy-walsy, piggly-wiggly, piggy-wiggy, ping-pong, pitter-patter, plip-plop, raggle-taggle, razzle-dazzle, rinky-dinky, rowdy-dowdy, rub-dub, scribble-scrabble, see-saw, shilly-shally, splish-splash, super-duper, teeny-weeny, teensy-weensy, tick-tock, ticky-tacky, tip-top, tippety-toppety, tootsie-wootsie, trip-trap, walkie-talkie, whing-ding, wibble-wobble, wig-wag, wiggle-waggle, willy-nilly, wishy-washy, yakety-yak, zig-zag.

Inspiring Writing

MYTHS

Just the names and titles of these epic Greek and Roman Goddesses and Gods is inspiring to the imagination. Make a list of two or three of your favorite characters and weave your own myth. Use the list of fantasy creatures and magic words to spice up your myth.

GREEK AND ROMAN GODS AND GODDESSES

GREEK	ROMAN	TITLE
Zeus	Jupiter	King of the gods
Hera	Juno	Queen of the gods
Rhea		Mother of the gods
Demeter	Ceres	Goddess of earth, agriculture
Gaea	Terra	Earth Mother
Apollo	Apollo	God of sun, music and medicine
Selene	Luna	Goddess of the moon
	Nox	Goddess of the night
Eos	Aurora	Goddess of dawn
Iris	Iris	Goddess of the rainbow
Poseidon	Neptune	God of the sea
Hephaestus	Vulcan	God of fire, blacksmith to gods

Pan	Faunus	God of flocks, pastures, forests and wildlife
Aphrodite	Venus	Goddess of love
Eros	Cupid	God of love
Hestia	Vesta	Goddess of hearth and home
Hygeia	Salus	Goddess of health
Panacea		Goddess of healing
Artemis	Diana	Goddess of the hunt
Athena	Minerva	Goddess of wisdom
Chloris	Flora	Goddess of flowers
Dionysus	Bacchus	God of wine
Hypnos	Somnus	God of sleep
Morpheus		God of dreams
Hebe	Juventas	Goddess of youth and cupbearer to gods
Nike	Victoria	Goddess of victory
Enyo	Bellona	Goddess of war
Ares	Mars	God of war, wisdom, and crafts
Thanatos	Mors	God of death
Hades	Pluto	King of the underworld
Persephone	Prosepina	Queen of the underworld
	Janus	God of gates, doors & beginnings

FANTASY CREATURES

NAME	DESCRIPTION	CULTURE
Argus	hundred-eyed giant	Greek myth
Centaur	half-man, half-horse	Greek myth
Cerberus	many-headed dog	Greek myth
Chimera	fire-breathing part lion/goat/dragon	Greek myth
Cyclops	one-eyed giants	Greek myth
Devil	fallen angel	
Dracula	vampire (corpse AM, sucks blood PM)	English literature
Dragons	probably modeled on dinosaurs	
Dwarf	small person	English
Elf	small person	Irish/Scandinavian
Fairy	tiny, graceful, delicate creatures	
Frankenstein	manlike monster	English literature
Genie	a spirit	
Ghost	spirit of the dead	
Giant	huge manlike monster	
Gnome	a type of elf	
Goblin	ugly, mischevious elf	French
Gorgons	three female monsters (Medusa is one)	Greek myth
Griffin	half-eagle, half-bird	

Harpy	winged monster: woman's head, bird body	
Hydra	nine-headed serpent	Greek myth
Imp	devil's offspring, young demon	
Jabberwock	Lewis Carrol's famous poem	English literature
Leprechaun	shoe-making fairy	Irish
Minotaur	manlike monster with bull's head	Greek myth
Pegasus	winged horse	Greek myth
Phoenix	legendary bird	Egyptian myth
Pixies	souls of unbaptized dead babies	English folktale
Poltergeist	noisy fairies	German
Roc		legendary bird of Indian Ocean
Sphinx	woman's head, lion's body & paws, bird wings	Egyptian and Greek
Titans	huge giants with brute strength	Greek myth
Troll	ugly dwarf with magic powers	Scandinavian
Unicorn	head & body of a horse, hind legs of an antelope, tail of a lion, long twisted horn on forehead	Greek and Roman myths
Vampires	ghosts who leave graves to attack humans	European

MAGIC WORDS AND SUPERSTITIONS

abracadabra, amulet, anklet, bewitch, black cat, broken mirror, charms, cross, cross your fingers, curse, Druid, evil eye, four-leaf-clover, horseshoe, knock-on-wood, walk under ladder, luck, moon, mustard seed, occult, omen, opal, rabbit's foot, rainbow, rice, rites, ruby, snake, sneezing, soul, spilling salt, spirits, starts, step-on-a-crack, sun, taboo, toad, totem, triangle, voodoo, warlock, witch, zodiac...

POSSIBLE TITLES

If I Joined the Circus; Being Invisible; Sounds at Night; An Interview with a Famous Person; Ten Years from Now; Dear Santa; Riding Horses; Barefoot in the Mud; If I Lived Long Ago; Dream Vacation; A New Computer Game; My Dog Talks; Visit from Outer Space; Spending $1,000; If I Could Fly; The Day the Dinosaur Visited; My Favorite Season; My Favorite Age to Be; I Am Famous; New Flavors of Ice Cream; Designing a Ring for Me; A Day Without Gravity; How to Wash an Elephant; I Am the Parent: You Are the Kid; If Europeans had Left the Americas Alone; Where the White Goes When the Snow Melts; My First...; A Special Place; My Name; My Family; The Best Gift I Ever Gave (or Received); Swimming; Dancing; A Great Party; My Favorite Relative; Dying; An Embarrassing Moment; Me—the Famous Explorer; What My Teddy Bear Thinks of Life with Me...

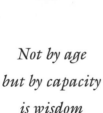

Not by age but by capacity is wisdom acquired.

—Lacydes
c. 241 B.C.

FIRST SENTENCES

It was the middle of the night, and everyone was fast asleep...

Once upon a time, long, long ago...

We were frightened when we saw the old house....

All the way home, I kept wondering how to explain it to my parents...

Waves thundered in toward the shore in an endless procession...

I stood stock still. My legs refused to move, and I broke out in a cold sweat...

MORE IDEAS

A Visit to Another Country (weather, food, transportation...)

Running Very Fast (running a race, running from something you fear...)

A Statue Comes to Life (Be a specific statue: Roman God, Pioneer, etc.)

I Am an Inanimate Object (stop sign, pair of socks, chair, etc.) What are your complaints?

A Famous Literary Character (Tom Sawyer, Mrs. Piggle-Wiggle, Scrooge, Superman) What do you do one day?

I Am a Wild Animal (How do you find food, protect yourself, where do you live?)

*True ease in writing comes
from art, not chance,
as those move easiest who have
learned to dance.*

—Alexander Pope

❧ Editing ❧

The CAPS System

1. Have someone else check your work.
2. Start with the first sentence and re-read your writing, asking CAPS questions for each sentence.
3. Mark your corrections with a red pencil or pen.
4. Rewrite your work (hopefully using the power of a computer) taking all the time you need.

The CAPS acronym stands for:

C: Capitalization

1. Are the first words of each sentence capitalized?
2. Are all proper nouns capitalized?

A: Appearance

1. Is the handwriting neat and legible?
2. Is the paper neat and attractive?
3. Are the first words of each paragraph indented?
4. Are the margins straight?
5. Are the sentences complete?

P: Punctuation

1. Is the right punctuation mark at the end of each sentence?
2. Are commas used when needed?

S: Spelling

1. First, have you eyeballed the word; does it look right?
2. Second, if you're still not sure, have you sounded it out?
3. Third, if still not sure, have you used the dictionary or asked for help?

No passion in the world is equal to the passion to alter someone else's draft.

—H. G. Wells

More on Editing

Here is a more detailed way to look at editing:

1. **Proofreading:** Check grammar, usage, capitalization, punctuation, spelling, paragraphing, and syllabication.
2. **Diction:** Are word choices appropriate, effective, and precise?
3. **Syntax:** Add or correct transitions, sentence structure and awkward word constructions.
4. **Accuracy of Text:** Check quotations, dates, and footnotes.
5. **Manuscript:** Check margins, headings, subheads, and paging.
6. **Semantics:** Make sure what you said is what you meant.

Writer's Self-Evaluation

Ask yourself these questions:

INFORMATION

1. Where, when, and with whom is the event happening?
2. Is your meaning clearly explained? Any confusing parts?
3. Are the scene and people described in a way that people can see and hear the story in their mind's eye?
4. Do people talk in the story? Are there quotation marks when they do?
5. Are examples used to show meaning?

TOO MUCH INFORMATION

1. What parts aren't needed?
2. What is the piece really about? Do all parts stick to the theme?
3. Is it more than one story?
4. Is there too much conversation?

BEGINNINGS

1. Does the beginning bring the reader right into the action or main idea of the piece?
2. Where does the piece get going? Can you cross out the first paragraph?

ENDINGS

1. Does the ending leave the reader wondering? (This can be good or bad.)
2. Does the ending go on and on?
3. How does the reader feel at the end?
4. What do you want the reader to know at the end?

TITLES

1. Does the title fit the piece?
2. Does it grab the reader and make her want to read the piece?

STYLE

1. Is something said more than once?
2. Are the words *and, then,* or *said* used too much?
3. Are sentences too long or too short?
4. Does the voice telling the story stay the same—I, he, or she?
5. Does the verb tense remain the same—past, present, or future?

I have rewritten—often several times—every word I have ever published. My pencils outlast their erasers.

—Vladimir Nabokov

Responses to Writing

✦ First read the piece without correcting any grammatical or spelling errors.
✦ Point out creative examples, picturesque descriptions or descriptive words, your understanding of the idea, good handwriting or printing, humorous incidents, good ideas, thoughts expressed well.

Helpful Remarks

✦ "Tell me more about..."
✦ "How..." and "Why..." questions (to elicit more details).
✦ "What part of the story (or piece) would you like to work on?"
✦ Finally, if this is a piece of writing to be shared outside the family, "Let's re-read this and check for spelling (or punctuation or capitalization)."

Listening Tapes

Tape record your writings and share them with family and friends. Send tapes to faraway friends and relatives.

Drama Productions

Convert your writing into plays and present them to family and friends. Have a drama night.

Read Aloud

Read your stories to others. Have a literary night or a poetry reading.

Getting Published

Here are some magazines that publish children's writing:

Cricket/ PO Box 300/ Peru, IL 61353
Dynamite/ 730 Broadway/ New York, NY 10003
Stone Soup/ PO Box 83/ Santa Cruz, CA 10003
Highlights for Children/ 803 Church St./ Honesdale, PA 18431

The end of writing is not the finished book, the end of writing is the reader.
—*Anonymous*

No tears in the writer, no tears in the reader.

—*Anonymous*

❧ Handwriting ❧

Holding a Pen or Pencil

There is a generally accepted "correct" way to hold a pencil, and just as many people who have variations on the "correct" way. The main point of penmanship is to produce legible handwriting and feel comfortable when writing. The generally accepted way to hold a pencil (pencil resting on the first joint of the third finger, and thumb and second finger pinching the top as shown here) is usually less fatiguing because the movement of the pencil is produced in the fingers. In other styles, the pencil's action is 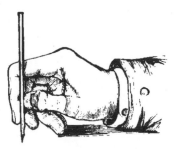 produced by the wrist, which causes the writer to tire more quickly because more muscles are being used. If the way your child holds his pencil tires him out, then he will probably grow to dislike writing. Younger children (4 to 8) tire more quickly of writing than older ones.

In *What Do I Do on Monday?* John Holt says,

> *There are other ways to hold pencils, and some of them, for children with small and weak fingers, might at first be a good deal better than the one we try to teach them. Given the right kind of pencil or pen (like a ball-point), it is really very easy to write with the pen gripped in the whole fist.*

Printing

THE FOUR STAGES OF WRITING:

✦ **Scribbling:** (first two years) for the joy of movement and the delight of seeing a hand-made mark on the paper.

✦ **Scribble-Writing:** scribbling across the page.

♦ **Mock Writing:** wavy lines, circles, etc.

♦ **Creation Writing:** Mixture of real and created letters. Kids like to write the "letters" and have you "read" them.

Cursive

John Holt says that cursive writing developed from copper engraving. Then someone got the great idea that everyone should learn cursive because it was a faster way to write. Not true. Almost all adults I know have developed their own style of combined printed and cursive writing. Alas and alack! As with any form that we want to break free from, we must first learn the original before we can give it up.

...(some overqualifying words like somewhat, rather, very, little, sort of are:) leeches that infest the pond of prose, sucking the blood of words.

—E. B. White

These are the basic strokes of cursive handwriting:

1. A short, curved upstroke.
   This stroke makes these six letters:

   ii rr uu vv ww xx

2. A "hump" shape.
   This stroke makes these three letters:

   m m n n s s

3. A *c* shape.
   This shape makes *c's* and *a's*:

   c c c a a a

4. A tall loop above the line.
   The tall loop makes:

   l l l b b b k k d d h h

5. Long loop below the line, to the left.
Makes:

gg jj yy zz

6. Long loop below the line, to the right.
Makes:

fff ppp qq

7. The last three letters are *e*, which is a short, rounded loop; *t*, which is a tall *i* that is crossed; and *o*, which is round, like the *c* shape, but closed at the top:

ee tt oo

POINTS TO WATCH

1. Slant all letters the same way for a neat appearance.
2. Short letters should be half the size as tall ones, except *t*, which is half way between the two.
3. Watch for unnecessary backstrokes in *c* based letters and loopy *t*'s.

PRACTICE SENTENCES THAT USE ALL THE LETTERS OF THE ALPHABET

Use these sentences to practice printing and cursive handwriting.

The quick brown fox jumps over the lazy dog.

The spy squaw mixed a dozen jugs of black veneer.

Joe packed my sledge with five boxes of frozen quail.

Pack my box with five dozen liquor jugs.

John had my big quiz trick of six cap vowels.

Quiet gadfly jokes with six vampire cubs in zoo.

Picking just six quinces, new farm hand proves strong but lazy.

Back in my quaint garden, jaunty zinnias vie with flaunting phlox.

Jumpy zebra vows to quit thinking coldly of sex.

Exquisite farm wench gives body jolt to prize stinker.

CALLIGRAPHY

Calligraphy handwriting was regarded by the ancient Persians and Chinese as an art of equal importance to painting. Before Gutenberg's revolution of the printing press, all books were made by hand, and the calligraphers were in great demand.

English is a remarkably clear, flexible, and useful language. We should use it in all of our communications.

—Daniel O'Neal, Jr.

Italic handwriting is a modified system of calligraphy that can be done with an ordinary pen or pencil. For workbooks for all ages in Italic Handwriting, please write: Portland State University Continuing Education Press P.O. Box 1394 Portland, Oregon 97207.

❧ HANDWRITING GAMES ❦

Squiggle Color Designs

The wastepaper basket is a writer's best friend.

—Isaac Bashevis Singer

When I was in school, I used to make designs like this when I was bored. They're fun to do with someone else. Make a free-form design in the middle of the paper, and take turns with your child in drawing concentric designs. Use a variety of colored pens for the lines. Peggy Kaye's book, *Games for Learning* gave me the idea of using this common game to foster small motor control.

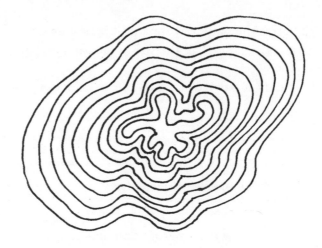

The Bee and the Flowers

Make a game board like the one shown. Explain that the bee has left his hive and must go to each flower to get honey. The bee may not cross over any lines and must return to his nest after collecting the nectar. (Adapted from The Farmer and his Crops in *Games for Learning* by Peggy Kaye, © 1991.)

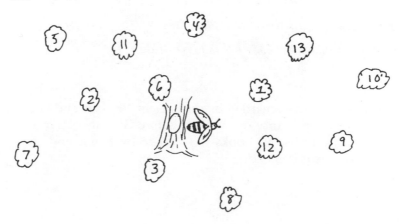

Decorated Letters

Choose an expression from the list below, (notice that the words begin with the same letters (alliteration) or make up your own crazy one, or try your name. Take **colored pencils,** trace around the word, go over each letter one or two times, or make circles, triangles or squares out of the letters. You can also decorate the words any way you please. Below are some words to decorate.

sleepy salamander
salty soda
radiant radio
magic milky marbles
pink pear

House Letters Game

Print all the letters of the alphabet on a piece of handwriting paper as shown, and then ask your child the following questions: Which letters live in the whole house? Which letters live just downstairs? Which letters go all the way to the basement?

Thinking is the activity I love best, and writing to me is simply thinking through my fingers.

—Isaac Asimov

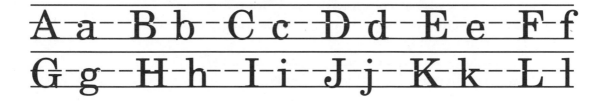

❧ GRAMMAR AND SPELLING ❦

Mind and muscles thrive on challenge but not frustration.

—Don H. Parker

There are people who are born good spellers (it seems to have something to do with a photographic memory) and there are people who struggle to learn rules and memorize correct spellings. When we try to read misspelled words, it can slow us down and make it harder (but not impossible) for us to grasp the meaning of the writing. A writer who is a poor speller may not impress the reader with her ideas, no matter how profound, and a poor speller may be judged as being ignorant and careless. In actuality, it is only important to use correct spelling when you wish to share your work with others.

Now-a-days, with spell checkers built into computers, people can free themselves from the tyranny of spelling lessons and concentrate on the higher task of writing. As Richard Gentry, Ph.D. wrote in his book *Spel is a Four Letter Word:*

"Make an honest attempt to spell werds wright. Right the write werd when you no it. When u don't, hook it up. (That is, hook up your computer, type in your message and turn on the spelling check.)...Don't feel bad if you're a terrible speller. Bad spellers can do almost anything. For proof, just look at this list of bad spellers: Queen Elizabeth I, George Washington, Andrew Jackson, Thomas Edison, Albert Einstein, Bruce Jenner, Cher."

Remember this:

+ People of great intelligence can have trouble with spelling.
+ Too much focus on "correctness" is bad for spelling.
+ Copying words and focusing on mechanics won't necessarily make you a good speller.
+ Writing with purpose can help in learning to spell.
+ Kids learn to spell by using invented spellings.

Invented Spelling

Most children begin writing by using *invented spelling*, which means they make up the spelling of a word as they write. I find invented spelling delightful and usually phonetically correct. Children leave most of those pesky vowel sounds out when they use invented spelling. (Who needs them, anyway?)

It is important to validate this type of creative writing. If you want to share the correct spelling with your child, point out how closely her invented spelling comes to the traditional spelling. Most of the time it's only a letter or two off anyway.

In fact, spelling phonetically (spelling a word the way it sounds) is a method that can help in "real" spelling. For example, a pesky word such as Wednesday, pronounced phonetically, is *Wed-ness-day,* so that the *d* and *s* are heard, thus giving the speller a way to remember the spelling. Island is another good candidate for phonetic pronunciation: *Iss-land.*

The problem with using spelling books is that the words the child studies in the spelling book don't relate to other subjects that the child is studying and perhaps writing about. Success in spelling will come if spellers work with a variety of methods. Have them learn words that come primarily from their own writing needs or the current topic of study.

Ideas for Spelling

- ✦ Let the children pick out their own spelling words for study, maybe 12 to 18 words a week.
- ✦ Keep a personalized **Spelling Dictionary**. Divide a sheet of paper into 32 sections and label each section with a letter of the alphabet. In the last eight sections, list those pesky diphthongs (two consonant letters found together that make one sound when pronounced): *wh, sh, ch, th,* etc. Then, each time your child asks you how to spell a word, have him write it in his Spelling Dictionary, and he will create his own list of spelling words.

The High-Utility 500

Over the years researchers have carefully tabulated the most frequently used words. Spelling instruction, with the goal of helping students become better spellers in their daily writing, should focus exclusively on these high-utility words.

The following list of words was compiled initially from the American Heritage Word Frequency Study (Caroll, Davies, Richman). These words were cross-checked with other respected studies.

In 1985, Milton Jacobsen analyzed the compositions of over 22,000 students in grades 2-12 to determine the validity of these and other word-frequency studies. The results of this intensive analysis indicated that students continue to use the same basic core of high-frequency words in their writing. All spelling instruction should focus on high-use writing words. Teach the kids to use the dictionary or computer spell checkers for words that are not on this list.

I don't give a damn for a man that can spell a word only one way.

—Mark Twain

500 Words Spelling List

One way to use this list is to pick out four to six words from one of the groups of 100 and take turns telling or writing short stories or sentences using all the words that you picked.

THE FIRST 100

the, of, and, a, to, in, is, you, that, it, he, for, was, on, are, as, with, his, they, at, be, this, from, I, have, or, by, one, had, not, but, what, all, were, when, we, there, can, an, your, which, their, said, if, do, will, each, about, how, up, out, them, then, she, many, some, so, these, would, other, into, has, more, her, two, like, him, see, time, could, no, make, than, first, been, its, who, now, people, my, made, over, did, down, only, way, find, use, may, water, long, little, very, after, words, called, just, where, most, know

THE SECOND 100

get, through, back, much, go, good, new, write, our, me, man, too, any, day, same, right, look, think, also, around, another, came, come, work, three, must, because, does, part, even, place, well, such, here, take, why, help, put, different, away, again, off, went, old, number, great, tell, men, say, small, every, found, still, between, name, should, home, big, five, air, line, set, own, under, read, last, never, us, left, end, along, while, might, next, sound, below, saw, something, thought, both, few, those, always, show, large, often, to-gether, asked, house, don't, world, going, want, school, important, until, form, food, keep, children

The heart of our trouble is with our foolish language. It doesn't know how to spell and it can't be taught.

—Mark Twain

THE THIRD 100

feet, land, side, without, boy, once, animals, life, enough, took, four, head, above, kind, began, almost, live, page, got, earth, need, far, hand, high, year, mother, light, country, father, let, night, picture, being, study, second, soon, story, since, white, ever, paper, hard, near, sentence, bet-ter, best, across, during, today, however, sure, knew, it's, try, told, young, sun, thing, whole, hear, example, heard, several, change, answer, room, sea, against, top, turned, learn, point, city, play, toward, five, himself, usually, money, seen, didn't, car, morning, I'm, body, upon, family, later, turn, move, face, door, cut, done, group, true, half, red, fish, plants

THE FOURTH 100

living, black, eat, short, United States, run, book, gave, order, open, ground, cold, really, table, remember, tree, course, front, American, space, inside, ago, sad, early, I'll, learned, brought, close, nothing, through, idea, before, lived, became, add, become, grow, draw, year, less, wind, behind, cannot, letter, among, able, dog, shown, mean, English, rest, perhaps, certain, six, feel, fire, ready, green, yes, built, special, ran, full, town, complete, oh, person, hot, anything, hold, state, list, stood, hundred, ten, fast, felt, kept, notice, can't, strong, voice, probably, area, horse, matter, stand, box, start, that's, class, piece, surface, river, com-mon, stop, am, talk, whether, fine

THE FIFTH 100

round, dark, past, ball, girl, road, blue, instead, either, held, already, warm, gone, finally, summer, understand, moon, animal, mind, outside, power, problem, longer, winter, deep, heavy, carefully, follow, beautiful, everyone, leave, everything, game, system, bring, watch, shall, dry, within, floor, ice, ship, themselves, begin, fact, third, quite, carry, distance, al-though, sat, possible, heart, real, simple, snow, rain, suddenly, leaves, easy, lay, size, wild, weather, miss, pattern, sky, walked, main, someone, center, field, stay, itself, boat, ques-tion, wide, least, tiny, hour, happened, foot, care, low, else, gold, build, glass, rock, tall, alone, bottom, walk, check, fall, poor, map, friend, language, job

John Holt on Spelling

I deeply believe that all this messing with spelling is foolish. If children read for pleasure, and to find out things they want to find out, and write in order to say what they want to say, they will before long spell better than most people do now…. Meanwhile, if we must give spelling tests, let the children correct them by looking up each word, as they spelled it, in the dictionary. If they can't find it, either they are using the dictionary wrongly or they can't spell the word.

(*What Do I Do Monday?* John Holt Associates, 1994.)

Common Misspelled Words

accommodate, accumulate, acknowledgment, all right, believe, calendar, consensus, definite, describe, embarrass, existence, February, forty, fourth, government, grammar, inoculate, iridescence, irrelevant, judgment, liaison, lightning, maintenance, meant, miscellaneous, necessary, nervous, ninety, occasion, occur, prerogative, pseudonym, recommend, reconnaissance, rhythm, sense, separate, succeed, success, surprise, through, truly, Wednesday, weird, unnecessary

Homographically-Spelled Words

accept-except, affect-effect, already- all ready, choose-chose, its-it's, lose-losing, prefer-preferred, principal-principle, procedure-proceed, receive-receiving, stationary-stationery, than-then, there-they're, to-too-two, weather-whether, write-writer-writing

Words With Silent Letters

Gh, silent gh: ghastly, ghetto, ghost, ghoul, bought, caught, dough, eight, flight, high, right, sleigh, sigh, taught, thought

Gn, silent G: gnarl, gnash, gnat, gnome, gnu, align, arraign, feign, reign, sign

Kn, silent K: knack, knapsack, knave, knead, knee, knew, knife, knight, knit, knob, knock, knot, know, knowledge, knuckle

Wr, silent W: wrap, wreath, wreck, wren, wrench, wrestle, wring, wrinkle, wrist, write, wrong, wrote

Mb, silent B: bomb, climb, comb, crumb, jamb, lamb, limb, numb, thumb, tomb

Spelling Games

If survival depended solely on the triumph of the strong then the species would perish. So the real reason for survival, the principle factor in the "struggle of existence," is the love of adults for their young.

—Maria Montessori

ERASERHEAD

This game is a variation of *Hangman*. On a sheet of paper, draw the figure of Eraserhead and all the letters of the alphabet. Then draw letter frames (see picture) for the word you want to play with. Have your child guess the letters, crossing out each one as she goes. If she is right, fill in the blanks. Wrong guesses, and Eraserhead becomes slowly erased. (Text and graphics adapted from Eraser in *Games for Learning* by Peggy Kaye, © 1991.)

a b c d e f
g h i j k l
m n o p q r
s t u v w x y z

(for the word "elephant")

SILENT E

Write some of the following pairs of words on 3 x 5 index cards, using a different color for each word in the pair, then draw or cut pictures from old magazines to illustrate the words, if possible.

bit/bite	grad/grade	quit/quite	ton/tone
can/cane	hat/hate	rid/ride	tub/tube
cap/cape	hid/hide	rip/ripe	twin/twine
cod/code	hop/hope	rob/robe	van/vane
con/cone	Jan/Jane	Sam/same	wad/wade
cub/cube	kit/kite	sham/shame	win/wine
cut/cute	mad/made	slat/slate	
dim/dime	man/mane	slid/slide	
fad/fade	not/note	slop/slope	
fin/fine	pal/pale	spit/spite	
fir/fire	pin/pine	strip/stripe	
gal/gale	plan/plane	tap/tape	
glob/globe	pop/pope	Tim/time	

GUERRILLA SCRABBLE

Players sit around a table and place Scrabble pieces face down around the edge of the table. Everyone begins turning over tiles on the word *go*. Look for words. When you see one, shout it out (play with a four letter minimum if desired) and place the word in front of you. Other players may steal the letters from you by adding to your word as long as the new word is not based on your word (i.e., you could add *ar* to *doll* but not *s*). However, you may add on to your own word. Players may rearrange letters to make new words. Winner is first person to make ten words.

HIDE YOUR WORDS IN ART

Draw all spelling words with crayons or other markers. Make the letters large, small, fat, skinny, round, squiggly, or 3-D. Next, hide the words by drawing abstract designs around them.

BILLBOARD

Design an ad for your word. Try to sell it to your friends.

WORD BLOCKS

Fold a piece of paper four times to make sixteen squares. Try to fit sixteen spelling words into each square.

SPELLING COLLAGE

Cut and paste spelling words from letters in magazines or look for pictures that represent the spelling words.

CROSSWORDS

On centimeter **graph paper**, try to make a crossword puzzle from the list of current spelling words.

WORD DOMINOES

Cut **heavy paper** or **tag board** into 2" x 4" rectangles. Divide each rectangle into 2" squares. In each square write a spelling word. Each word must be used twice, once in manuscript writing and once in cursive. A word must never appear twice on the same card. Play as in regular dominoes. Turn over all the cards face down. Turn them up one-by-one and try to match the cursive and manuscript versions of the same word.

> *Education is what you have left over after you've forgotten everything you've learned.*
>
> *—Unknown*

Grammar Games

PARTS OF SPEECH

Construction Sentences   A simple formula for sentence construction. Have kids add their own sentences:

Adjective	Noun	Verb	Adverb	Preposition	Noun
Small	boys	run	quickly	to	candy.
Delightful	flowers	smell	sweetly	in	spring.

ADVERB ACTING

#1 (YOUNGER KIDS): Pre-write verbs and adverbs on small cards. Have each person draw two cards and act out the verb and adverbs on the cards:

VERBS: Smile, twirl, eat, gallop, write, drink, read, laugh, skip, run, hug, leap, jump, hop...

ADVERBS: Merrily, warmly, quietly, slowly, drowsily, quickly, sadly, noisily, nervously, happily...

#2 (OLDER KIDS): Person who is *It* leaves the room and the rest of the group thinks of an adverb for *It* to personify. When *It* comes back, she asks people to do things "in the manner of the adverb." i.e., "Josh, give a drink (or walk) to Richard in the manner of the adverb."

ADVERBS: lavishly, doggedly, secretly, amicably, illegally, accusingly, freely, wildly, caressingly, malevolently, modestly, wonderfully… (Check a thesaurus for more suggestions.)

PUNCTUATION

Read the following sentences out loud. Notice how the punctuation changes the meaning of the sentence:

There is no such thing as a genius. Some of us are less damaged than others.
—Buckminster Fuller

Take that little baby.
Take that, little baby!

We'll be there on time.
Well, be there on time!

Marie and I told you yesterday.
Marie, and I told you yesterday!

Give it to her son.
Give it to her, son!

Give it to me!
Give it to me?

Let's eat daddy.
Let's eat, daddy.

Mr. Jones, the criminal, has been caught.
Mr. Jones, the criminal has been caught.

Seven people knew the secret, all told.
Seven people knew the secret; all told.

Shakespeare played with punctuation in *Othello*:

CASSIO: Dost thou hear, my honest friend?

CLOWN: No, I hear not your honest friend; I hear you.

In Egypt, there is a city named Said, that is pronounced Sah-eed. Punctuate the following sentence to make sense:

Said I said you said I said said said he how said I said you said said I said said is said said said is not said said.

HYSTERICALLY FUNNY PUNCTUATION GAME

(This idea comes from pianist/comedian Victor Borge.) Pick a story with plenty of dialogue in it and assign a sound to each punctuation mark. Read the story out loud, substituting the sounds at every punctuation mark. (Funny crrk funny crrk funny whht ptt.)

Suggestions:

1. period: Ptt
2. comma: crrk
3. question mark: crrk, ptt

4. exclamation point: whht, ptt
5. hyphen: spp
6. apostrophe: chtt
7. quotation marks: chtt chtt

PUNCTUATION PICTURES (AND GENERAL USAGE)

Draw pictures using only punctuation marks:

Period [.] Use: End of sentences, abbreviations

Comma [,] Use: Breathing in sentences, words in a series, beginning or ending quotations.

Question Mark [?] Use: When asking questions.

Exclamation Point [!] Use: To show excitement.

Quotation Marks [" "] To show when a person is speaking (dialogue), title of a story, poem, or song.

Semicolon [;] Use between independent clauses (parts of sentences).

Colon [:] Use: before a list, summary, or long quotation.

Apostrophe ['] Use: to indicate possession, or missing letters.

Parentheses [( )] Use: to de-emphasize a secondary explanation.

Ellipses: [...] Use: To indicate an omission within a quote.

*Those who love their own children
about them; and who are therefore in
earnest, will see to it that a right school
is started somewhere around the
corner, or in their own home.*

—J. Krishnamurti

Numbers

✤ THE SIGNIFICANCE OF NUMBERS ✤

Numbers are magical. Immersed within their depths, we can truly experience the divine that is all around us; indeed, the concept of infinity is found here. Numbers display infinite kaleidoscopic interweavings and beautiful yet logical arrangements. With their great sense of higher order, they continue to amaze even the staunchest of atheists: it's almost as if they are here to make us all believers. Numbers symbolize a greater reality than the one that our five senses bring us. Some numbers, like the numbers 9, 11, 1, and 0 are just plain fun to work with because of their patterns. I especially love the 9s family. In the Dark Ages, young scholars were forbidden to study math because numbers were developed in the pagan lands of Arabia!

Do not worry about your difficulties in mathematics. I can assure you that mine are still greater.

—Albert Einstein

In school, most students will spend about 2,400 hours over a twelve-year period trying to learn various aspects of math. In our everyday lives, most of us will call upon basic math skills of addition, subtraction, multiplication, and division. For some (like bookkeepers and accountants), skills in working with percentages and fractions may be useful. Carpenters and builders need a general awareness of geometry, measurement, and fractions. It makes life easier to have these basic math facts committed to memory. However, with calculators abounding, it is certainly not a necessity.

Do we need much more? Yes— if we want to be scientists, engineers, or architects, but no—if we don't aspire to these careers. The only arguments in favor of studying mathematics in depth is that one, it develops skills of reasoning and logic, and two, it "exercises" the brain. (The brain, like all of our muscles, thrives on stimulation, and puzzles for the mind are good for it, although many other activities also stimulate the brain.) Logical skills are certainly desirable, but these skills are not the exclusive property of mathematical studies.

Remember that *no one* really *teaches* math (or anything) to kids, rather we provide experiences for kids in which they will learn about math. That's why it is best to learn basic math skills through games and working with manipulatives and using math in real-life situations. Most kids *need* to touch, count, see, and move around objects to understand how math works. Use a minimum of math textbooks and workbooks. Spend the time saved on watching a sunset. That is unless of course your child *loves* doing pages of math, then go for it, Einstein! (who, by the way, flunked math in school.) Carl Jung and Beethoven (who never learned to multiply or divide) were also terrible at math.

Manipulatives

Manipulatives are hands-on objects that children can manipulate with their hands to learn various mathematical ideas. The following is a list of my personal favorites.

CUISENAIRE RODS

Cuisenaire rods are wonderful manipulatives. They are little colored rods that are fun to play with—even one- and two-year-olds enjoy using them. The rods were invented by George Cuisenaire in Belgium over 35 years ago. George is a trained composer and was seeking to show his math students how notes on a musical scale match the relationship of numbers to one another. He came up with a "keyboard for mathematics"—a set of carefully designed rods (in metric scale) constructed in graduated lengths and selected colors. The rods represent abstract number concepts by means of physical models. The rods can teach everything from addition and subtraction to fractions, place values, associative property, factoring, and algebra. Write (or call) for the Cuisenaire catalogue at:

> Cuisenaire Company of America, Inc.
> PO Box 5026
> White Plains, NY, 10602-5026
> (800) 237-3142

CHIP TRADING

Chip trading teaches the concept of place value. (Place value is the idea that numbers are worth more if they are farther to the left in a number.) Some kids would play the game with me *forever* if I let them. I made my own board and I use poker chips for markers. So can you.

Making and playing the chip trading game

1) Make a **board** by dividing a piece of **paper** (one for each player) into at least four equal columns.
2) Obtain **poker chips** of at least four different colors. On the top of the paper, **tape** (or color) one color of each poker chip for each column.
3) Choose what your **base number** will be (five and ten are the most common).
4) Choose one player to be the banker.
5) Roll one or two **dice**. Each player gets as many colored chips (matching the color of the right hand column on the playing board) as are shown on the dice.
6) If more chips are in the right-hand column than are in the base number, players may count out that number of chips and trade them to the banker for the next color of chips. For example, in base ten, every ten chips collected in the right-hand column may be traded in for one chip of the next color to the left. (Below number 125 is represented.)
7) Play until everyone has a chip in the farthest left-hand column.

Bless us,

Divine numbers.

—Plato

Geoboards

Geoboards are square boards with twenty-five pins nailed into them at regular intervals. Rubber bands are placed in various geometric configurations on the nails. Activities with geoboards invite kids to use a hands-on approach to learning about geometric shapes, area, measurement, estimation, percentage, fractions, multiplication, division, and graphing.

You may purchase geoboards through the Cuisenaire Company.

Cards

A deck of playing cards is a fantastic tool to use in developing various math skills. Please see the section on number games for specific card games.

Beans or Small, Polished Pebbles

Beans (or pebbles) make terrific counters for kids that are just learning numbers. Beans are a mainstay in the CDA math system (see below), but can be used as a supplement with any math work. They're easy to get and very cheap. When you're done, you can cook them up and use them in tacos. (The beans, that is!)

Math Textbooks

Observe how system into system runs.

—Alexander Pope

There are tons of math texts and math systems available. I have chosen two of my favorite to review, although there are many other noteworthy ones out there. If you use a math textbook, don't feel your child has to do every problem on every page and don't feel that you have to go in order, either. Especially don't force them to do pages and pages of problems with concepts that they have already mastered. Use textbooks with discretion, and instead encourage kids to become involved in real life math problems such as cooking, buying things, writing checks, balancing a check book, figuring out tips and sales taxes. Opportunities abound.

CDA Math

The *Pattern and Problems* books available through CDA is a very enjoyable workbook. Younger grades learn concepts of mathematics through work with beans and "bean sticks" which are tongue depressors with beans glued on them. If you have never used CDA math, it would definitely be wise to buy a teacher's manual. Write for one at:

Curriculum Development Associates, Inc.
PO Drawer 2320
Monterey, CA 93942

or

Suite 414, 1211 Connecticut Ave, NW
Washington, DC 20036

Real Math

Open Court's *Real Math* books are best for their dice games. They use specially numbered dice, so you would either need to buy or make some to play the games. They also have stories to develop critical thinking skills, in which kids have to solve math problems created by the characters in the stories.

> Real Math
> c/o Open Court Publishing Company
> Box 559
> Peru, Illinois 61354

LEARNING MATH WITH TRADE BOOKS

There are three outstanding trade books on math that cover basic math skills through use of exciting games and projects:

1) *Family Math* by Jean Kerr, Virginia Stenmark, and Ruth Cossey, 1986
2) *I Hate Math* by Marilyn Burns, 1975
3) *Games for Math* by Peggy Kaye, 1987

I do believe that these three books cover every aspect of the seven math strands (see below). One could easily skip all the boring math textbooks and receive a fine basic education in math by using these. The books present mathematical concepts in exciting, intriguing ways. All three books are a must for homeschool libraries. In addition, *Games for Learning* by Peggy Kaye, contains both math and reading games that make learning fun.

Mathematics is the queen of the sciences.

—Carl Friedrich Gauss

Aims

AIMS (Achievement in Math and Science) combines the fields of science and math. Learners explore these subjects through activities and experiments such as finding out how many drops of water fit on the head of a penny (which involves math skills of estimation and graphing) and the result (which demonstrates the scientific principle of surface tension). For more information please write:

> AIMS Education Foundation
> PO Box 8120
> Fresno, CA 93747

Math Dictionaries

As you and your children explore math concepts, you can record new math terms you come across in a personal math dictionary. (See curriculum guides for a list of math vocabulary words in each grade level.) For fun, you might like to make a "daffynition" of the word before writing the real one, such as:

octagon:
1. October's all gone.
2. A polygon having eight sides and eight angles.

parallel lines:
1. Two lions from Lell.
2. Two lines continuing in the same direction but never meeting.

Math Strands

About thirty years ago, California educators developed the concept of math strands to help broaden the concept of math. The strands are all interconnected and most number problems involve a combination of strands. Currently, the strands are:

1. Numbers
2. Measurement
3. Geometry
4. Functions
5. Statistics and Probability
6. Logic
7. Algebra
8. Discrete Mathematics

However, Rudy Rucker in his book *Mind Tools* (Houghton Mifflin Co. 1987) divides numbers into five levels with corresponding psychological roots:

1. Number (including measurement)= Sensation.
2. Space (Geometry) = Feeling.
3. Logic (including Statistics and Probability) = Thinking.
4. Infinity (Patterns and Functions) = Intuition.
5. Information.

The following sections of the Numbers chapter will deal with each strand separately and present a variety of games and ideas that aspire to make learning about math more fun. However, the Discrete Mathematics is not included in the discussion, as it was a "new" strand I discovered two weeks before this book's deadline.

❧ NUMBER SYMBOLS ❧

Most math instruction concentrates at least 50–60% on teaching how to manipulate numbers. Learning about numbers means learning how to read and write them, how to count them, how to place them in order, and learning about place value. It also means learning the basic skills of addition, subtraction, multiplication, division, fractions, and decimals. Each number has a different quality and shape associated with it. These basic number qualities are at once both subjective *and* universal.

one: the number of unity and the Great One…

two: duality and polarity: night/day, mother/father…

three: triad (considered lucky), mother/father/child, physical/mental/spiritual, Vishnu/Shiva/Brahma, Father/Son/Holy Ghost, Jupiter/Neptune/Pluto, give three cheers, …

four: the square, fairness and perfection, foundation, house, four elements (earth, air, fire, water), square deal, square accounts…

five: the pentagon, or human shape, five senses (seeing, hearing, tasting, touching, feeling), symbol of marriage between the male (2) and female (3)…

six: hexagon, the "perfect" number because $1 + 2 + 3 = 6$; Star of David, protection: two actions, or three twice…

seven: heptagon, the joining of three (action or mind) with four (matter), considered a lucky number, seventh heaven, seven days of the week, seven major planets…

Number nine, number nine, number nine…

—John Lennon

eight: the octagon, a "fresh start" $(7 + 1)$, is the balance of two fours…

nine*: the nonagon, is 3^2 (action on three planes), or 4 (matter) + 5 (people), (dressed to the nines, cat has nine lives, a stitch in time saves nine…)

ten: decagon, $5 + 5$, the completed human cycle, ten digits.

*Herb Kohl writes about number nine in his book *Mathematical Puzzlements* (Schocken Books, New York, NY, 1981):

> *"…Nine generates some unexpected and interesting number patterns…. Nine always returns to itself, which is why it was regarded as the symbol for indestructible matter in ancient times."*

Herb's book is a must-have for older children (and keen younger ones). His book covers tilings and tesselations, symmetry, fractals, number patterns, knots, maps, connections, logic, and strategy. It invites exploration into the playful, mystic, and thought-provoking world of numbers.

In the arithmetic of love, one plus one equals everything, and two minus one equals nothing.

—Mignon McLaughling

POEM FOR WRITING NUMBERS

A line straight down is lots of fun,
That's the way to make a 1.
Around the railroad track and down...
Toot Toot straight in comes number 2.
Around the tree, around the tree,
That's the way to make a 3.
Down and across and down one more,
That's the way to make a 4.
Down and around; put a hat on top;
And see the 5 you've found.
A curve and a loop,
A 6 throws a hoop.
Across the sky and down from heaven.
That's the way to make a 7.
Make an S, but do not wait;
Climb back up to make an 8.
First a circle, then a line;
That's the way to make a 9.
Circle around to make a zero;
And you will be a great big hero.

—AUTHOR UNKNOWN

❧ COUNTING AND NUMBER GAMES ❦

NUMBER BOOK

Create a scrapbook of numbers. On each page write a number up to 10 or 20, and have your child write a number on each page. He can then illustrate things that come in that number (such as a pair of shoes for two or a triangle for three) and write as many math problems as possible whose answer is the chosen number. This is a modified technique of one that is used in Waldorf schools (known as Illustrated Lesson Journals), except that in traditional Waldorf schools the children copy into their books what the teacher writes on the blackboard.

Addition Games

DOMINO ADDITION

Instead of matching like pieces, players must make matching **dominoes** add up to six or any other number that is choosen.

PYRAMID

This is a classic game I used to play as a kid. This version, which changes the goal number to ten and removes picture cards, was developed by Peggy Kaye.

Pyramid is played with a **deck of cards**. First, remove all the picture cards and the tens, then arrange 21 of the remaining cards into a six-row pyramid. Place the remaining 19 cards face down in a pile. The **object of the game** is to *remove cards in groups that add up to combinations of ten*. Cards must be fully exposed to remove. If ten can't be made, then turn over the pile of 19 cards to help make matches. Put these cards, if not used, face up in a discard pile. You may only play the top card in the discard pile. The game ends when you've turned over all 19 cards in the pile. Your score is the number of cards remaining in the pyramid, the lower the better.

Classic version: Play with a full deck and start with a row of 7 cards to build the pyramid. Try to remove cards with the sum of 13. Jack = 11, Queen = 12, King = 13.

Roll-a-Number Bowling

Although this game takes a bit of preparation, it is a wonderful game for the active types.

Construct a board out of **plywood** or **cardboard** as shown. The board may be any size you wish. It's nice to have a board with all the numbers 0-9 on it, but not necessary. Players take turns rolling 2 or 3 small **tennis balls** onto the board. (Board is tilted down.) **Object of the game:** *Player wins if the score is under 21 or over 11.* Rules may be changed if desired.

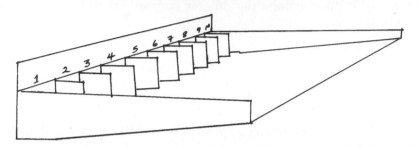

Number Line Games

Construct a **number line** like the one shown below and write the numbers from 1-20 on it. Numbers should be a few inches apart. Place **beans** or **small rocks** randomly on the number line. Take turns throwing a pair of **dice**. Choose one of the numbers on the dice and move your **marker (paper clip, rock, etc.)** that number of spaces.

Object of the game: Players try to pick up as many objects from the number line as possible.

Variations:

#1: Begin on number 10. Each player then decides whether to move up or down on the number line.

#2: Cut 12 **index cards** in half (saves paper) and write the numbers from 1-12 twice. Give one set to each player and have players determine which number to use each turn to "pick up" a bean or rock.

#3: Make up rules such as "name two more than..." then name that number. The next person names a number that is two more than the first one. Use a number line at first.

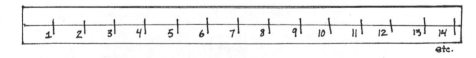

STORE

Playing store is lots of fun. Supply plenty of props for the kids to use, and let them do the rest. Encourage one person to be the buyer and one to be the seller. Play with them. Here is a list of items to stock in your store:

✦ toy cash register, egg carton, or plastic tray
✦ stick-on labels for marking items

A mathematician, like a painter or a poet, is a maker of patterns. If his patterns are more permanent than theirs, it is because they are made with ideas.

—Godfrey Hardy

- ✦ items for storage such as empty food boxes and cartons
- ✦ ink pad and rubber stamp
- ✦ sales receipts or small note pad
- ✦ old wallets and purses
- ✦ play dollars (draw a picture of a regular bill on green construction paper and decorate)
- ✦ play coins (bottle caps, buttons, poker chips)
- ✦ other money ideas:
  - ▼ Make coin rubbings with **crayons** and **paper.**
  - ▼ Make printed coins with **tempera** paints. Paint directly onto coins and then make prints of them. Cover coins with clear **contact paper.**
  - ▼ Make an enlarged **photocopy of a dollar bill**, obscuring the face and amount. Let children draw their portrait on the bill and the amount.

TARGET NUMBERS

On a large (2' x 3') piece of sturdy **cardboard**, draw a target with five circles. Label the numbers as shown. For younger children, draw identical pictures that represent each number. Using two **art erasers** or **dice**, take turns throwing the pair onto the target. For written practice, write out and solve each problem. For mental arithmetic this is a good way to teach younger children the concept of **counting on**. Let's say the numbers are 6 and 8. Have children pick the larger of the two numbers (8). Now, you hold up the remaining number of fingers (6). Have the children start *counting on* from number 9 until they count all your fingers.

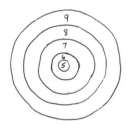

TRIANGLE NUMBERS

Use **counters** such as beans, small polished rocks, or tiles. Lay them in successive rows and keep adding each row on numbers together. Do you see the pattern that emerges in the numbers?

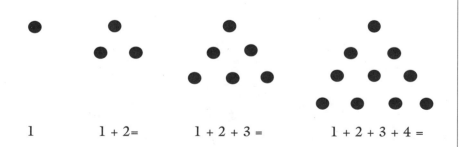

1   1 + 2=   1 + 2 + 3 =   1 + 2 + 3 + 4 =

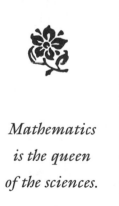

Mathematics is the queen of the sciences.

—Carl Friedrich Gauss

On Numbers

"Numbers have a definite existence as patterns underlying the thoughts and objects that surround us. Depending on the complexity of the pattern from which they are drawn, numbers fall into four rough size ranges: small, medium, large, and inconceivable. *Small numbers*—the numbers, let us say, from 1 through 1,000—code up simple, universal archetypes. These numbers have the solidity and definiteness of naturally occurring crystals. *Medium numbers*—the numbers from 1,000 up through a trillion or so—are used to stand for various collections of discrete objects: the number of trees in a forest, the number of people on earth, the number of books in a library, the gross national product in dollars, and so on. These numbers are hard to visualize "all at once," and they have a more abstract quality than do the small numbers. *Large numbers* are the numbers lying out at the fringes of our ability to come up with number names. "Googol" is one of the smallest large numbers. Googol is written as a 1 followed by a hundred 0's: 10, 000, 000, 000, 000, 000, 000, 000, 000, 000, 000, 000, 000, 000, 000, 000, 000, 000, 000, 000, 000, 000, 000, 000, 000, 000, 000, 000, 000, 000....*Inconceivable numbers* are the numbers that, while not infinite, are nevertheless so large and complex that we have no clear way of thinking about them."

(Excerpt from *Mind Tools* by Rudy Rucker. Copyright ©1987 by Rudy Rucker. Reprinted by permission of Houghton Mifflin Company. All rights reserved.)

Subtraction Games

TARGET NUMBERS

(For older children) Remove all the 10's and face cards from a **deck of cards**. Shuffle cards and deal each player four cards, then turn over two and put them in the middle. That is the target number. The **object of the game** is to arrange the cards two-by-two so that when you subtract them, your number will be closest to the target number. For example, let's say the **target number** is 53. You draw an ace (1), 5, 6, and 9. You would want to make up the problem 96 – 51 = 45. By doing this, it would bring you closest to the target number of 53. Next, you would subtract your number from the target number 53 – 45 = 8. Eight would be your total for that round. Person with the *lowest* score wins.

 Variation: Players may wish to play by trading their cards among themselves.

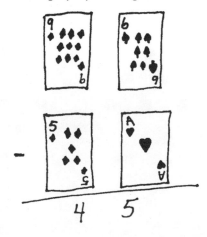

(Adapted from *Family Math* by Jean Kerr, et al. ©1986. Used by permission.)

Subtraction War

Play war in the conventional manner with this twist: when both players turn over their cards, the one who wins the trick is the one who can call out the correct answer to the subtraction problem of the two cards. Ace = 1, King = 12, Queen = 12, Jack = 11.

Mixed Operation Games

SPIDERS

Put a number on your paper and draw a circle around it. Take turns thinking up as many problems as you can that make up that number:

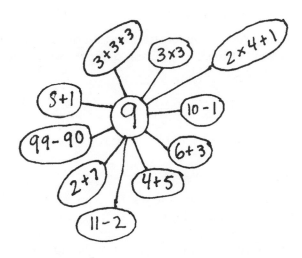

FROGS

On **index cards**, write the numbers from 0-15 (or 0-25 or 21-50 for older children). Tape them to the floor with **masking tape.** Take turns being frogs (you may want to make "mistakes" so your children can "catch" you) and jump around on the numbers saying things like:

"Hop to the four."

"Now hop to the number that's one less than four."

"Skip to the number that's one more than thirteen."

"Count backwards from sixteen to nine and hop on each number as you go."

"Can you get to seven in one jump?"

"Run to the number that's two more than eight."

(Adapted from Grasshopper in *Games for Math* by Peggy Kaye, © 1987.)

All the pictures which science now draws of nature and which alone seem capable of according with observational fact are mathematical pictures...From the intrinsic evidence of his creation, the Great Architect of the Universe now begins to appear as a pure mathematician.

—Sir James Jeans

WHAT'S DIFFERENT NOW?

Place 3 to 10 **beans** in your hand. Show them to your child, then have him close his eyes while you add or subtract a few items. When your hand opens again, have him guess what you did.

(Adapted from What Did I Do in *Games for Math* by Peggy Kaye, ©1987.)

How can finite grasp infinity?

—Joseph Butler

CATALOG SHOPPING

This is a good game for older students. Math skills include working with decimals, percentage, and four-digit addition in columns.

Choose your favorite catalog from the junk mail. You have $300. Order anything you like from the catalog. Add up the items and figure out tax and shipping if you want.

THE ROUNDABOUT NUMBER

Let me introduce you to the most interesting number I know: 142,857. Multiply this number by 2, 3, 4, 5, and 6. Now divide it by 2 and 5. Split the number in two and add:

```
 142
+857
```

Next, try multiplying 142,857 by 7. Are you surprised?

LUMBERYARD

This game was invented by Ruth Caswell when she was six years old in 1991. Since then, many homeschoolers have enjoyed playing it. You need a set of **cuisenaire rods** and some real or pretend **money** to play.

Choose one player to be the **builder** and one player to be the **lumber seller.** First, the lumber seller straightens up the piles of "lumber" (rods) from ones to tens and the buyer straightens up the money. Next, the builder asks the buyer for lumber, saying such things as, "Give me four rods that are two longer (or shorter) than five (or yellow)." Or, "Give me two rods that are half as long as orange (or ten)." Next, the lumber seller selects the rods and quotes a price. If you have enough money, you can even make it so that change has to be made. The builder then proceeds to build her house, while the lumber seller grows rich.

Place Value Games

Here is a little chart that helps in remembering place value. It's easy to see that the numbers we are used to dealing with are so very small! Googol or googolplex (which is one of my son Josh's favorite words) means the number one followed by a hundred zeros. The name was made up by the nephews of Edward Kasner who was solving difficult math problems at the age of eight.

HUN	(DRED)	100
THOU	(SAND)	1,000
MIL	(LION)	1,000,000
BI	(LLION)	1,000,000,000
TRI	(LLION)	1,000,000,000,000
QUAD	(RILLION)	1,000,000,000,000,000
QUIN	(TILLION)	1,000,000,000,000,000,000
SEX	(TILLION)	1,000,000,000,000,000,000,000
SEP	(TILLION)	1,000,000,000,000,000,000,000,000
OCT	(TILLION)	1,000,000,000,000,000,000,000,000,000
NON		(Well, you get the idea!)
DEC		

TENS AND HUNDREDS

Draw a Collect Ten game board as shown. Fill a small bowl with dried **beans** (about 200) and have on hand **20 paper cups.** Roll a **die.** That number of beans (determined by the die number) gets placed on the game board. Each group of ten beans collected goes into a cup. The goal of the game is to collect 100 beans and fill up all the cups. (Adapted from Collect Ten in *Games for Learning* by Peggy Kaye, ©1991.)

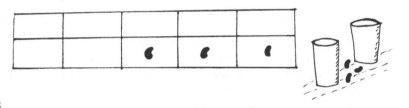

POTS

Place three (or four) **pots** (plastic containers) on the floor. Label them ones, tens, and hundreds (and 1,000, if you use four pots). Establish a base line. Players take turns throwing nine **beans** into the containers. When all beans are in place, tally up how many hundreds, tens, and ones (and 1,000's) you accumulate. Write the number on a score sheet (for younger children write three or four dashes for them to write their numbers on).

MONEY TOSS

Get three empty **yogurt containers.** Label one pennies (1¢), one dimes (10¢), and one dollars ($1.00). Now get at least **fifteen pennies, fifteen dimes**, and **ten green chips** or beans to represent dollars. Next, try to toss coins into their proper containers. When all coins and chips have been tossed, count the number of coins or chips that landed in each container. If the pennies or dimes exceed ten, then trade them in for the next highest coin or chip. Finally, record your money score on a piece of **paper.** Play until you make a certain amount of money.

(Adapted from Three Pots from *Games for Math* by Peggy Kaye, ©1987.)

The mathematical sciences particularly exhibit order, symmetry, and limitations; and these are the greatest forms of beauty.

—Aristotle

Multiplication Games

Fizz Bizz

An old standby—good for car trips or while dish washing.

Players decide which multiple will become *fizz* and which one will become *bizz*. For example, choose all multiples of 5 to be *fizz* and all multiples of 7 to be *bizz*. Each player takes a turn counting out loud: *One,* (says the first player), *two* (says the next), then *three, four,* fizz, *six,* bizz, *eight, nine,* fizz…

Grids

Use a grid with the numbers 1-100 drawn on it. Take turns throwing a **die** and use **counters** to cover any number on the grid that is a multiple of the number that you threw. (If you throw 4, for example, you may cover 4, 8, 12, 16, 20, 24…)

Circles and Stars

Start with a blank piece of **paper** and a **pencil**. Players go one at a time. On the first round, roll one **dice** and mark your paper with that number of circles. Next player follows fashion. On the second round, each player rolls the dice and puts that number in each of the circles. This picture represents a multiplication problem. (Adapted from Star Count from *Games for Math* by Peggy Kaye, ©1987.)

Box Multiplication

Make a box, like the one shown, on a sheet of **paper**. Let's say we are going to multiply 25 x 13. The diagonal line in each box separates the 1's column from the 10's, the bottom triangle for the 1's, the top for the 10's. Multiply 5 x 1 for the top left-hand box, putting the 5 in the bottom triangle. Next, multiply 5 x 3, putting the answer in the bottom left box, the 1 (tens) on top, the 5 (ones) on the bottom. Multiply the 2 on the top by the 1 and the 3, then add up the numbers *diagonally*, beginning in the bottom left-hand corner. If the answer is over 10, regroup (carry) the number into the next left-hand column of the next diagonal. Neat trick!

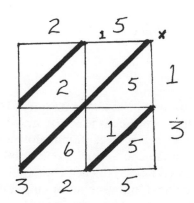

FINGER MULTIPLICATION (9's)

Hold both hands in front of you. Let's say we're multiplying 9 x 5. Count off from left to right until you reach your fifth finger. Bend it down: the four fingers to the left of the bent one are the 10's (40) and the 5 to the right are the 1's: the answer is 45. Another "magic" property of nine is that no matter what number you multiply by nine, the sum of the numbers in the answer will always be 9! (9 x 5 = 45; 4 + 5 = 9!)

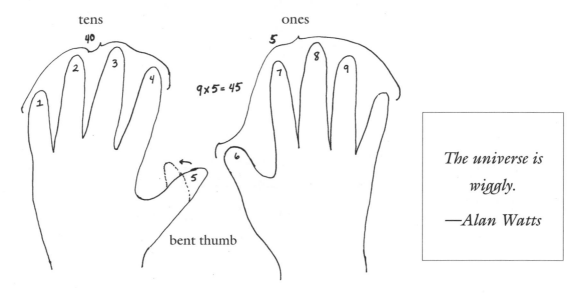

The universe is *wiggly.*

—*Alan Watts*

BOXES

This game uses graph paper. On the first roll of a dice, the number thrown determines the length of the player's box. (For example, if you roll a 3, make a line three spaces long.) The next throw determines the height of the box, and with that information, the box can be completed. Next, add up the number of squares enclosed in the box. This is your score. Scores can be expressed in multiplication equations (there are two for each box).

(Adapted from Lots of Boxes in *Games for Math* by Peggy Kaye, © 1987.)

HOW MANY?

Use your multiplication to determine how many basic multiplication facts have answers in the 40's, then find the facts for the 50's, 60's, 70's and 80's. You may be surprised!

NUMBER LINE MULTIPLICATION

Construct a **number line** that goes all the way up to 99. Take turns throwing a **dice** (or choose a number) and have each player **draw** or use a **marker** to mark that many skips all the way down the number line. One player draws marks above the line, the other below.

Count the Dots

Pick out all the aces, twos, threes, fours, and fives from a **deck of cards** (Ace=1). Shuffle the deck and pick one card at a time. If you pick a four, draw four parallel vertical lines on a sheet of paper. Pick a second card (let's say it's a three) and draw three parallel horizontal lines on your paper. Then, make a dot at the point of intersection between the two sets of lines. Count the dots to get your answer. (Note: you may also roll two dice.) (Adapted from the game Count Your Points in *Games for Learning* by Peggy Kaye, ©1991.)

> *Whatever*
> *you teach,*
> *be brief.*
>
> —*Horace*

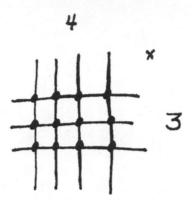

Six to Nine Chart

The most difficult multiplication factors to memorize are the factors of six through nine. This "game" (from John Holt) focuses on these factors.

Draw a **chart** like the one below. With a **pencil,** write in the multiplication products for each pair of factors. Before you begin to play, point out that each pair of multiplication factors (with the exception of the square or doubled numbers) has a *reciprocal* partner, cutting in half the total number of problems to memorize. Randomly point to the numbers in the outside rows and columns on the chart and have your child say the multiplication factor of the two numbers. After a while, start erasing the answers. Keep randomly choosing pairs of numbers. If the answer doesn't come easily, re-write the answer on the chart. Game ends when the whole chart is blank.

	6	7	8	9
6	(36)	42	48	54
7	42	(49)	56	63
8	48	56	(64)	72
9	54	63	72	(81)

Dot-to-Dot

Create a dot-to dot drawing using number factors from one set of multiplication facts. (For example, if you chose the four's table, you would dot-to-dot 4, 8, 12, 16, 20...) Have your child connect the dots in order. You may color in the resulting abstract pictures—they make lovely designs. (Adapted from Number Drawing in *Games for Learning* by Peggy Kaye, © 1991.)

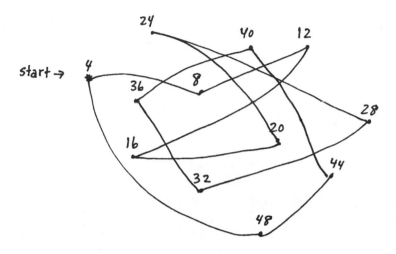

Times Tables Spirals

1. Cut about a 2" strip off the end of a piece of **lined paper.**
2. Starting with 0, write the numbers between the lines.
3. With the numbers on the outside, roll up the strip into a cylinder.
4. Loosen or tighten the roll so 0 lines up with 4.
5. With a **pencil,** push the cylinder up to make a spiral. You should now be able to read all the factors of the 4's times table.
6. To read other tables, line up the cylinder with a new number.

Division Games

> *A little learning is a dangerous thing; drink deep, or taste not the Pierian spring: there shallow draughts intoxicate the brain, and drinking largely sobers us again.*
>
> *—Alexander Pope*

Division Rap

I got this in an educator's magazine and didn't save the source, so thanks to the anonymous teacher out there that wrote this rap. It's great for remembering the steps it takes to do division.

> I'm Dr. P. and I'm on the scene,
> With my division rap and it's truly mean.
> It goes "Divide, Multiply, Subtract, and Bring Down."

Now we can do it wrong, or we can do it right,

But if we do it wrong, we'll be here all night.

So let's Divide, Multiply, Subtract, and Bring Down.

Again, Divide, Multiply, Subtract, and Bring Down.

First, we Divide, and then like 1-2-3,

Step 2 is Multiply—sometimes that socks it to me.

Step 3 is Subtract, and it's a natural fact

That you Bring Down the next digit, and then go right back.

To Divide, Multiply, Subtract, and Bring Down.

That's Divide, Multiply, Subtract, and Bring Down.

Left Outside

This game helps children learn about remainders.

Both players pick a number between 10 and 30. Let's say you pick 12 and your child picks 28. On your paper, you draw (in ink) 12 *x*'s and your child draws 28 on his.

Next, you both make fists. Pound on the table while chanting "One, two..." and on "three," stick out between one and five fingers. Add up the total amount of fingers, (let's say it was 7) and loop your *x*'s (in pencil) into sets of 7. The "winner" is the person with the *least* number of *x*'s outside a set. If you draw the *x*'s at random, you may erase the penciled loops each time and reuse the *x*'s.

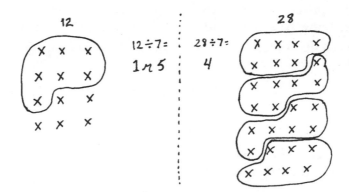

(Adapted from The Outsiders in *Games for Learning* by Peggy Kaye, ©1991.)

Lima Bean Circles

Count out twelve **lima beans.** With **paper** and **pencil,** draw two circles. Divide the lima beans into the circles. Now, try it for 3, 4, 5, 6, and 7 circles.

Fraction Games

APPLES

Cut an **apple** into two pieces. Explain that each part equals one half, and together they make a whole. Then cut another apple into quarters, and another into thirds.

COOKING

Use any recipe and cut it in half. A great and tasty way to explore fractions. Recipes abound in fractions. You can also double or make it 1½ times the size of the original recipe.

Mathematics is the alphabet with which
God has written the universe.

—Galileo

Percentage Game

PERCENTAGE PICTURES

On **graph paper**, outline several 10 x 10 squares. Draw a picture in the square, and then count the boxes to determine what percentage of squares you used.

Variation: Choose the percentage *before* you draw your picture, or tell your child to color in a varying amount (such as 25%, 50%, or 5%) of the squares.

Proof is an idol before which the mathematician tortures him or herself.

—Sir Arthur Eddington

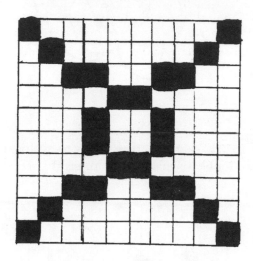

24%

47 %

Prime and Square Number Games

TILES

I learned this game from a fellow homeschool teacher Joe Wagner, affectionately known as "Mr. Math." (But you should hear him play bass…)

For this game, you need to get some **ceramic tiles** from the local tile shop, or make 25-100 1" x 1" squares out of heavy **cardboard**. (Note: You may also use 25-100 Cuisenaire "one" cubes.) Now, beginning with three tiles (one and two are special cases) ask your child if she can arrange them into even squares or rectangles that are at least two rows wide. If you can only arrange the tiles in one row, then that number of tiles represents a **prime number**. If the tiles make perfect squares, then that number represents the **square numbers**. Children will also see graphic representation of all **multiplication products** and **division quotients**.

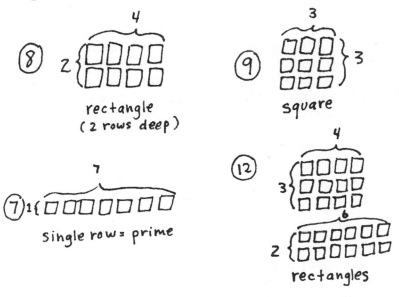

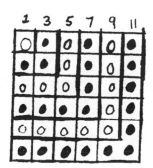

To show that square numbers are based on the addition of adjacent prime numbers, start counting the numbers as shown below. Try adding triangle numberswith the square numbers for yet another amazing series of number patterns.

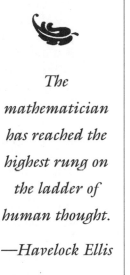

The mathematician has reached the highest rung on the ladder of human thought.

—*Havelock Ellis*

Mathematicians are artists of the imagination.

—*Michael Guillen*

❧ MEASUREMENT ❦

Measurement Overview

Measuring activities are usually fun because they're hands on. Be sure to include metric measurements in your studies because everybody else in the world uses metric.

There was a time when we measured things with parts of our bodies: feet, hands, and arms. This measuring system would work fine if we were all the same size. Still, it is the base of our standard measuring system!

Because standard measurements reflect natural body measurements, they seem more natural to us than metrics. Problems arose with standard measurements when they were used for things like buying cloth. From the tip of the nose to the end of an outstretched hand is about one yard, but whose arm would measure the cloth; the weaver's or the buyer's? Some people even measured a yard by the length of a man's belt. So in England, it was King Henry I (in the 1100's) whose feet and hands (naturally) were first used as measuring standards. In the 1300's King Edward II tried to standardize an inch by declaring that an inch was equal to three grains of barley laid end-to-end.

The metric system was developed in France in 1790. French scientists measured the distance from the North Pole to the equator and based the metric system on one ten-millionth of that distance, which they called a meter. Metrics is a preferred method for scientists because metrics (which is based on cycles of ten) is much easier to compute than Standard measurement (which is based on cycles of twelve and eight). Also in metrics, one cubic centimeter of water equals one milliliter equals one gram, and one cubic decimeter of water equals one liter equals one kilogram. Unfortunately, the instruments used to measure the distance from the North Pole to the equator weren't very accurate, so the calculations are a bit off.

The most interesting thing to measure is our narcissistic selves: height, weight, running speed, heart beat, which can be measured sitting, standing, after running, after jumping, and then compared to each other in a graph. Don't most families have a wall that marks the youngsters' and family friends' heights? More uses of measurement at home can include sewing, carpentry, cooking, and art.

Measurement begins with comparisons—big/small, warm/cold, and the like. It progresses to non-standard measurements (footsteps, arm lengths), and finally to standard systems such as metrics, units of time, distance, angle, temperature, and weight.

> *"I only took the regular course."*
>
> *"What was that?" enquired Alice.*
>
> *"Reeling and writhing, of course, to begin with," the Mock Turtle replied: "and then the different branches of Arithmetic —Ambition, Distraction, Uglification and Derision."*
>
> *"I never heard of Uglification," Alice ventured to say. "What is it?"*
>
> —Lewis Carroll, *Through the Looking Glass*

Measurement Games

RIBBON MEASURING

Use **ribbon** and **scissors** to measure different parts of your body such as foot, ankle, wrist, neck, nose, mouth, waist, etc. Make a chart of the results. The results may include writing the standard or metric measurements. (Adapted from Ribbon Me in *Games for Math* by Peggy Kaye, ©1987.)

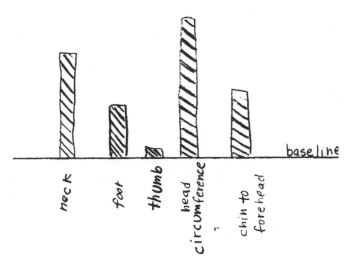

Understanding is nothing else than conception caused by speech.

—Thomas Hobbes

MEASURING HIKE

Use a tape measure to find each of these measurements:
1. Circumference of the biggest tree.
2. Circumference of the smallest tree.
3. Distance between any two trees.
4. Length of a leaf that is almost as long as your nose.
5. Length of a shadow.

PORTABLE RULER

These measurements are what Standard measurements are based on:

One inch (1")	= first thumb knuckle to thumb tip
Four inches (4")	= (a "hand") width of the closed hand (used in measuring horses)
Six inches (6")	= width of hand with fingers spread out
1 foot (1')	= a foot (on an adult male) or two spread-out hands, fingertip to fingertip
1 yard (1 yd.)	= distance from fingertip to the nose
1 fathom (6')	= arms stretched out wide
1 cup (1 c.)	= two hands cupped together
1 mile (1,000 paces)	= from Roman *mille*—1,000

Try measuring the length from your elbow to your wrist. Now compare it to the length of your foot.

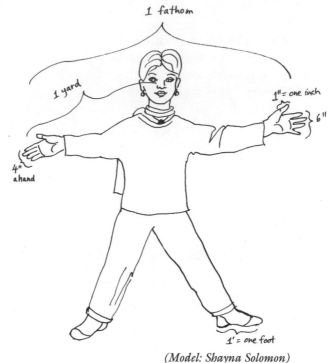

(Model: Shayna Solomon)

Non-Standard Measuring

Pick a large object like a couch. Measure it in various ways such as: normal walking pace, heel-to-toe, hand span (fingers spread out), palm (fingers together).

Spring Scale

Take a 6" piece of **rubber band** and make a loop at each end. Open a **paper clip** and insert it through one of the loops. Find a **cardboard** rectangle and **tape** the rubber band to the top length of the cardboard.

Now you have to *calibrate* the scale. Mark a horizontal line on the cardboard where the rubber band lies slack. Now hang a **spoon** from the hook, and mark the lowest point that the rubber band now hangs. This space is one *interval*. Continue to mark the cardboard at equal intervals, numbering from zero on up. Use your scale to weigh objects such as pencils, rulers, and knives.

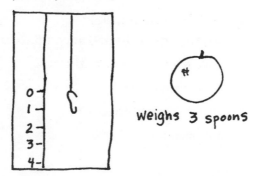

weighs 3 spoons

❦ GEOMETRY ❦

Geometry Overview

Geometry is the study of shapes in 2-D and 3-D space: lines, curves, shape, arear, volume, angles, points, and surfaces. The earliest use of geometry was for measuring land and materials. The Greeks searched for the secrets of nature through the study of geometry. They noticed that God geometrizes in nature. For two thousand years, Euclid's geometric truths served our needs, and they still do, in the limited area of the tiny sphere we occupy, but new models of geometry, such as Einstein's famous theory of relativity, were needed. For example non-Euclidean geometry rejects the idea that parallel lines never meet. Indeed, they may well bend and intersect in endless space. Geometry is my favorite subject in math because it comes closest to art.

Geometric lines also affect our feelings: horizontal lines and gentle curves tend to fill us with feelings of rest, contentment and ease. These lines are found in rolling meadows, crescent-shaped sand dunes, and calm ocean movement. Jagged angle lines, such as shark's teeth, great mountain ranges, volcanoes, and spears are associated with violence and unrest. Spiral lines that continuously change directions tend to be stimulating.

*Geometry...
the only science
that it hath
pleased God
hither to bestow
on mankind.*

*—Thomas
Hobbes*

Geometric Formulas

EINSTEIN'S THEORY OF RELATIVITY

$E = MC^2$ (Energy = Mass x Speed of Light squared)

(Great amounts of energy result from a small mass if it is completely changed into energy. This theory helped produce atomic energy.)

PERIMETERS

Rectangles: $P = 2\,l + 2\,w$ (Perimeter = 2 x length + 2 x width)

Squares: $P = 4s$ (Perimeter = 4 x side lengths)

Triangles: $P = a + b + c$ (Perimeter = side a + side b + side c)

AREAS

Circle: $A = \pi\,r^2$ (Area = pi x radius squared)

Square: $A = s^2$ (Area = side squared)

Rectangle or Parallelogram: $A = bh$ (Area = base x height)

Triangle: $A = \frac{1}{2}\,bh$ (Area = ½ base x height)

Ellipse: $A = \pi\,(\frac{1}{2}M \times \frac{1}{2}\,m)$ (Area = pi x [½ major axis + ½ minor axis])

Trapezoid: $A = (h \times b^1 + b^2) \div 2$ (Area = [height x base 1 + base 2] ÷ 2)

TOTAL AREAS

Square or Cube: $A = 6e^2$ (Area = 6 x edges squared)

Rectangle or Cube: $A = 2\,(lw + lh + wh)$ Area = 2 x (length x width + length x height + width x height)

Cylinder: $A = \pi\ dh + 2\ \pi\ r^2$ (Area = pi x diameter x height + 2 x pi x radius squared)

God ever

geometrizes.

—Plato

VOLUME

Cube: $V = s^3$ (Volume = sides cubed)

Rectangular Solid: V = lwh (Volume = length x width x height)

Cone: $V = \frac{1}{3}\ \pi\ r^2\ h$ (Volume = $\frac{1}{3}$ pi radius squared x height)

Cylinder: $V = \pi\ r^2\ h$ (Volume = pi x radius squared x height)

Sphere: $V = \frac{4}{3}\ \pi\ r^3$ (Volume = $\frac{4}{3}$ x π x radius cubed)

Pyramid: $V = \frac{1}{3}\ bh$ (Volume = $\frac{1}{3}$ base x height)

CIRCLE CIRCUMFERENCE

$C = \pi\ d$ (Circumference = pi (3.14) x diameter)

Geometric Games

PROTRACTOR SUN CLOCK

That sometimes clear...and sometimes vague stuff...which is ...mathematics.

—Imre Kakatos

On a piece of **cardboard** (or use a **paper plate**), use a **felt-tip pen** to trace the outline of a **protractor.** Mark the following angles on the circle: 0°, 30°, 60°, 90°, 120°, 150°, and 180°. Flip the protractor over and mark the same degrees on the other side except 0° and 180°. Write the numbers 1-12 around the circle as seen on a clock. Take the clock outside on a sunny day and place it on the ground. Insert a **pencil** into the middle of the circle so that it is straight up and down. Rotate your clock so that the shadow of the pencil falls on the correct hour of the clock.

TOOTHPICK SHAPES

Soak some **dried peas** in some water. When they are soft, stick them onto the ends of **toothpicks** to make a variety of geometric shapes.

ANGLE BOAT RACE

Experiment with angles and speed. See how design affects movement. On some **stiff paper** draw and cut three **triangles** about 1" high. Make one triangle a right angle (90°), one an acute (less than 90°) angle, and one an obtuse (more than 90°). Cut a small notch in the base of each triangle. Fill a **cookie sheet** with **water**. Take **toothpicks** dipped in **dish soap** and touch the water just inside the notch on each boat. (You need at least two people to "push" all three.) Which boats move the fastest?

SHAPE COLLAGE

This is a classic way to introduce young children to shapes. Peggy Kaye has an original version of this idea in *Games for Math*.

With **colored construction paper, scissors,** and **glue**, cut out different sizes of triangles and make a collage from the various shapes. You may use other geometric shapes such as circles, squares, rectangles, and hexagons, or make a collage from a variety of shapes.

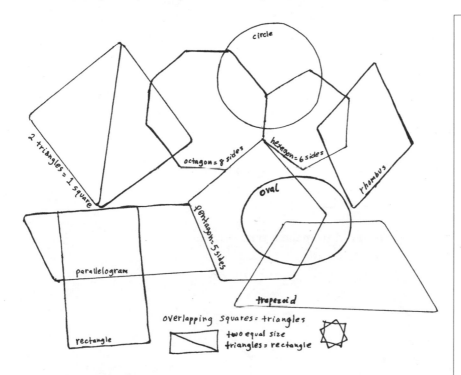

ORIGAMI GEOMETRIC FUN

Introduce young children to basic geometric shapes with origami. As you make simple origami objects with your child, talk about the various shapes you are folding. The following activity is taken from *Games for Math* by Peggy Kaye.

Cat:

Begin with a **square** piece of **paper.** Fold the square to make a **triangle**.

Fold the top point of the **triangle** down and forward.

*If triangles
had a god
s/he would have
three sides.*

—Montesquieu

Fold the two bottom points up and forward.

Turn the paper over. Draw a cat face on the **pentagon**-shaped face.

Dog:

Begin with a **square**. Fold to make a **triangle**.

Fold top corners of the **triangle** down and forward. (This makes a **diamond** shape in the middle with two **triangular** flaps.)

Fold the top *and* bottom of the **diamond** down and backward.

Draw a doggie face.

PLAY DOUGH

Cut out different geometric shapes from play dough such as circles, squares, rectangles, stars, and triangles.

JUNK SCULPTURES

Make sculptures out of junk, using **cylinders** from paper towels and toilet paper, **rectangular bricks (cuboids)** from cereal boxes, butter containers, and other objects.

SYMMETRICAL SQUARES

Use a piece of **grid paper**. Divide the paper in half. One person colors a square on her side, and the other one colors the mirror image (symmetrical) of it. Take turns. You may color more than one square at a time. If you use different colors, it creates more of a challenge for the other person.

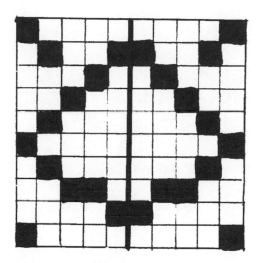

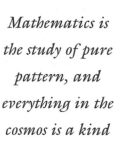

Mathematics is the study of pure pattern, and everything in the cosmos is a kind of pattern.

—Rudy Rucker

SYMMETRICAL PAPER CHAINS

Fold a piece of **paper** into a fan-fold of about 1" squares. Draw a half-person on the folded paper, making sure the arm extends to the edge of the paper. Use **scissors to** cut out your figure.

MIRROR IMAGES

Tape a small **mirror** to the edge of a **shoe box**. Write your name on an **index card** and place it under the mirror. Now take another card and try to write your name so that it will appear correctly in the mirror.

Geometry/Yantra Pictures

Staple 20 sheets of 8 ½ x 11" paper together width wise, using two pieces of **construction paper** as covers. With a **protractor, draw** a circle on each page. On the first page, divide 360 (degrees in a circle) by 3. Using that answer, (180) mark off those intervals on the circle. Connect the points with solid lines and color if desired. Continue dividing the circle into geometric configurations for the next 20 numbers. Below is an octagon drawn by my daughter Genessa.

The science of pure mathematics, in its modern developments, may claim to be the most original creation of the human spirit.

—Alfred North Whitehead

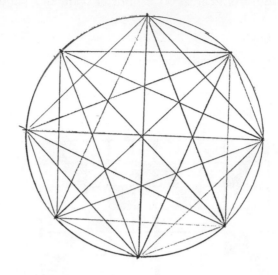

Toothpick Number Patterns

Get out the toothpicks. Make some patterns with them using only two toothpicks. Next, make up some with three, and finally try four.

Road Signs

Make a guessing game about trying to name the shapes of various road signs. See how many different shapes you can find.

❧ ALGEBRA ❧

Algebra Overview

Algebra is one of the main branches of science. The word comes from the Arabic word *Al-jabara,* meaning "binding things together," or "bone setting." Algebra helps "…make the specific universal, describe situations, and derive relationships with elegance and power," according to the *Mathematics Framework* of California.

In *Mind Tools,* Rudy Rucker says, *"Algebra provides a way for logic to connect the continuous and the discrete…. Knowing algebra is like knowing some magical language of sorcery—a language in which a few well-chosen words can give one mastery over the snakiest of curves."* Science is written in the language of algebra and it is sometimes called the *language of mathematics.* Scientists, civil engineers, chemists, electrical engineers, mechanical engineers and physicists use algebra everyday in their line of work. Business and industry have many uses for algebra.

Skyscrapers and steam shovels are constructed with algebraic formulas. Telephones, radios, TV, CD's, and computers need algebra for construction.

Briefly, algebra is working with unknown numbers (usually) represented by letters, most commonly x and y. Learning algebra means learning to apply the operations of addition, subtraction, multiplication, and division to *letters* as well as numbers. The letters may stand for more than one number, as in the statement $x + y = 12$. The advantage of using letters is that it allows us to use *formulas* and apply number variables to the letters written in the formula, such as *distance equals speed multiplied by the time of traveling* (d = s x t). We can name any speed we choose (*s* stands for speed) and any length of time we choose (*t* stands for time) to find distance (*d*).

To order clear, concise, inexpensive workbooks on algebraic concepts, fractions, percentages, and geometry please write:

Key Curriculum Press
PO Box 2304
Berkeley, CA 94702

Algebra Games

MY DAD'S FAMOUS 2=1 AND 4=5

Even after I had my dad explain this to me two or three times, I still don't get it—but by gum, it works on paper!

$2 = 1$:

$A = B$

$A^2 = B^2$

1. $A = B$
2. $A^2 - A = B^2 - B$
3. $A^2 - B^2 = A - B$
4. $(A + B)(A - B) = A - B$
5. $A + B = 1$
6. $1 + 1 = 1$
7. $2 = 1$

The problem is in line four. It looks alright, but try dividing by 0. When you divide by $A - B$, if you said the numbers were not equal then your equation would be right. Try plugging in "real" numbers. My dad says: "You are right, $A - B = 0$ if $A = B$. Any number divided by 0 is zero."

Next,

$4 = 5$:

1. $20 = 20$
2. $-20 = -20$
3. $16 - 36 = 25 - 45$
4. $16 - 36 + {}^{81}/_4 = 25 - 45 + {}^{81}/_4$
5. $(4 - {}^9/_2)(4 - {}^9/_2) = (5 - {}^9/_2)(5 - {}^9/_2)$
6. $(4 - {}^9/_2)^2 = (5 - {}^9/_2)^2$
7. $4 - {}^9/_2 = 5 - {}^9/_2$
8. $4 = 5$

The "mistake" is in line seven. You cannot take the square root of a negative number. Dad says $\sqrt{-{}^1/_2}$ = indeterminate.

❧ LOGIC AND LANGUAGE ❧

Logic and Language Overview

Logical thinking means making sense out of things in an organized fashion: the outcomes of cause and effect; the science of correct reasoning. The California Mathematical Framework says, "The logic and language strand focuses on the power of careful reasoning carried out in natural language to show things that are important but not obvious."

Of all the classes I ever took, the one that perhaps confused me the most was my college Logic class, (I got a solid "C") so I'm not even going to pretend to be an expert in this area. However, one of the best ways to learn about logic is through **jigsaw puzzles** and I just happen to enjoy an occasional jigsaw puzzle in my "leisure" time. Intuition tells me that logic develops by trial and error and through experimentation.

Logic includes:

1. Categorization: Being able to sort things out by character (like bottles or cans).
2. Predictions: Thinking ahead about what the results of an action might be (cause and effect).
3. Estimations: Listen to your child's explanations of how they *think* they think, and listen to them talk about different strategies for solving problems. It is important for children to verbalize this process so they can transfer strategies.

Other skills include the ability to compare, hypothesize, perceive, extrapolate, and reach conclusions.

Don't forget that **jigsaw puzzles, chess, crossword puzzles,** and many **computer** and **video games** will help develop logical skills. Lecture on logical theory can take us just so far from one problem to another.

"Contrariwise," continued *Tweeldedee, "if it was so, it might be; and if it were so, it would be; but as it isn't, it ain't. That's logic."*

—*Lewis Carroll*
Through the Looking Glass

Logic Games

THE REFRIGERATOR DOOR

Everyone in the family estimates how many times the refrigerator door is opened in one day and writes his guess down on a piece of paper. Tape the paper to the fridge. The next day, everyone makes a **tally mark** each time he opens the door. (Adapted from *Family Math* by Jean Kerr, et al. ©1986. Used by permission.)

GUESSTIMATIONS

Only your imagination should limit you as to what to guesstimate: grains of rice in a teaspoon, jellybeans in a jar, how much money you will spend at the grocery store (a very practical estimation), how much it will cost to buy all the toys you want, how long a minute is (have the children tell you when to start, then tell you when they think a minute is up).

Fancy Guesstimation: How many kernels of uncooked popcorn will fill a cup? How many pieces of popped corn will fill a cup?

TAPATAN

Peggy Kaye says this traditional game is the brainy Filipino version of tic-tac-toe.

Draw the following board on **heavy paper** and use three markers for each player (markers can be pennies and nickels, red chips and blue chips, etc.). The idea is to arrange your three markers in a row horizontally, vertically, or diagonally on the points. Take turns placing markers on the board one at a time. When all pieces are on the board, take turns sliding markers from point to point along the board lines. You cannot jump over another marker, nor share a point with any other marker.

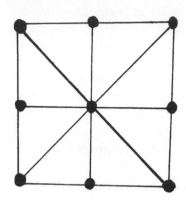

(MY DAD'S FAMOUS) LOGIC PROBLEM

If a hen-and-a-half lays an egg-and-a-half in a day-in-a-half, how long will it take one hen to lay a dozen?

It took me thirty years to get this one down. See if you can figure it out by using this chart: Nope, I'm not giving you the answer in the book.

HEN	EGG	DAY
$1\frac{1}{2}$	$1\frac{1}{2}$	$1\frac{1}{2}$
1	1	$1\frac{1}{2}$

(When asked late in life why he was studying geometry)

If I should not be learning now, when should I be?

—Lacydes
c. 241 BC

❧ FUNCTIONS ❦

Functions Overview

Functions is all about discovering the concise beauty of number patterns; number mandalas. The concise definition of function is "a mapping of all members of one set to members of another," and the broad definition is "the many kinds of relationships among quantities and the manner in which those relationships can be made explicit—but not necessarily symbolic. California Mathematics Framework used to include Patterns in this strand, but it was eliminated because "the role of patterns in mathematics is too important and too broad to link with one particular strand." An earlier version of the California Mathematical Model Curriculum Guide stated: "Looking for patterns helps bring order, cohesion, and predictability to seemingly unorganized situations. The recognition of patterns and functional relationships is a powerful problem-solving tool that enables one to simplify otherwise unmanageable tasks and to make generalizations beyond the information directly available."

Functions encompasses symmetry, counting by twos, fives, relationships between sets of numbers, rounding off numbers, finding means and averages, rounding off numbers, and the Cartesian plane (coordinate graphs).

Functions Games

PATTERNS

On a piece of **paper**, draw a series of shapes in a pattern, or use Cuisenaire Rods to make a pattern. Have your child guess which shape comes next. Then have him draw or design a pattern for you.

MISSING NUMBERS

On a piece of **paper** write a series of numbers omitting a few numbers (1, 2, 3, __, 5, 6, __, 8, __, ...) See if your child can fill in the blanks. For middle aged children, write patterns in twos, fives, threes, or tens. For older children, give sequences involving square numbers and fractions.

PATTERNS IN NATURE

Take a walk and examine objects such as leaf pattern or number of petals in a flower.

My grandmother wanted me to have an education, so she kept me out of school.

—Margaret Mead

SECRET CODES

On a piece of centimeter **graph paper**, set up a Cartesian plane graph of ordered pairs as shown below. Write one letter for each point on the plane. Then, write a secret message to your child using ordered pairs. Have him locate the ordered pairs to read the message. Let him send a message back to you.

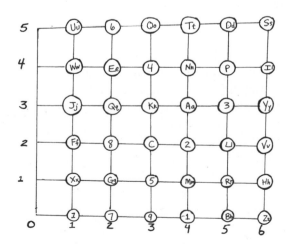

(Used by permission from *Family Math*, Jean Kerr et. al..)

BATTLESHIPS (OR BUMPER CARS*)

On **graph paper,** each of two players draws two identical ten-square-by-ten-square playing fields (see illustration). One area is marked **Home Fleet,** the other **Neighbor Fleet.** On the Home Fleet area, each player marks out his battleships: **1 battleship** (four squares long), **2 cruisers** (three squares long), **3 destroyers,** (two squares long), and **four submarines** (one square). The battleship squares must be all in a row and at least one square must separate each battleship. Players separate their papers by standing a thick book on end between them.

Next, players take turns calling out the names of any three squares (for example: B-2, C-4, and J-10) and marking them on the enemy fleet area. If any of the squares called out are hits, the other player must state how many and what kind of boats were hit. To sink a ship, every square that makes up the ship must receive a hit. If a boat is sunk, the play indicates this on the home fleet area by shading that area. [**Note**: for peacetime Battleships play Bumper Cars, using Cadillacs (4 spaces), Chevys (3 spaces), Fords (2 spaces), and Hondas (1 space). Play as above.]

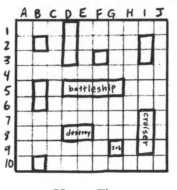

Home Fleet

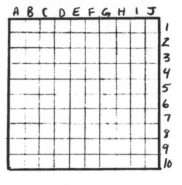

Neighbor Fleet

Really, universally, relations stop nowhere, and the exquisite problem of the artist is eternally but to draw, by a geometry of his own, the circle within which they shall happily appear to do so.

—Henry James

BURIED TREASURE

This is a simpler version of Battleships. Each player marks on a piece of nine-by-nine **graph paper** as in Battleships (mark letters A–I, numbers 1–9). Next, on small slips of paper, write the letters from A to I, and the numbers from 1 to 9 and turn them face down. Each player takes four letters and four numbers. Players begin to take turns by asking the other player whether she holds a certain letter or number. If the answer is *yes*, then the player shades that area on her graph. To trick the opponent, players may ask about a number or letter they hold. Game ends when there is one square left uncovered, the "buried treasure."

CRYSTALS

Try to "grow" crystals on graph paper (using colored pencils) that have two lines of symmetry, visualized by drawing four axes through the center of the crystal: horizontal, vertical, and two diagonals. Thus, it is possible to fold the crystal on any axis and produce mirror images of the crystals

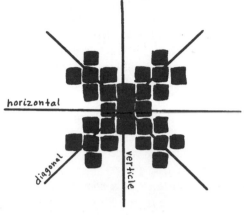

FUNCTION MACHINES

Make *function machines* for your child to complete. List numbers under *N* and have her find *N + 3* or whatever addition or subtraction problem you want.

N	N+3
5	8
3	6
10	13

❦ STATISTICS/PROBABILITY ❦

Statistics deals with number manipulations. First people collect the information (data or analytical statistics) then they record it (descriptive statistics). Scientists use statistics to chart information whenever an element of **probability** is involved. Probability involves the likelihood of an occurrence. Statisticians strive to create a mathematical model (using **graphs** and **pie charts**) of the information. Generally, the wider base of observation and less bias the scientist has, the more accurate the statistics will be.

> *There are three kinds of lies: lies, damned lies, and statistics.*
>
> *—Mark Twain*

Probability is chance and it teaches us humility. Not all physical laws apply to all circumstances. Variables exist. Statements that are true about objects cease to be true if the objects are exceptionally huge or tiny.

It has been said that if one knows where, how fast, and the direction of each atom, one could predict the future of eternity. That, unfortunately, is not the case. There's just no way to determine movement of individual electrons. This is called the Principle of Uncertainty, or to some, the Laws of Chance (*"Now," sputtered the White Rabbit, "if a chance had a law, it wouldn't be a chance, and it'd have to go to jail for breaking the law, wouldn't it, perchance?"*)

Most of us use statistics and probability for interpreting graphs and pie charts in magazines and newspapers. However, it is extremely difficult for statisticians to produce unbiased surveys because most statistics are born with a desire to "prove" something. Unfortunately grievous wrongs are committed by people who continue to manipulate numbers to serve their own personal interests.

The bones of statistics and probability involve systematically collecting, organizing, and describing data and constructing, reading, and interpreting tables, charts, and graphs. Descriptive statistics helps us "learn to collect and organize information in a variety of graphs, charts and tables to make those data easier for…others to comprehend." (*Mathematical Framework for California Public Schools, 1992.*)

Graphing Games

LEAF GRAPH

Pick some **leaves** and paste them onto a sheet of **graph paper**, or measure them, drawing a line on the paper to see which leaf is longest.

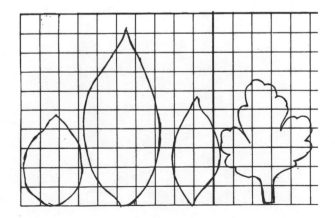

BEAN GROWTH BAR GRAPH

Line a **drinking glass** with **paper towels**. Wad up some more towels and fit them snugly into the glass. Evenly space four **pinto beans** about 1" (2.5 cm.) from the top of the glass. Keep the glass moist, not wet, every day. When the beans begin to grow, mark their position with a piece of tape. Then, with a **ruler**, measure the growth of the bean each day and record the results (use graph paper) on your **bar graph.**

God not only plays dice, (S)he also sometimes throws the dice where they cannot be seen.

—Stephen Hawking

MARBLE DERBY BAR GRAPH

Set up the derby by placing six sheets of **paper** edge-to-edge on the floor. Put a **book** at one end of the paper road and place one edge of a **ruler** on the book, the other on the paper. Hold a **marble** at the top of the ruler and let it go. As soon as the marble touches the paper, start timing seconds. As each second passes, mark the position of the marble on the paper. Fill in a **line graph** as shown to record your data.

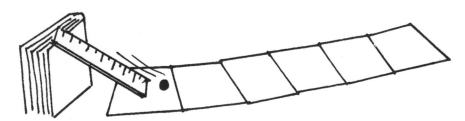

PENNY TOSS PICTOGRAPH

Place a small plastic **bowl** inside a larger **bowl**. Toss pennies into the bowl and record your results using a pictograph. See sample chart below. (Adapted from In and Out in *Games for Learning* by Peggy Kaye.)

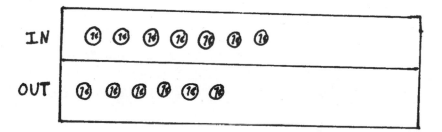

CIRCLE OR PIE GRAPH

Get out **100 peanuts.** Have everyone eat as many as they want. Record the results on a **pie graph.**

Probability is the very guide of life.

—*Joseph Butler*

BAR GRAPH: THINGS TO GRAPH

Interview about 10 to 20 people, and record your data on **graph paper.**

HOW MANY...? People in your family, brothers and/or sisters, rooms in your house, buttons do you have on, letters in your name...

WHO'S YOUR FAVORITE...? Movie or TV star, rock group, book character, singer...

WHAT'S YOUR FAVORITE...? Ice cream flavor, book, holiday, color, animal, movie, song, food, musical instrument...

OTHERS: What would you like to be in the future? What is the length of your right thumbnail?

MACHINE BAR GRAPH: Graph a list of all the machines you or your family used yesterday according to how they were used: for *play, work,* or *transportation.* Machine examples include: alarm clock, remote control TV, refrigerator, dishwasher, vacuum cleaner, computer, heater, radio, CD player...

RUNNING GRAPHS: This is a great thing to graph. John Holt, in *What Do I Do Monday* (John Holt Associates, 1994) has a way to extend this idea further: calculate average running speed in feet and seconds. Next, using the formula: **44' per sec. = 30 mph**, work out individual average speeds.

You can also compare your record to the fastest human at **100 yds. in 9.1 sec.** (which is also ¾ of 30 mph, or 22 mph), or the speed of light: 186,000 mph.

In the small number of things we are able to know with any certainty...the principal means of ascertaining truth are based on probabilities.

—*Pierre Simon de Laplace.*

Here are some more of John's ideas.

How fast can you go in 100 yards:

1. Carrying another person of equal weight piggyback.
2. Hopping on one foot.
3. Jumping with both feet tied together.
4. Running backwards.
5. Running sideways without crossing feet.
6. Going on hands and knees.
7. On hands and feet backward.
8. Crab walk: hands and feet with back facing ground.
9. Skipping.
10. Skipping backward.
11. Going along a straight chalk line.
12. Going along a curved chalk line.
13. On a course made of bricks, jumping from brick to brick.
14. A slalom course, zig-zag around or between various markers.
15. Figure Eight: 10 times around 2 markers 5 yards apart.

❧ COMPUTERS ❧

Biased Operator

You are looking and reading the computer work (about two years' worth) of a former computer hater. Like many others, I believed computers were a sinister means of controlling the populace, and an expensive and unnecessary toy for people who didn't have "real" lives.

Then I wrote a songbook (by hand) and spent my whole book advance on a used Macintosh computer. When we brought it home, we were afraid to turn the beast on. When we did, we treated it like an alien from outer space. Four years later, I've come to know that my computer, Max Baby (short for Maxine) is a good electronic "friend." When I'm not working with her, I could be reading a computer book, editing work produced by the computer or attending a computer class. So much for having a real life!

In the beginning, computers were born out of a desire to "number crunch"—increase the speed of mathematical calculations. Essentially, the computer is a sophisticated abacus.

Opening Doors

Computers help us process the vast amounts of information we have accumulated in our complex society. They have led us to the door of ultimate simulation experiences such as virtual reality, which essentially creates a computer-induced reality. Jerry Garcia says, "Technology is the new drug." Boot up, jack in, and get virtual.

A computer is like an artificial brain. Cyborgs—part human, part machine—loom on the horizon of the future. John Perry Barlow suggests we put a Cray (a giant mega-computer) in every cranium. Wouldn't it be delightful to have all that computer information surgically implanted in your brain? We could all be walking encyclopedias!

However, getting that Cray inside our brains will be no easy feat. The human brain contains 10,000 million neurons. In computer terminology, our hard disks (brains) contain a "mere" 117.4 *billion* megabytes of RAM. For a computer to have this much memory, well, you would need a 100-cubic-foot room to hold all the memory chips! To try and stuff a Cray that big in our brains... well...let's just say we would be fairly brain-heavy. Besides, most computers process information in a serial fashion, not in a parallel fashion like we do. Even if we could build that 100-cubic-foot computer that's as sophisticated as our brain, it would take the monster three weeks to search its memory for *one* four-letter word!

Let's talk about vision. Pixels are the tiny dots that make up images on computer screens. Our eyes have three million pixels crammed into a tiny space the size of a marble. The best video screen on the market, presumably at least a 12" screen, has a resolution of one million pixels.

Computers can open doors into all realms of human experience. Like dogs, computers are without prejudice and judgments. They will be your friend as long as you feed them (they love electromagnetic energy). Computers supposedly save us time. (Oh yeah?) They

In no dimension of education has there been more explosive developments in recent times than in educational media .... The important thing is not just that these resources are available but that learners use them proactively rather than reactively.

—Malcolm Knowles

If humans are most distinguished from other organisms by the elaborateness of their communications, then the coming of new levels of world communications implies the arrival of something more than human. Cyborg civilization, maybe, or a cognitive planet.

—Stewart Brand

are whizzes at numbers and help writers by making it easy to edit their work. Musicians and artists have interacted with computers and created new art forms.

Most of the world's indigenous peoples will probably never use, need, or see a computer. In the "civilized" world, they are fast becoming necessities. People seem to be both lured to the computer's siren call and distrustful of these murky electronic devices. Even people who don't use computers can have confidence that their name is out there somewhere on someone's computer database.

Computers could ultimately put our entire reality into "real" time—an artificial, magnetically created realm. However, long ago, when writing became vogue, Socrates understood that when we learn something indirectly it cannot replace our direct involvement: *information should not be confused with experience.* Computers create artificial realities, but they don't have babies, get married, or celebrate holidays. I love my computer, but it doesn't love me.

Computers in Education

Computers are creating a revolution in education. It is very difficult to analyze data about computer use in education, because the field is so new and its parameters are changing so rapidly. Currently, there is one computer for every thirty kids in the United States. It's been said if we sold just one Phantom Bomber, each kid in the U.S. could have his or her own computer!

Homeschooling and computers seem to be a happy marriage. Homeschoolers can take advantage of *modems,* which allow them to send computer-generated information over ordinary phones, and *networks,* which are groups of computer users linked with common interests.

In classrooms, kids usually use computers in their "free" time to play games. Some teachers hook up their computers to video screens or overheads and use them for group experiences.

Computers can empower kids and give them self-confidence as they learn to master these devices. Computers can help kids cooperate and collaborate with each other. They can help teach a way of thinking that expands the mind's capacity to solve problems. With computers, curriculum comes more from the child than from the topic. In our home, we have some computer games, such as *Where in Time is Carmen San Diego* that our kids enjoy playing. They learn history from this program and look stuff up in the dictionary to play the game!

In the future, teachers, (yes, even we homeschool parent-teachers) will become more the facilitators and collaborators and less dispensers of information. Computers can dispense information for us. Children will still need us to learn social skills, values, and ethics. Anyone know of a software program that teaches these skills?

Many folks still distrust technology, and who can blame them? Electromagnetic toys are expensive, potentially hazardous to the health, addictive, and the power needed to run them comes from earth-polluting sources. Yet the computer's power in education is awesome and incredibly revolutionary.

Seymour Papert, a wizard from MIT, has been working with computers in inner-city Boston schools since 1985. He invented the popular LOGO computer language for children and believes that as children learn how to program in LOGO, they also learn to understand their own thought processes. Using computers, he wants to change learning from a passive to an active atmosphere. He claims children can *"feel the flexibility of the computer and its power. They can find a rich intellectual activity with which to fall in love. It's through these intellectual love affairs that people acquire a taste for rigor and creativity, and they see games right away that are fun to play."* (Quoted by permission.)

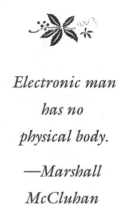

Electronic man has no physical body.

—Marshall McCluhan

Dr. Gordon Pask and Susan Curran, in their book *Microman: Computers and the Evolution of Consciousness*, say:

> A major advantage of computers is that they can indicate what topics are to be learned, how they are connected together, and (having picked up information about your style of learning) how you might learn them most expeditiously.... As an institutional necessity most schools have periods, classes, examinations, curricula, and syllabi. Certain topics are supposed to be taught in particular settings and at particular times. These institutional requirements echo the hierarchical concept of knowledge; they are the outward expressions of the well-worn notion that easy topics should be learned first and difficult ones later. But there is no good evidence that learning in general proceeds in this way, even if teaching sometimes does.
>
> [In the future] youngsters today can learn their facts and figures at home, or in their friend's apartment, or (if they prefer) around the globe. Schools still exist. One of their major roles is one the computer cannot fulfill: to teach social skills, maturity, and general demeanor. The computer's special role is to teach you how to learn. Learning to learn is the vital skill. Computers teach us to innovate, to take and combine different viewpoints, to find out information and fit it together. With this skill under their belts, youngsters are fitted for a lifetime of self-education.

Do they sound as if they're talking about homeschooling?

My Little Mac

I have a bias towards Apple Macintosh computers because they have it all over IBM in the graphics department and they're "user friendly." (Ha!) However, since Apple and IBM are realizing the financial advantages of working together, we are now seeing less difference between the two types of computers.

If you do buy a Mac, I recommend *The Little Mac Book* by Robin Williams. The book is concise, witty, and full of sparkling gems of information. I had Robin as a teacher for five computer classes. She answered zillions of my questions about these magic and powerful machines. She has also written *The Mac Is Not A Typewriter,* and *Pagemaker 5, An Easy Desk Reference*. Her latest book, *Jargon* is a dictionary of computer terms. Next, she is working on a book about font technology. She knows her stuff.

Computers are fantastic learning tools, and they're here to stay. Any young person in our society who is not computer literate will be facing a severe handicap in the "real" world. In addition, computers are especially useful to homeschoolers who generally pursue most academic subjects alone. With over 20,000 software products on the market, there are programs that do just about anything. Again let me remind you: beware of using computers exclusively; they are not warm and fuzzy, and they don't like pizza.

[Computers can help]… strengthen children's creativity, their gift for fantasy and imaginations … their curiosity and their hunger for exploration, discovery, and experimentation.

—Fred D'ignazio

Commonly Used Programs

1. **Word Processing:** For word processing, you can't beat a computer. Word processing programs are the computer's typewriting programs. Using one of these programs, you can edit text, choose from a variety of formats (such as bold, italic, outline), check your spelling, check your grammar, have access to an on-line thesaurus, paste in pictures, and much more. I usually use *Microsoft Word,* but *MacWrite, Word Perfect,* and *Write Now* are also good programs.

2. **Bookkeeping:** Bookkeeping programs usually include two programs: *data base* helps you make lists such as addresses, phone numbers, book lists, and other information. Then, the computer can manipulate the data to do such things as alphabetize, find everyone on the list who lives in California, or who is over 40. *Spreadsheets* are designed to number crunch, which is what computers love to do. I like *Microsoft Works,* but have read many favorable reviews of *Claris*.

3. **Desktop Publishing:** These programs let you create anything from brochures to newspapers to magazines and books. My favorite is *Pagemaker,* but others like *Quark Xpress* and *Ready Set Go*.

4. **Paint:** These are the computer-generated art programs. We use *Superpaint*. Other drawing programs include *MacPaint, Kid Pix* (great fun for the little ones), and *Mac Draw*.

5. **Games:** Includes everything available from shoot 'em up to cops 'n robbers to highly educational programs that teach reading and math skills, geography, logic, and more. Our favorite games come from Broderbund Software (1-800-521-6263) and MECC (1-800-228-3504).

Educational Networks and Software

If you are interested in the Internet, you will need the following: telecommunications software, computer, modem, phone line, and Internet provider. Your provider company will give you access to the Internet, which is a network of networks. Each company has different perks to lure you. Some give away free communications software, others offer no startup fees, or free hours a month (every time you dial out to a network using your computer you will more than likely be charged the cost of a long distance phone call). Some companies offer toll-free dialing numbers.

Networks provide their subscribers with things like specialized information, electronic mail service, electronic bulletin boards, and on-line on-going open conferences with other computer users. There are currently about 4 million people signed up for on-line computer services.

NETWORKS

FrEd Mail Project
San Diego County Office of Education
Linda Vista Rd.
San Diego, CA 92111
(619) 292-3639

Cooperative education messaging network. Two on-going conferences: Ideas, teaching exchange ideas, and Kidwire, an electronic bulletin board that posts students' work.

Institute for Global Communications
3228 Sacramento St.
San Francisco, CA 94115

Dedicated to global peace and environment issues, users in over 70 countries. Conferences include PeaceNet, EcoNet, *and* ConflictNet.

Kids Network
National Geographic Society
17th and M St.
Washington, DC 20036

Students share hands-on science project through the network.

News Access
2179 Hannah Lane
Tucker, GA 30084

News via Week in Review *for students.*

Prodigy
445 Hamilton Ave.
White Plains, NY 10601

On-line information on weather, news, and sports. Educational services include The Club, *an electronic bulletin board for kids.*

CompuServe
P.O. Box 20212
Columbus, OH 43220
(800) 848-8990

Perhaps the biggest network around...not specifically for kids.

WELL (Whole Earth 'Lectronic Link)
(415) 332-6106

This network is run by the people who produce the Whole Earth Catalog. *Definitely an alternative network, and not specifically for kids.*

KidTech (Educational Software)
5261 Prospect Rd.
San Jose, CA 95129

Computer Learning Foundation
PO Box 6007
Palo Alto, CA 94306-007

Guide for parents and teachers: Everything You Need to Know (But Were Afraid to Ask Kids) About Computer Learning.

High/Scope Foundation
600 North River St.
Ypsilanti, MI 48198

Write to them for their Survey of Early Childhood Software *invaluable review of over 400 programs.*

R.R. Bowker
PO Box 762
New York, NY 10011

Publishers of Only the Best: An Annual Guide to Highest Rated Educational Software

INTERNET PROVIDERS

Netcom
(800)501-8649

Dial n Cerf
(800) 876-2373

PSI International
(800) 774-3031

America Online
(800) 227-6364

Nature

Nature (science) is the study of the natural world around us. The two main branches of nature are:

Physical Science

Chemistry (food analysis, chemical reactions, acids, bases, alloys —a combination of metals—, compounds, elements)

Physics (mechanics, work, energy, solar power, simple machines, matter, heat, sound, light and optics, electricity, magnetism)

Astronomy (sun, moon, stars, planets, comets, meteors, telescopes)

Geology (earthquakes, rocks, volcanoes)

Biological (Life) Science

Botany (plants, ecology)

Biology (anatomy, human behavior and intelligence, hypnotism, parapsychology, psychiatry)

Scientific Fields

Anatomy (study of the human body)

Archaeology (study of the past by identifying and interpreting material remains of human culture)

Architecture (art of building, combines art and engineering)

Astronomy (study of outer space)

Audiology (science of hearing)

Bacteriology (study of bacteria)

Biochemistry (study of the substances occurring in living things and their reactions)

Biology (study of living things: plants, animals, and humans—biology has many related fields of study)

Biophysics (branch of biology in which principles of physics are applied to biological studies)

Botany (study of plants)

Chemistry (study of the elements—chemicals—and compounds and reactions between them)

Dentistry (study and care of the teeth)

Earth Science (study of the Earth including topography and earthquakes)

Engineering (planning, designing, management, or construction of things such as machinery, roads, bridges, or dams)

As art is a habit with reference to things to be done, so is science a habit in respect to things to be known.

—William Harvey

Forestry (management of forests, especially for production)

Genetics (study of heredity and genes)

Geology (study of rocks)

Mathematics (a primary branch of science: study of numbers, geometry, algebra, logic, etc.)

Medicine (art and science of healing)

Metallurgy (study of metals)

Mining (extracting ores and minerals from the earth)

Nursing (care of the sick, injured, or developmentally disabled)

Nutrition (study of how living organisms utilize food nutrients and how foods affect the body)

Occupational Therapy (treatment of the mental and physical ailments produced by work)

Oceanography (study of the ocean)

Optometry (study of the eyes)

Osteopathy (a system of treating disease based on the belief that it results from displaced bones)

Parasitology (study of parasites)

Pathology (study of diseases)

Pharmacology (study of drugs)

Pharmacy (preparation or dispensing of drugs)

Physical Therapy (also called Physiotherapy—a system of physical treatment for disease or disability)

Physics (study of the interaction of matter and energy)

Physiology (study of the function in living organisms)

Public Health (practice and organization of preventative medicine)

Speech/Language Pathology (study of disorders in speech)

Veterinary Medicine (medical care of sick animals)

Zoology (study of animals)

The caduces, symbol of the medical profession, represents the staff carried by the Greek god Hermes, and the snake entwined represents human energy rising toward spiritual enlightenment.

Recommended science books can be found at the end of the chapter. See next chapter on Body World for more information about the human body. It is not within the scope of this book to provide a complete curriculum for the study of nature. However, I have included a few ideas as a basis to begin nature studies.

Nature Games

ROOM DECORATIONS

Decorate children's rooms with live plants or pictures of plants, live animals, or posters of nature such as the solar system or insects. Collect special rocks or shells to create a nature-rich environment.

SCAVENGER HUNT

This is a group activity that could also be a great idea for a birthday party game. You can supplement the hunt with magazines such as *National Geographic* or *Natural History*. If players can't find the item outside, use a magazine picture as a substitute. You may choose to "score" bonus points for an item that fits into more than one category, or not to use items in more than one category.

General List

Find:

1. Something older than you are
2. Something younger than you are
3. Something flammable
4. Something non-flammable
5. Something solid
6. Something liquid
7. Something gaseous

Textures

Find one each of the following: something that is rough, smooth, hard, soft, sharp, bumpy, ridged or grooved, uneven, geometric, symmetrical.

Shapes

Find one each of the following: something that is circular, triangular, square, rectangular, heart-shaped, star-shaped, spherical, cylindrical.

Sequoia

Nearness to nature...keeps the spirit sensitive to impressions not commonly felt, and in touch with the unseen powers.

—Ohiyesa

Specific List

Find:

1. a maple leaf
2. a piece of granite
3. a fly
4. a caterpillar
5. a bird's nest (just observe, don't take unless it's been abandoned)
6. a wildflower
7. a seed
8. a bird feather
9. a cocoon or an eggshell
10. a snail shell
11. a vine
12. something that doesn't belong outside

Sensory Walk

Find something on a hike that:

1. Smells good
2. Makes a noise
3. Feels bumpy
4. Looks wrinkled
5. Is likely to change the way it looks

RUBBINGS WALK

With a piece of **paper,** make a rubbing of something: smooth, gritty, grooved, ridged, or patterned. Anything else? Make a mystery rubbing of something and think of two clues to help people guess what it is.

BIRD, MUSHROOM, FLOWER, TREE, OR LEAF WALK

Take a walk and observe a specific plant or animal. If appropriate, you may wish to collect specimens.

(For more nature ideas, please see Earth Games.)

A child should have mudpies, grasshoppers, waterbugs, tadpoles, frogs, mud turtles, elderberries, wild strawberries, acorns, chestnuts, trees to climb, animals to pet, hay fields, pinecones, rocks to roll, sand, snakes, huckleberries and hornets—and any child who has been deprived of these has been deprived of the best part of his or her education.

—Luther Burbank

❧ PLANTS ❧

The plant kingdom is divided into four main groups, or phyla:

1. **Thallophytes:** Plants with no leaves, roots or stems: algae, fungi, and lichens
2. **Bryophytes:** Mosses and liverworts
3. **Pteridophytes:** Ferns and their relatives, horsetails
4. **Spermatophytes:** Seed plants, including angiosperms (flowering plants), and gymnosperms (cone-bearers)

✦ The best way to learn about plants is to **grow them**. Even if you live in an apartment, you can plant a mini-garden in a big pot. Science concepts abound in gardening. You'll learn about such subjects as fungi, bacteria, ecology, soil chemistry and composition, cover crops, rotating crops, composting, biological control of pests, and climate. In the field of chemistry, you can learn about pH (acid/alkaline).

✦ Cut off the tops of plants such as **carrots, pineapple,** and **sweet potatoes,** stick them in a **dish of water**, and watch them grow.

✦ Make a **seed chart**, with seeds and pictures of the plants that they make.

✦ Grow **sprouts** and eat them. Put seeds in a mason jar that has a mesh screen in place of the lid and soak seeds in water overnight. Rinse and drain the seeds and place upside down in the drainboard. Rinse once or twice a day. Try sprouting lentils, rye, wheat, mung beans, fenugreek, alfalfa, sunflower, radish, or clover.

FLOWERS

There are about 200,000 kinds of flowers divided into 300 families.

✦ Make a book of pressed flowers. To press flowers, lay them between the sheets of old comic books and weigh them down with heavier books. They will be dry in about two to four weeks. Flowers that press well include clover, daisies, buttercups, delphiniums, celandine, and cow parsley.

✦ Label one of the dried flowers by parts.

✦ Test the pigment of flower petals by mashing some petals in a bowl and adding enough **rubbing alcohol** to make a runny mixture. Hang a strip of **blotting paper** over the bowl and leave it in an airy place for an hour.

TREES

✦ Go outside and sit under a tree. Draw a big outline of the tree on your **paper**. Now draw whatever animals or plants (like moss or lichen) that you see in the branches of your tree. Next, draw what you see at eye level, and last what you see at the base of the tree.

✦ Collect and label leaves, seeds and seed pods from trees.

Science increases our power in proportion as it lowers our pride.

—Claude Bernard

No occupation is so delightful to me as the culture of the Earth, and no culture comparable to that of the garden.

—Thomas Jefferson

❧ CREATURES ❧

The animal kingdom has two major groups. *Invertebrates,* animals without backbones, and *vertebrates,* animals with backbones.

Invertebrates include sponges, worms, centipedes, mollusks, and insects. More than half of all living things in the world are insects. Over 500,000 different kinds have been classified. There are about 25,000,000 insects on every square mile of land. The major groups of insects include *anthropods* (which means six legs), *hymenoptera* (membrane-winged, such as bees), *arachnids,* which includes spiders, mites, ticks, scorpions, and daddylonglegs. Butterflies and moths are also classified as insects.

Vertebrates are animals with a backbone and cranium (brain case). There are seven living classes of vertebrates. All vertebrates are bilaterally symmetrical, that is, left and right sides of the body are alike. Most vertebrates have a bony backbone, called a spinal column, but some have cartilage rather than bones.

1) **Mammals:** There are about 4,000 kinds of mammals. They give birth to live babies, feed their babies with milk, and they all have four legs, or two arms and two legs. They also have fur or hair on their bodies. There are a few "primitive" animals, the *monotremes* (such as the anteater and duckbill platypus) that lay eggs but feed their young, and the *marsupials* (such as opossum, kangaroo, and koala) whose babies are born alive, but underdeveloped, then are placed in a pouch in the mother's fur and nourished there.

2) **Reptiles:** These animals are characterized by being cold-blooded and covered with scales or shells. They lay eggs and then leave the young to fend for themselves. Examples of reptiles are turtles, alligators, crocodiles, lizards, and snakes.

3) **Birds:** Most birds fly and have feathers. They hatch their young from eggs and usually make a nest to protect the eggs, which must be kept warm in order to hatch. There are approximately 14,000 species of birds.

Animal Study Games and Ideas

✦ The best way to learn about animals is to **take care of them**. Classic household pets include dogs, cats, goldfish, parakeets, hamsters, rats, and turtles. (Our family has taken care of one dog, two cats, two parakeets, one hamster, and one goldfish… but that's nothing. Our neighbors Don and Nan have a *zoo*— bunches of horses, goats, one dog, at least fourteen cats, chickens, doves, a rabbit, parakeets, *and* a snake.) Animals teach us about nurturing and nurturing animals is great preparation for learning how to take care of babies. Pets can also help children develop self-confidence, teach them greater sensitivity in understanding non-verbal communication, and console them from family or life stresses.

✦ Collect a **cocoon**. Put it in a safe place to observe the chrysalis transforming into an emerging butterfly.

Among scientists are collectors, classifiers, and compulsive tidiers-up; many are detectives by temperament, and many are explorers; some are artists and other artisans. There are poet-scientists and philosopher-scientists and even a few mystics.

—Sir Peter Brian Medawa

✦ Make an **ant, worm,** or **snail** farm. Put some snails on black paper to observe their trails. Have a snail race. Remember to return insects to the wild when you are done observing them.

✦ Take a piece of **yarn** about a yard long and tie it in a knot. Spread it into a circle and place it on a section of grass. Observe the kingdom before you.

✦ A robin makes a nest out of dried mud and bits of straw and twigs. To understand why the nest doesn't crack, find two large **jar lids.** Fill one with **plain mud** and the other with **mud** mixed with bits of **straw.** As the mud dries, the straw-mud should not crack. If it does, add more straw.

✦ Make a **bird feeder** and observe.

❧ EARTH ❧

The study of the earth includes the study of soil, rocks, fossils, and ancient animals.

Soil is divided into five main parts, with each of the five main parts combining with the others plus minerals to make a variety of soil types:

1) **Clay**: very fine and light in color, sticky when water is added.
2) **Gravel**: coarse, with pebbles in it.
3) **Sandy**: gritty feeling, you can see grains of sand in it.
4) **Loam**: mixture of sand and clay.
5) **Humus**: dark and loose, made from bits of decayed plant and animal material with very little rock.

Rocks are made up of minerals. Most rocks contain more than one mineral. Each mineral has its own crystal pattern in varying sizes and shapes. The *types* of rock are:

1) **Sedimentary rock**: always in layers.
2) **Sandstone**: formed from sand.
3) **Shale**: formed from clay.
4) **Conglomerate**: pebbles cemented together with sand.
5) **Limestone**: ground up shells, skeletons of sea creatures, or lime that settle to the bottom of a body of water from the water itself.

The *kinds* of rock are divided by the method of their formation:

1) **Igneous rocks**: formed by the cooling of magma below the surface of the earth. An example of this is granite.
2) **Sedimentary rocks**: formed from bits of sediment worn away from old rocks, water, wind, and grinding action of rock against rock. This material is deposited in layers and then formed under great pressure over a long time.
3) **Metamorphic rocks**: formed when the other two kinds of rocks receive great pressure and heat over a long period of time. *Meta* means change, and *morphic* means form.
4) **Fossils:** are the preserved remains of plants or animals inside sedimentary rocks. Most fossils found are from extinct plants and animals.

Earth Games

✦ Make a **rock** or **crystal display** of various rocks.

✦ Do lots of **hiking.** Climb a mountain or climb to the top of a tree.

✦ **Earth Day**, celebrated April 22, is a perfect time to learn more about ecology and the earth. *Kids for Saving the Earth* is an international club whose goal is to help kids be active participants in saving the earth. For a guide book that includes activities, suggestions, facts, and resources write to: Kids for Saving the Earth /PO Box 47347 /Plymouth, MN 55447.

✦ Make your own **fossils** by putting damp **clay** into the bottom of a small box. Press a **shell, bone,** or **seed pod** into the clay, making a print. The empty mold is one kind of fossil.

✦ Launch a toy boat in a creek and follow it.

✦ Follow a night sound (cricket, frog, owl) to its source.

✦ Make a **soil sampler.** Determine soil texture. Moisten a sample, rub it between your fingers, and compare it to the descriptions above.

✦ Make **crystals**:

    #1: In an old **pie pan**, crumble up a few **charcoal briquettes.** Add two tablespoons *each* of: **salt, water, ammonia,** and **bluing.** As the liquid evaporates, crystals will form.

    #2: (Directions by Genessa at age 9) **What you need:** 1 cup of **water**, 2 cups of **sugar**, a medium **jar**, a **string**, a **paper clip**, a **pencil**, and a **pot.**

    What to do: Tie the string onto the middle of the pencil and tie the paper clip onto the bottom of the string. Then mix the sugar and water in the pot and boil the water. Wait until the sugar water is clear, and then put the sugar water into the jar. Put the pencil in the jar and wait about two months. Hint: It's better if the string touches the bottom of the jar.

Other substances that form crystals include: salt, borax, Epsom salts, copper sulfate, and sodium hyposulfite. Be careful when using these potentially harmful substances!

✦ Lead someone on a **blindfold walk** through the forest.

✦ Observe the mini-kingdom defined by a three- to five-foot piece of **string** laid in an interesting spot. Use a magnifying glass.

✦ **Photograph** the same spot through the seasons.

✦ Keep a **journal** of the natural changes that happen over a year: the first autumn rain, migrating birds, first cricket of summer, fall leaf colors, first snow…

Experience, the universal Mother of Sciences.

—Miguel de Cervantes

❧ OCEAN ❦

The ocean is where we come from. It is home to the beginning of the food chain, which starts with the one-celled diatom. The diatom is so small that there may be a million in one quart of seawater! This simplest form of algae is called **protozoa**, and together, protozoa make **plankton**, which feeds the tiny shelled animals called **crustaceans**, which are eaten by **herring**, one of the most abundant fish of the sea. The largest mammal of the world, the blue whale, lives exclusively on plankton. The different species that live in the ocean are:

1) **Mollusks**, a group of 90,000 different animals. They have a flat, muscular foot, and a mantle that forms the shell. They're divided into *univalves* or *gastropods* (meaning belly-footed). Examples are periwinkles and limpet. The other group is called *bi-valves*, and they have a two-part mantle to form two shells, fastened at the back with a strong hinge. They are well developed, with gills for breathing and a wedge-shaped foot for digging. Mussels, oysters, scallops, and clams are bi-valves.

2) **Echinoderm**, a family of 5,000-6,000 members. Its members have spiny skins, and include sea urchins, sand dollars, and sea cucumbers. They are built on a wheel plan (all their marking go out from the center like the spokes of a wheel) and have no heads or tails.

3) **Crustaceans** are animals whose skeletons are on the outside of their bodies. This skeleton does not grow with the animal, but splits open and is discarded so a new one can grow in its place. The best known crustaceans are: lobsters, crabs, and shrimp.

4) There are 25,000 species of **fish**. Their common characteristics: they are cold-blooded, completely aquatic, they have vertebrae (backbone), breathe by means of gills, and have two-chambered hearts.

5) **Seaweed** are algae and belong to the same group as the diatoms. They have no true roots, leaves, or stems, flowers, or seeds.

Amphibians means "double life," that is both water and land. Amphibians begin life as gill-breathing water creatures; in their adult stage, they breathe air with lungs and live on land or in and out of the water.

Ocean Activities

- ✦ Exhibit different kinds of **shells**.
- ✦ Make frequent **outings to the ocean** and **explore tide pools**.
- ✦ Make a **chart of seaweed**.
- ✦ **Cut open a dead fish** and identify the parts.
- ✦ Go **fishing**.
- ✦ Go **surfing, body boarding** or **body surfing**.
- ✦ Go **boating, canoeing,** or **rafting**.
- ✦ Build a **sandcastle** and make up a story about the creatures who live there.

- Build a **secchi disk** (8" metal disk quartered and painted in opposing sections of black and white tied in the middle to a 50-foot cord knotted every foot) to check the depth of the water off a pier.
- Send a **message in a bottle**. The Woods Hole Oceanography Institution in Massachusetts releases 10,000 to 20,000 bottles annually to try and determine the speed and direction of ocean currents.
- Go **whale watching**.

❧ WATER, AIR AND LIGHT ❧

Water

Water is the true staff of life. It covers about 75% of the earth and is sometimes called the universal solvent because it will dissolve so many things. Water is never used up or destroyed, merely recycled through evaporation and condensation. About $\frac{1}{3000}$ of all water is evaporated by the sun each year and becomes water vapor in the air, which in turn becomes rain when warm air meets colder air and condenses.

Clouds

Clouds are made up of water vapor or tiny bits of ice. Not all clouds are rain clouds. Fog is a cloud that forms at ground level. The seven basic types of clouds are:

1) **Cumulus**: white, puffy cotton-like.
2) **Cirrus**: thin, white, wispy curls, formed by ice crystals, moving about 200 mph at about 25,000 feet.
3) **Stratus**: layers, thin, grayish-white, covering most of the sky.
4) **Nimbus**: long, flat clouds with ragged edges, dark gray, covering a large part of the sky.
5) **Cumulo-nimbus**: thunderheads, towering heaps of cumulus turning from light gray to dark gray.
6) **Nimbo-stratus**: heavy layer of thick, dark gray clouds.
7) **Cirro-cumulus**: small, fluffy with clouds fairly high in the sky.

Rain and Snow

One inch of rainfall on an acre of ground weighs 113 tons. Raindrops fall 15 to 25 feet a second. Snow is formed when water vapor changes from a gaseous form into solid crystal.

Science is the search for truth—it is not a game in which one tries to beat his opponent, to do harm to others. We need to have the spirit of science in international affairs, to make the conduct of international affairs the effort to find the right solution, the just solution of international problems....

—Linus Pauling

Air

Air is a mixture of gasses: 78% nitrogen, 21% oxygen, .93% argon, and .07% other gasses. Air also carries water vapor and solid matter, ranging from 15,000 parts per cubic inch over the mid-Pacific to 5 million parts per cubic inch in city smog. Air occupies space, and the layer of air surrounding the earth creates 14.7 pounds of pressure per square inch at sea level. This pressure is what holds things together. At 10,000 feet, the pressure drops to 10.2 pound per square inch.

> *Science is built up with facts, as a house is with stones. But a collection of facts is no more a science than a heap of stones is a house.*
>
> —*Jules-Henri Poincaré*

AIR, SUN, AND LIGHT GAMES

Paper Airplane Games

A good way to learn about aeronautic design and wind currents. Good for parties, too.

1. See which plane flies the farthest. Launch planes from the same place and at the same height.
2. With a **watch**, fly your plane three times. Take the best of the three flights to record.
3. Hold an **Airplane Race** by choosing a course: around a baseball diamond, track, or house. Start by launching the plane. Wherever it lands, pick it up and launch it again. Whoever makes it in the *fewest* launches can have everyone take her out for pizza. (Or just try to better your own record.)

Celsius Temperature Pictures

1. Fold a **paper** into quarters. Write the names of the seasons in each quarter, then write the corresponding Celsius temperatures: 0° for winter, 10° for fall, 20° for spring, and 30° for summer.
2. **Draw** pictures of what you would be wearing for each season.
3. Older children might enjoy using a formula for converting Celsius into Fahrenheit: $\frac{9}{5}$ x centigrade (Celsius) temperature + 32. ($10°$ c = $\frac{9}{5}$ x 10 + 32 = 50)

Solar Box Cooker Plans

Write to:
Solar Box Cookers International
1724 Eleventh St.
Sacramento, CA 95814

Making Colors

#1: Take a **styrofoam egg carton** and fill each section with **water**. Into three of the sections, put in **blue, yellow,** and **red food coloring**. With a **medicine dropper**, encourage kids to make different colors in the remaining sections. (Or use a bunch of clear plastic cups.)

#2: Warm up about 1 to 2 cups of **milk.** Add some **dish detergent.** (Dawn or any heavy-duty grease cutter works well.) Drop 1 to 2 colors of **food coloring** in the solution. (Scientific principle: detergent emulsifies [breaks down] the fat in the milk.)

Books must follow sciences, and not sciences books.

—Francis Bacon

🌿 GEOGRAPHY 🌿

Geography is the branch of science concerned with the surface of the earth and the distribution of life on it. Geographers study maps. The main branches of geography are: biogeography (distribution of life), economic geography, mathematical geography (size, shape, and motion of the earth), physical geography, political geography, regional geography, historical geography, and applied geography which combines all aspects of geography, in order to solve social and economic problems.

Geography Games

WEATHERVANE GAMES

One person acts as the Wind. The rest of the players stand together, facing the Wind. The Wind then calls out, "The wind blows...south!" Everyone then turns to the south.

The Wind may help the players at first, but then she may twirl around and end up facing the wrong direction to confuse everybody.

Make a more difficult game by adding northeast, southwest, etc. If a player faces the wrong direction ten or twenty times, he's out.

TREASURE MAP

Making treasure maps is an excellent way to introduce children to geography and map making skills. Make a map of your backyard or neighborhood and have kids hunt for hidden treasure using the map. For authenticity, we always wrinkle the map, rub some dirt on it, and burn the edges a bit.

GEOGRAPHY SONGS

Sing songs such as *Home on the Range, This Land Is Your Land,* and *Wabash Cannonball* to learn about U.S. geography. Use folk songs from other countries such as *Guantanamera, La Cucaracha, Tongo,* etc. to learn world geography. Get out the globe and find the country where the song originates.

LICENSE PLATE GAME

Almost every child has played this game on a long trip. The object of the game is to find license plates from as many states as possible. Buy a blank U.S. map from a teacher supply store and have kids color in the maps as they find each state.

❧ OUTER SPACE (ASTRONOMY) ❧

> *Astronomy compels the soul to look upwards and leads us from this world to another.*
>
> —*Plato*

> *Nature composes some of her loveliest poems for the microscope and telescope.*
>
> —*Theodore Roszak*

As a child, I went to Girl Scout camp in the summer, and our camp director was an enthusiastic amateur astronomer. She would have the entire camp sleep outside every night, then she would come around with her flashlight and point out different constellations to us. We would even make up our own constellations and invent corresponding myths to go with them. Lying under the stars night after night like that was good for our young souls, and helped us put things into perspective. I still enjoy sleeping outside in the summer.

Astronomy is one of the oldest sciences. The ancients learned to tell time by studying the position of the sun in the sky and the shape of the moon. Astronomy encompasses the study of the sun, moon, planets, comets, meteors, nebula, stars, and other miscellaneous flotsam and jetsam of our universe.

Space extends in all directions and has no known limits or boundaries. Space begins when the air on earth has so little density that it no longer affects objects passing through it. Space is characterized by the absence of light and air and extreme cold. The planets are the heavenly bodies that make up our solar system. Also included in the study of outer space is the study of rocket ships and astronauts.

Astronomy Activities

✦ The best way to explore the sky is to **lie out on a starry night**. Better yet, sleep outside all summer. My children's grandparents, Jack and Marie Drechsler (who are in their 80's) have been sleeping outside every summer for at least fifteen years! Children are usually fascinated by outer space and enjoy stargazing. (Write to Superintendent of Documents, U.S. Government Printing Office, Washington, D.C. 20402 and ask for *Stars in Your Eyes* for an inexpensive constellation book.) A flashlight works well to point out individual stars.

✦ Going to local **observatories** is another good way to learn about outer space. I grew up in the astro-scientific community of Pasadena (home of the Jet Propulsion Laboratory and Cal Tech). Even the junior college I attended had an observatory that Albert Einstein dedicated.

- Build **models** of the sun and the planets and hang them from your ceiling.

- Purchase a Farmers' Almanac and learn when to **observe meteor showers**. There are several spectacular displays that happen annually. They are usually named after the constellation where most of the meteor activity seems to appear. One night I was sleeping out and watched in awe as a *huge* meteor streaked across the night sky, leaving an orange glowing tail. I was positive the earth was going to quake when the behemoth landed! (It didn't.)

- If you ever get a chance to **observe a total solar eclipse** DO IT! In 1991, I was lucky enough to be in Baja California for this magical event. Our son Joshuwyn was three at the time, and still remembers this special event. If you can't observe a total one, chances are that you will be near to a partial eclipse or even a moon eclipse. Check with your local librarian or pick up a copy of *Celestial Delights, The Best Astronomical Events through 2001* by Francis Reddy and Greg Walz-Chojnacki.

- Make a **balloon rocket**. Tie 50 feet of **fishing line** and mark off 5-foot intervals. Tie one end high up to a tree branch. Thread a **drinking straw** on the end of the line, blow up a **balloon,** and **tape** it to the straw. Let it go and record its flight. Experiment with differently shaped balloons.

Electricity, Magnets, and Machines

There is nothing in nature that is not in us.

—*Naum Gabo*

Electricity is all around us. It is perhaps our most useful form of energy. **Electricity** is a stream of moving electrons, which are the nucleus of atoms. They are carried through wires, just as water is carried through hoses. **Magnetism** is generated by the motion of electrons or electrical currents. It is characterized by the attraction exerted on certain substances, such as iron. **Machines** are any devices that change the amount, speed, or direction of a force. Tools are operated by the force of a person and include digging tools (shovels), pulling tools (winches), cutting tools (scissors), smoothing tools (sandpaper), spreading tools (paintbrushes), piercing tools (needles, nails), and gathering tools (rakes or brooms). The eight kinds of energy are: mechanical, electrical, chemical, moving air, moving water, solar, atomic, and radiant.

Using the Scientific Method

Introduction: Give relevant facts or background information.

Problem: Identify and state the problem.

Hypothesis: State the hypothesis (unproven theory). If a hypothesis stands the test of new data, then it becomes a theory. A theory is an explanation, supported by data, that makes the most sense of a problem. Theories may change as new evidence becomes available.

Materials: List all material used in the experiment.

Procedure: What you did to gather and record data.

Results: State results of data gathering and observations.

Conclusions: Analyze data and draw relevant and appropriate conclusions.

NATURE MOVIES

Watch films such as: *Call of the Wild,* and *Never Cry Wolf.* For more films contact *Bullfrog Films* 1-800-543-FROG

NATURE BOOKS

Going Green by John Elkington, et al.
Earth Book for Kids by Linda Schwartz
Save the Earth: An Action Handbook for Kids by Betty Miles
Planet Earth by Martyn Bramwell
50 Simple Things Kids Can Do to Save the Earth by the Earth Works Group
My First Green Book by Angela Wilkes
My First Science Book by Angela Wilkes
Environmental Science: 49 Science Fair Projects by Robert Bonnett
The Way Things Work by David Macaulay
A Brief History of Time: From the Big Bang to Black Holes by Stephen Hawking

LITERATURE BOOKS ABOUT NATURE

Miss Rumphius by Barbara Cooney
The Wind Blew by Pat Hutchins
The Carrot Seed by Ruth Krauss
What the Moon Saw by Brian Wildsmith
Mousekin's Close Call by Edna Miller
Unicorn and the Plow by Louise Moeri
Everybody Needs a Rock by Byrd Baylor
Moon Song by Byrd Baylor
Fish is Fish by Leo Lionni
The Magic School Bus (Series) by Joanna Cole
The Lorax by Dr. Seuss

NATURE/SCIENCE CATALOGS

Animal Town, PO Box 485, Healdsburg, CA. 95448. *Many cooperative and scientific games. You'll love their catalog!*

Edmund Scientific Company, 101 E. Gloucester Pike, Barrington, NJ 08007-1380. *Send for the Annual Catalog for Technical Hobbyists.*

Jerryco, Inc. 601 Linden Place, Evanston, IL 60202.

Nasco Science Catalog, 901 Janesville Ave., Fort Atkinson, WI 53538-0901. *A major school supplier.*

Learning Things, Inc., P.O. Box 436 Arlington, MA 02174. *Ask for the Science/ Math/Technology catalog.*

Carolina Biological Supply Company 2700 York Rd. Burlington, NC 27215. *This catalog is 1300 pages long!*

The Exploratorium 3601 Lyon Street, San Francisco, CA 94123. *A catalog of terrific science books.*

OTHER RESOURCES

Growing trees from seed: *Trees For Life, 1130 Jefferson St., Wichita, KS 67023.*

Information on Organic Gardening: *The New Alchemy Institute, 237 Hatchville Rd., East Falmouth, MA 02536.*

Recycling Paper: *Conservatree Paper Co., 10 Lombard St., Suite 250, San Francisco, CA 94111.*

Environmental Songbook: *Citizens' Clearinghouse for Hazardous Waste, PO Box 926, Arlington, VA 22216.*

Picture of Planet Earth: *World Federalist Association, United Nations Office, 777 United Nations Plaza, New York, NY 10017.*

It is not half so important to know as to feel.

—Rachel Carson

❧ *Body World* ❧

Teaching kids how to take care of their bodies requires us as parents to do what we say. Teach your children that the body is the temple of the soul. Good health is the most precious thing we can possess. Not only does a healthy body honor the soul within the body, but people with healthy bodies feel good and have more zest for life.

Physical fitness includes cardiorespiratory endurance, muscle strength, flexibility, and body composition. Factors of physical wellness include mental alertness, nutritional habits, stress reduction, relaxation, sleep, rest practices, injury prevention and care, personal activity program, and personal hygiene. Movement skills encompass perceptual-motor skills, motor skills (both fine and gross), movement qualities, and posture. The following information will help remind you of the importance of good health and of being healthy role models for your kids.

❧ BEING WELL: TAKING CARE OF THE BODY ❧

> *If anything is sacred the human body is sacred.*
>
> —*Walt Whitman*

Wellness is an ongoing process. Very simply, it is a combination of:

- ✦ FOOD: healthy eating habits
- ✦ SLEEP: sleeping long enough to recharge the brain
- ✦ WATER: drinking enough to be properly hydrated
- ✦ EXERCISE: regular heart-pounding physical exercise
- ✦ ATTITUDE: a positive attitude helps us keep healthy
- ✦ CLEANLINESS: soap and water

Exercising the Body

> *Nature, time and patience are the three great physicians.*
>
> —*Anonymous*

Healthy body, healthy mind. Bodies need movement every day. The brain's food is oxygen, and exercise is like a feast for your brain. Twenty-five percent of all oxygen intake goes to feed the brain, which is only 2% of the body's weight.

My personal favorite sports include (in no particular order):

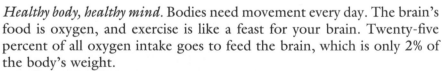

- ✦ gymnastics
- ✦ yoga
- ✦ swimming
- ✦ hiking
- ✦ surfing/body boarding
- ✦ dancing
- ✦ biking
- ✦ running
- ✦ gardening
- ✦ carrying wood
- ✦ making love
- ✦ friendly non-competitive games where winning is incidental to camaraderie

Exercise is also beneficial to the brain. The brain eats up our energy, consuming 20% of the body's total energy needs. During a workout, we increase the formation of new blood vessels in the cerebellum, the walnut-shaped structure at the base of the brain that controls muscle movement. Thus, improving the brain's ability to respond better to one form of exercise also helps the brain to better handle other physical activities as well. Growth of blood vessels in the brain occurs in response to the cerebellum's need for more air and sugar (oxygen and glucose), and its need for getting rid of wastes produced by increased physical activity. Regular physical activity should include two or three one-hour sessions a week at the *minimum*. Engage in activities that enhance flexibility *and* involve sustained endurance. Sustained endurance is any activity that makes the heart beat over 120 beats per minute for 20 minutes. These types of activities include walking, swimming, jogging, and bicycling. The benefits of sustained activity may include:

- ✦ More efficient functioning of the heart and lungs
- ✦ Reduction of chronic back fatigue
- ✦ Better posture
- ✦ Reduction of stress and tension
- ✦ Lower cholesterol levels
- ✦ Increased muscle response with greater energy
- ✦ Reduced chances of contracting heart disease
- ✦ Easier weight control
- ✦ Ability to sleep soundly

Posture

The simple health practice of keeping our skeletons upright (spinal alignment) reaps tremendous benefits. Good posture is a subtle yet profound influence on our health. Good posture indicates mental and emotional strength and control. Poor posture indicates defeat and discouragement. Posture is perhaps a person's most conspicuous overall indicator of the state of body, mind, and spirit.

Next time you're about, look at all the people walking around you. Look at their shoulders. Are they slumped and hunched over? Are they erect? Are most people standing tall and proud or are they hunched over and looking discouraged?

Standing erect is an instant pick-me-up, far better than sugar, coffee, or cigarettes. Remind youngsters (and yourself) to stand up straight with a gentle hand on the back, or remind them to think of a ribbon attached to the top of their heads pulling them up to the sky. Hold the pelvis vertically as if it were being pressed between two panes of glass. Pull back the shoulders. *(As I straighten my hunched-up computer back!)*

Sitting up straight keeps the spinal vertebrae in alignment. Hindu beliefs recognize that the spine is the dwelling place of our *chakras*, centers of spiritual energy. Don't you think it might be the most important mind/body/spirit practice of all?

Nobody can be in good health if he does not have all the time fresh air, sunshine, and good water.

—Flying Hawk

Now this *baby has good posture!*

185

Sleep and Rest

We are all unique in our needs for rest, sleep, and relaxation. Time spent in the dream world is all at once fascinating, confusing, and refreshing. It's our connection to other worlds. Enjoy. Kids need more sleep than adults, roughly 10 to 12 hours a day, and babies need one to two naps on top of this. Most of my babies stopped taking naps around age three or four. In our house, we usually begin putting kids to bed around 8:00 or 9:00, and more often than not, they're not asleep until 9:00 or 10:00 or so. For us, this works out, because they usually sleep until 7:30 or 8:00. Once, eight-year-old Genessa wrote a letter to the then First Lady Barbara Bush about homeschooling. Her letter began: "Homeschooling is better than you think. We don't have to get up early…" One of the hidden blessings of homeschooling is unhurried mornings and being able to sleep in if you are tired.

Routine sleep and rest will also help the brain function at an optimum level. Disruption of your sleep routine will reduce mental efficiency. And of course *everybody* knows never to wake a sleeping baby.

> *The health of nations is more important than the wealth of nations.*
>
> —*Will Durant*

Teeth

When Amarina, my oldest, was born, I thought that once I showed her how to brush her teeth she'd get it right away. Was I ever naive! This is probably the best analogy I know that demonstrates how slow the process of acquiring knowledge can be. Habits and skills require countless repetition. Teach kids to brush their teeth a lot (ideally after every meal), to floss, and to avoid overeating sweets.

Hearing

Hearing is the second most important sense. Hearing gives pleasure and can warn of danger. Hearing can be vital to communication and to intellectual, emotional, and social development.

Sound is a form of energy produced by vibrating objects. It has to have a medium, such as air, gas, liquids, or solids to travel through. It travels faster through warmer mediums, and travels about a mile a second. Pitch depends on the number of vibrations per second of the sound: the more vibrations, the higher the pitch. Musical sounds have regular wave patterns, noise has irregular patterns. Loudness is measured in decibels.

Hearing impairments in children are usually noticed around the age of two. Signs of being verbally challenged are lack of speech, slurred or muffled speech, and/or chronic ear infections. Try a simple hearing test: rub your finger and thumb together and see how far away your child can still hear the sound. Examine both ears, and test your own ears for comparison.

Vision

Vision is the most important sense and is closely linked to art. Our eyes give us the most direct clues to our surroundings. For sighted folks, vision is directly linked to reading. Being able to interpret symbols indicates a readiness to begin reading pure alphabet symbols. Even though our son has eaten at McDonalds' only a few times, he can easily identify the golden arches.

The eye functions just like a camera, or should we say the camera functions just like the eye. Clues to visual problems include straining the eyes to read (eyes might look pinched, strained, squinty, or book might be held too close), eyes might show redness or soreness, or the person may complain of blurred vision.

When one sense is impaired, it is important to encourage the development of the remaining senses. Most people who have challenges in one sense develop extraordinary powers with their remaining senses. If you pretend you're blind, you don't really need to use flashlights outside on a dark night...try it sometime.

Food

You are what you eat. Many factors affect our choices of food including customs, traditions, and historical influences of different countries and cultures. I tell my kids that the best foods to eat are the ones that come from Mother Earth: fresh organic fruits, vegetables, nuts, seeds, seaweed, beans, and grains. I believe if a person wants to eat animals (who feed upon this bounty) then they should be able to kill the animals and process the meat themselves.

Diet affects learning, not only in food *content* but also in food *consumption*. After eating a big meal, blood flows to the stomach to aid in digestion. This leaves the brain feeling sluggish. It's a fact that more accidents happen on the job right after lunch. As far as food content goes, carbohydrates make you sleepy, protein increases alertness, and fat dulls mental performance.

The variation of diet helps the family adapt to season, activity, and environment. Food can help us adapt to seasonal weather, activity, and environment.

Health and intellect are the two blessings of life.

—Menander c. 342-292 BC

Laughing

LAUGHING CAN KEEP YOU HEALTHY

Laughing causes the lungs to expel carbon dioxide more efficiently. The eyes are cleansed, muscles relax, and the flow of adrenaline increases slightly. More endorphins, the chemicals produced in the brain to relieve pain, are released into the bloodstream.

We all know that the immune system helps fend off harmful diseases. When we are anxious or afraid, our bodies produce stress hormones that prepare us to act quickly. These hormones can suppress our immune systems and make us more likely to get sick. Laughing helps us make more germ-fighting hormones called *Immunoglobulin A (IgA)*. Also, like anything that we practice repeatedly, the more we do it, the better we get at doing it. The more we laugh, the healthier we will be.

We Feel Better About Ourselves When We Laugh

If you can laugh at something that is bothering you, it won't bother you so much. In addition, people make more mistakes and have more accidents when they are tense or uptight. By laughing at ourselves, we release the tension. Thus, we won't make as many mistakes.

Laughing Can Help You Make Friends

People who laugh a lot seem more friendly, confident, and accepting. When you laugh with another, you may suddenly feel closer to that person because when two people laugh together, their hearts beat in rhythm and they begin to breathe as one.

Woman, in your laughter you have the music of the fountain of life.

—*Rabindranath Tagore*

•

He who laughs, lasts.

—*Mary Pettibone Poole*

•

Humor is the shortest distance between two people.

—*Victor Borge*

People With a Sense of Humor Do Better Work

People who have a sense of humor tend to be more creative and willing to experiment. When you work, you can perform better with laughter because laughing can give you more energy and make you feel less tired.

Laughing Is Good Exercise

When we laugh, we increase our heart rate, work the muscles of our faces and stomachs, improve the circulation of blood throughout our bodies, and breathe faster. Ten seconds of belly laughing raises a person's heartbeat as much as ten minutes of rowing a boat! A good laugh also gives the lungs more oxygen because we exhale more air than normal and bring in more fresh oxygen. Laughing *feels* good! What's more, after we laugh and our bodies enter a relaxed state, our blood pressure, breathing, and heart rate all fall below normal levels, and muscle tension disappears.

Mental and Emotional Health

The goal of mental and emotional health is to be able to recognize and successfully deal with the gamut of human emotions. We also must be able to know which ones are righteous and which ones aren't. Nurture children in right emotions by modeling them. *It is what we do, not what we say that children follow.* Here are a few guidelines for developing healthy emotional attitudes in children.

- ✦ Point out the things they're doing right.
- ✦ Keep expectations realistic, and don't have unspoken expectations.
- ✦ Discuss what it means to have empathy toward others.
- ✦ Practice acceptance of self and others.
- ✦ Point out positive emotions of love, ecstasy, joy, contentment, peace, satisfaction, and happiness when they happen.

(More information on the development of positive emotions and values can be found in the sections on Family Meetings and the section on the Inner World.)

Games to Play

Playing games, whether they are quiet or active, are important ways to learn a variety of social and personal skills.

Through physical activity, we can learn social skills such as:

+ respect
+ appreciation for individual styles
+ playing fair
+ cooperating
+ leadership skills
+ assistance
+ camaraderie

All this may be summed up in the old proverb: *It's not whether you win or lose, but how you play the game.*

Movement creates positive self-esteem through:

+ developing optimum body conditioning
+ physical confidence
+ developing skills of grace, agility, strength, stamina, flexibility, balance, coordination, and a sense of rhythm

Physical activities enhance self-realization by developing:

+ self-appraisal
+ self-control
+ self-direction
+ self-expression
+ harmony
+ creativity
+ will power
+ the aesthetics of human movement
+ concentration
+ risk taking
+ sense of optimum well-being through the gratification and exhilaration of top-notch physical performances

Physically, strenuous activities release a hormone called *endorphin* into our bodies. Endorphin produces a sense of well being, and is known by runners as the "runner's high." The dictionary says endorphin is "any of several peptides secreted in the brain that have a pain-relieving effect like that of morphine."

The health of the people is really the foundation upon which all their happiness and all their powers as a state depend.

—Benjamin Disraeli

Inside Games

INTRODUCTIONS

These are good games to play when people are meeting for the first time.

Line up according to:

+ shoe size
+ birthdays
+ alphabetical order of last names
+ hair length

Gather in groups by:

+ sock color
+ number of brothers and sisters
+ favorite ice cream flavors

NO WAY!

Sit in a circle. First player says a sentence. Next player says, "No Way!" and changes *one* word in the sentence. (i.e., "The baby crawled on the floor." "No way! The baby crawled on the elephant." "No way! The baby peed on the elephant.")

BODY PARTS

Players combine in groups of two (or three if need be). One leader calls out the names of two body parts (*nose to elbow)* and partners must touch those body parts together. (NOTE: You may play that *both* players have to touch *both* body parts together, or that one player touches one part, and the other one the other.) If the leader yells *Scramble!*, then everyone changes partners, and the one remaining player becomes the leader.

> *It is a happy talent to know how to play.*
>
> *—Ralph Waldo Emerson*

SMILES

Players stand or sit in a circle. *It* goes to each player, one by one, and says, "Smile if you love me." The player answers, "I love you but I can't smile." Of course *It* does everything possible to get a smile going. If a player smiles, s/he joins *It*.

BLANKET GAME

One or more people sit on the floor, legs crossed. Put a large blanket over each person and tell him to "take off the most unnecessary thing you have on." (It's the blanket!)

CHARADES

The person who is *It* tries to get the other players to guess what he is acting out:

> ✦ First, show what you are acting out. *Book*: hold a pretend book in your hands, *song*: pretend to be singing, *movie*: turn the "crank" of a camera).
>
> ✦ Next, show how many words are in the title by holding up that amount of fingers.
>
> ✦ Use hand signals to help with clues.
>> *Syllables:* lay proper amount of fingers (from one hand) onto the wrist of the other hand.
>> *Sounds like:* tug your ear.
>> *Small word:* hold thumb and first finger a small distance apart.
>> *Longer word:* pull hands apart.

MAGAZINE SCAVENGER HUNT

Make a list of ten or so items to find in a **magazine**, such as: a pencil, a car, a surfer, or whatever. Players then have ten minutes to find the items, which they list on a piece of **paper** (or cut out and paste). Players may wish to work in groups of two or three. VARIATION: Announce a letter of the alphabet, and list or cut out as many objects in the magazine that you can find that begin with the same letter.

Outside Games

MOMMY OR PAPA

A referee oversees the game. Everyone else, standing in a random fashion, closes his eyes. Silently, the referee picks one person to be the mommy (or papa). On the word, *"Go!"* players mill around, and when they touch someone else, they shake hands, and ask, *"Mommy?"* If the person doesn't answer, he or she is the Mommy. The player joins hands with the Mommy and continues playing. The game ends when everyone is holding hands with the Mommy or Papa.

> *The human body is an instrument for the production of art in the life of the human soul.*
>
> —*Alfred North Whitehead*

WONKER DUCKS

- ✦ Group divides into two teams.
- ✦ One group forms a circle (corral) around the other group by holding hands. Two players in the circle drop hands to create a gate.
- ✦ Then, players in the middle (wonker ducks) close their eyes, bend over and grab their ankles and begin walking backwards, trying to find the gate. When one player finds the gate, he begins to cry, "Wonk, wonk, wonk!" so all the other ducks can find the gate.
- ✦ Meanwhile, all the corral people are singing a song such as *Six Little Ducks* at the top of their voices to drown out the wonker birds.

You can do anything with children if you only play with them.

—Otto Von Bismarck

PICKLE

A fast-moving variation of baseball.

Three or four players stand on bases (**pieces of cardboard, rug scraps, etc.**). Other players (runners) run around from base to base while the players on base throw a **softball or tennis ball** between the bases. If a runner is tagged, then s/he becomes the person on base.

BUMPS

Two players stand next to each other. A third player throws a **sock-ball (rolled-up sock)** to them, and the two players try to catch it between them without using their hands.

HIT THE BUNS

Make soft balls out of old rolled up **socks**. Put the ball-socks on the ground. On the words "Hit the buns" each person tries to grab a ball and pelt the other players.

The weaker the body, the more it commands; the stronger it is, the more it obeys.

—Jean Jacques Rousseau

CIRCLE DANCE

Each player must have an old **carpet square** (or cardboard square) to play. Place squares in a circle close enough for players to hold hands with the person next to them. Everyone joins hands.

- ✦ As a group, slowly lower yourselves to a squatting position and back again.
- ✦ Sway from side to side.
- ✦ Jump from square to square. (A **drum** rhythm will help here.)
- ✦ When you're really good, try making a full turn before you jump.
- ✦ When you're really good, move the squares farther apart.

GROUP BOLA JUMP ROPE

Stuff a **tennis ball** into an old **sock**. Tie it to a 15-foot **rope**. Lie down on your back (or spin around in a circle) and spin the rope slowly in a circle. Everyone tries to jump the rope. Rope may speed up, players may hold hands, or the whole group may hold hands.

TANGLED MESS

All players (10 to 20 works best) gather into a tight circle with outstretched hands. Each player then randomly grasps two other hands from different people. Without letting go, try to untangle yourselves into a circle. Results may be either one big circle, a figure eight, two or more independent circles, or people may be facing out or in. One "tangle-aid"—a quick letting go and re-grasping of hands—is allowed per game.

HUG TAG

Play like regular tag with one exception. When you hug someone else, you're safe. Vary the rules by making it safe when three or four players are hugging!

THE BLOB

Play the blob like regular tag except that when you are tagged by *It,* you become part of the blob. When the blob is big enough, it can split in two.

STUCK IN THE MUD

Six (or so) players (with **sock-balls**–rolled-up socks) try to tag all the other players who, once tagged must stand with their hands on their heads and their feet spread apart. They may be freed if another player crawls through their legs. Game ends when all players are frozen.

BEAN BAG FREEZE TAG

All players have **bean bags** resting on some part of their body (all of them being on heads, shoulders, arms…). Three players are chosen to be *It,* and they chase the other players around with **tennis balls**. When others are tagged, they become *It* and take the tennis balls. If a player drops her bean bag, she is frozen until another player comes along and puts the bean bag back where it belongs. Players that are *It* can put their own bean bags back on if they are dropped.

CAPTURE THE FLAG

(NOTE: This game needs a rather large playing field.) Ten to thirty players divide into two teams. Divide the playing field into two sections. In each half, make two three-to-four-foot circles, one about fifteen-to-twenty-feet from the dividing line in the middle, as a place for the flag, and one five-to-ten-feet to the right of the flag area as a jail. (Use yarn, rope, rocks, or hula hoops for the circles.)

Next, each team chooses one of their players to guard the jail and one to guard the flag area. The **flags** can be bandanas, tennis balls, oranges, or similar objects.

Now the play begins. Each team tries to get across the dividing line and onto the opposing team's field to "capture" the flag. Opposing team members try to tag the other players who are on their side. A player who is tagged must go to jail. However, players are safe inside the flag circle.

First person across the divider with the opposing team's flag (without being tagged) scores one point for her team.

Let early education be a sort of amusement, you will then better be able to find out the natural bent of the child.

—Plato

193

LOG ROLL

In soft grass, players lie side-by-side on their stomachs. The **rider** gets on the "logs" (on her stomach) and the logs roll together to give the rider a ride. At the end of the ride, the rider becomes a log and the last log becomes the rider. Heavy players should support some of their own weight.

BLANKETBALL

Two teams (8 to 10 members each) hold on to two different blankets and try to toss a beach ball back and forth. Or, one team tosses the ball straight up and dashes out of the way to let the other team catch. If you get really good, teams can "juggle" two balls back and forth.

LEMONADE

Players divide into two groups. The size is not important. The field is divided in half. One group goes into a huddle and decides on something such as a tiger, a worm, a skyscraper to pantomime. Then, all players face each other in the middle. While one side panto-mimes, the other side guesses. When the correct guess is made, the guessing team chases the pantomiming team to their pre-determined finish line. If anyone is tagged before reaching the finish line, s/he must join the other team. Trade off chasing and pantomiming. (Game idea from Melissa Knight.)

ELBOW TAG

All players except two link elbows. If there is an extra player, three can link up. One person is *It,* and chases the other "loose" player. When the loose player links elbows with one of the people, the person who is *not* linked to the loose player now must become the loose player and *It* chases him. When the loose player is tagged, the roles reverse, and the new *It* counts to five and begins chasing the new loose player.

*Games bring you closer to a different reality, one
that comes naturally for children.*

—Melissa Knight

Outer World

The study of the outer world is the study of human life or social science. It includes two main areas: human culture and history, and human behavior. Disciplines include history, geography, anthropology, political science, economics, sociology, education, ethics, philosophy, psychology, criminology, law, and the humanities. These studies can be important in developing individual and social intelligence.

The true value in the study of the humanities is to understand the connection between *ideas* and *behavior,* and *values* and *ideals.* History should also expose us to issues dealing with *truth* and *justice.*

Traditionally, history is taught to develop patriotism and to develop, support, or overthrow a particular political regime, religion, economic system, or race.

Culture and History

History is a record of our past that is made by historians, *not* politicians or soldiers. Historians write about events of importance to *them.* What is important to them will depend on what kind of people they are. It is not possible for historians to keep their points of view from influencing what they write. In addition, people will have an entirely different outlook on history depending on where they live. Therefore, the study of history is one that should ultimately teach us to become discriminating thinkers and readers.

Man is a social animal.

—Spinoza

History can be broken down into:

+ local history
+ state history
+ national history
+ world history
+ contemporary history or current events

Not including pre-history, there are approximately three major eras of history: *ancient, medieval,* and *modern.*

Ancient History begins in most Western Eurocentric (i.e., the United States) countries in the Middle East. Historians traditionally begin their studies with the cultures of ancient Egypt, Sumeria, Babylon, and Assyria.

From there, further studies include Palestine, Phoenicia, and Persia. Next comes Greece, Carthage, and Rome. Finally comes the Far East: China, Southeast Asia, and Japan. Not much emphasis is placed on Far Eastern history.

Medieval History is thought to begin around 476 AD with the fall of the Roman Empire. The end of this period is thought to be around 1453, with the fall of the Byzantine Empire, while others believe it is 1492, when Columbus "discovered" North America.

Human Family (Socialization)

Human respect and dignity are the most important factors of socialization. Each individual has personal needs, but we all differ in what we think is important, so tolerance for other views is a key element for living in peace.

Inborn needs are food, water, and rest.

Acquired needs are learned from culture.

Social psychologists study the way culture and society are sources of social influence. The effects of societal influence can be seen in leadership, conformity, prejudice, attitude, childrearing, and morale.

We have **formal roles**, primarily dictated by society, for interactions between parents and children, husband and wife, teacher and student, and employer and employee. **Informal relationships** are formed by the interest of both parties. Informal relationships usually will not continue unless both parties are satisfied with the relationship whereas formal relationships, for various reasons, are obliged to be continued.

❧ SOCIALIZATION ❦

The social, friendly, honest man, Whate'er he be, 'Tis he fulfills great Nature's plan, And none but he!

—Robert Burns

Socialization is *the* question that always comes regarding homeschooling.

I call the homeschooler's style of socialization **tribal** or **natural socialization**. *Homeschoolers do not live in isolation from society.* They have opportunities to develop better social skills than their school counterparts. Here's why:

PUBLIC SCHOOL SOCIALIZATION

Public schools in California use a system they call ADA (Average Daily Attendance) to keep track of school attendance. ADA figures on approximately five hours of "schooling" a day (25 hours a week) for students from 1st-12th grade. If we divide the curriculum into eight general areas of study according to the theory of the *Rainbow-Colored Mind*, then our children should be socializing approximately 30 minutes each day, five days a week, 180 days (half) of the year. In school, children usually get about 20–30 minutes of recess each day, and a lunch break of 30–45 minutes. With approximately 60 minutes a day of pure social time, their socialization needs are more than being met, right? Wrong! This is why:

1) Kids are usually relating only in a **linear fashion** (i.e., 3rd graders socializing with 3rd graders, etc.).

2) In these linear classes, kids are fairly **isolated** within their class. They socialize almost exclusively with the same group of 25 or 30 kids for the entire school year.

3) In this situation, kids become **peer role models** for each other.

Homeschoolers, on the other hand, have their parents, *not* 30 other children and one lonely teacher (who views them as one in a group of 30) as their primary role models.

What most public school kids actually, and not even consciously, learn is a lop-sided social perspective, socializing in a linear fashion within a large group. Toddlers (who are usually in daycare) and elders (who are usually in rest homes) are seldom seen or welcomed into the schools.

Large gatherings of people (20 or more) are really only useful or necessary for musical and dramatic events, dances and sports events, religious gatherings, parties, peace demonstrations and the like. Other than that, socialization is best done in small groups of three to fifteen or so people.

Have you ever been at a gathering where you knew a lot of people there, only to feel disappointed at the end of the event because you didn't have a chance to talk to everyone? How many times have you been to a group meeting where confusion reigned, and you felt as if you should've brought your knitting or a Walkman? How many communication or socialization classes did *you* take in school? How many were required?

NATURAL TRIBAL LIFE

Homeschooling breaks away from this blatant separatism based on age and paves the way for more natural relationships to develop. Our personal homeschooling social activities fill up at *least* 5 to 8 hours a week— Ah! We meet our quota!—and during our activities, *the kids usually mix with people of all different ages.* Although no formal skills are being taught during these events, children who socialize in this manner naturally learn how to take care of babies, how to relate to the needs of toddlers, and how to play with kids of all different ages.

I am confident that homeschoolers living this lifestyle of natural tribal socialization are learning to become articulate, well-mannered, well-informed members of society. Natural socialization is simply not available to children when they are being schooled full time. Anyone with basic math skills can see that regular public schoolers can spend only 50% of their time in natural social situations.

HOMESCHOOLING AND MULTICULTURALISM

Homeschoolers don't have automatic built-in opportunities to seek out others of different backgrounds. This is perhaps the biggest drawback to full-time homeschooling and is one reason I believe in a home-and-school approach. Most alternative educators who believe passionately in public education do so because of the social mixing opportunities available to students, however limited they may be.

A valid point that comes up in regards to homeschooling (this can apply to private schools as well) is how do they gain a multicultural perspective? How do Asian-Americans, Euro-Americans, Mexican-Americans, and African-Americans learn to relate to each other?

The public high school I attended in Pasadena, California (John Muir) is unique in that there is no racial majority at the school. One of the first things my counselor told me was that she believed our school was the best social learning situation possible. Although I didn't really understand what she meant at the time, after two and a half years there, I had gained a clearer understanding of the whole concept of multiculturalism, and subsequently more tolerance for others. (However, the *real* roots of tolerance I learned at home.)

Multicultural tolerance is what makes America unique, and public schools, for better or worse, are perhaps the only places where the "tossed salad" of ethnic groups may truly become the melting pot of cultures.

> *Social prosperity means man happy, the citizen free, the nation great.*
>
> —Victor Hugo

> *Experience is the child of Thought and Thought is the child of Action. We cannot learn men from books.*
>
> —Benjamin Disraeli

❧ THE HUMAN FAMILY: LIVING TOGETHER ❦

The social state is at once so natural, so necessary, and so habitual to man, that...he never conceives himself otherwise than as a member of a body.

—John Stuart Mill

GROUPS

Activities that involve others include education, family relationships, childrearing, drama, religion, sports, economics and politics.

We are all members of various groups. If members of a group are strongly motivated to belong to the group, the group will have unity, and the group will more than likely conform to the norms of the group. Cohesive groups are inclined to get together more (which means they communicate more), and thus have a higher morale.

Conflicts arise in groups when needs of individuals in the group vary. We must be mutually accommodating to each other for our groups to function harmoniously. We all have to learn to 'go with the flow' and to make compromises. I find large group meetings rather tedious, and prefer action to talk.

CIRCLES

Ceremonial Circles by Joshua Halpern and Sedonia Calhill (1992) is a wonderful guide to "practice, ritual, and renewal for personal and community healing. Stanley Krippner calls it, "a guide and a manual for people starved for ritual, crying for community and yearning for sacred experience. Write to HarperCollins Publishers, 10 East 53rd Street, New York, NY 10022.

LEADERSHIP

Leaders must assist members in solving conflicts. Good leaders empathize with group members, and thus create respect. People follow leaders because they are wise or are experts in certain areas. The Iroquois name for chief, *Royaner*, means "person of good mind." Their leaders are expected to have "a skin seven times thick" when facing criticism and to exercise great control over negative thoughts and feelings. The Iroquois believe that a leader should be able to perceive the effects of his or her policies "down to the seventh generation." When a person becomes chief, he is told, "Now you are poorer than anyone. You have lost yourself and become a nation."

CHILDREN

Generally, children are "socialized" by their parents, especially during the early years. The closer the parents and children feel towards each other, the more the children will behave like the parents. The balance of affection and discipline from the parents will also influence the development of children's conscience, attitudes towards self, and relationships with friends. This reflects the child-as-mirror of the parent model; the apple never falls far from the tree.

It is my strong belief that if we, as a society, were to honor toddlers for their special needs (i.e., child-sized furniture, "crying" rooms in movie theaters and opera houses, special children's menus in restaurants, etc.), we would be on the right path to removing yet another source of societal discrimination. We need to take care of everyone who has special needs: babies, toddlers, elders, *and* developmentally or physically challenged folks.

VOLUNTEERS OF AMERICA

We can't turn our backs on the plight of the poor, the homeless, and the downtrodden, just because we homeschool and believe in alternative education. We need to be active, contributing members of society to help relieve the suffering of others. Most people I know, including myself, know that our dedication to our families is our most important commitment, but once our children are grown and our material needs are met, then it will be our time to give back to the earth and the people of the earth. There are enough causes to keep us busy for quite a while!

When I was a teenager, I traveled with a youth group to help paint an orphanage in Mexico. I remember the trip because it was fun being with my friends and I also remember feeling proud that I was doing something real to help these kids.

All children should have opportunities for community service. When you feel satiated with enough things, start giving your money away. Remember that by rolling up your sleeves and getting your hands dirty, you will be giving the best gift of all: yourself. Curiously, when we give of ourselves, we get the greatest wealth of all: peace of mind, and a deep, lasting satisfaction in our souls. The principles of individual freedom are the highest ideals society can strive for, yet unless *everyone* is free, the ideal is not met. Therefore, when we assist each other, we free ourselves. It has been pointed out that when people get greedy and the gap widens between the rich and the poor, the quality of life goes down for everyone. The wealthy suffer from paranoia and, in order to protect themselves and their wealth, lock everything up, procure elaborate security systems, and build bomb shelters to "protect" themselves. If they only realized that everyone in society is better off when the wealth is shared!

Social progress means a checking of the cosmic process at every step and the substitution for it of another, which may be called the ethical process.

—Thomas Huxley

MULTICULTURAL PERSPECTIVES

Besides volunteer work, homeschoolers can gain a multicultural perspective through travel, especially to other countries. They can visit Buddhist shrines, Jewish synagogues, Muslim mosques, Hindu temples, Christian churches, and other religious institutions. They can also study multiculturalism through magazines such as *National Geographic* and multicultural films. Check out your local county Office of Education and see if they don't have films on the country of your interest. For a powerful film from Grammy award winners Stephen Olssen and Scott Andrews, check out *Images of War*, a poignant documentary about five international journalists who were killed in the Afghanistan War.

CHANGING SEASONS (CELEBRATIONS)

A few years ago, I became very sensitive to the subtle difference in the light quality of each season: the soft, warm, clear light of spring, the deliciously warm, intense light of summer, the apple-scented rain-soaked mellow light of autumn, and the sharp, pine-filled, crispy clear light of winter. This recycling light is the reason for most celebrations, and each season (according to what place on the planet you live) has its special attributes to honor.

When people are busy celebrating, honoring the changing seasons and the sacredness of the earth, they are not fighting or scheming. They are with their families and loved ones, eating special foods and performing rituals of ancient origins. True, holidays can be times of stress and anxiety. This is directly due to over-commercialization. We don't need

A general definition of civilization: a civilized society is exhibiting the five qualities of truth, beauty, adventure, art, peace.

—Alfred North Whitehead

to spend a lot of money to create meaningful celebrations; a few candles, some special foods, songs, and loved ones are the essential ingredients.

Another book I have simmering in my computer is called *Planetary Holidays.* It will include information on holidays (one for every day of the year!), festive multicultural cooking, arts and crafts, songs, games, and holidays. Most celebrations are filled with ancient traditions that I feel in my bones. As the seasons change, it's as if my blood were also changing. Do you feel that too? Also, I like parties. The way I see it, around fifty celebrations a year is about right. Indeed, this fits the biblical tradition of honoring God by resting on the Sabbath. The reason that we're not supposed to work one day a week is because we're supposed to be celebrating and giving thanks for this magical creation. Celebrate by playing festive music, baking holiday foods, creating special art, playing games, going to temple or church, hiking in the woods, riding waves … oh there are just too many ways to celebrate! So, "Party on Garth, party on, Wayne!"

ON SERVING CHILDREN

The Eastern woman's mind is such that many are completely satisfied with being Mothers. It's as if in the West we forget to valorize "love." What did we do today? "We 'loved', nourished and directed our children."

From inside you can see what an accomplishment that really is. To love is to be near what is "real" in our life experience.

Western minds want to see a materialization of what has been done but if we watch from our heart we can see that loving has been done but gone unattached and returned to the source: the infinite. Om.

—Letter to Nan Koehler from Radha Malasquez 4.4.83

MEDIATION

This system of dealing with children's conflicts is quite effective and fair. Mediators do not take sides, but listen impartially and help children resolve their own conflicts. This method is useful for children from age four on up. It *does* take more time than just reprimanding the child for negative behavior, but in the long run, it is worth it. It teaches children to communicate their feelings in a direct, honest, and non-threatening way.

- ✦ Make sure you are at **eye level** with the children.
- ✦ Ask each child to **tell his or her side of the story,** while the other person listens. **No interrupting.**
- ✦ Ask each child to **repeat** the other person's story.
- ✦ **Summarize** what you think the children are saying.
- ✦ **Feelings:** ask each child to tell how s/he feels.
- ✦ Point out **areas of agreement,** such as: both are hurt, both have a problem, both want to solve the conflict.
- ✦ Have them **suggest ways of solving the problem** and help them evaluate their choices. Offer additional suggestions, if needed.
- ✦ Help them **reach a fair agreement.**

In conflicts, learn to:

1) **Use the other person's name** (as a sign of respect).
2) **Let her know how you feel** (how their action affected you).
3) **Identify the problem** (avoid focusing on blame, excuses, or personal attacks).

Examples:

"Ami, I feel angry when you call me names. Please don't."
Not: "Stop calling me names. I hate you, you big jerk!"

"Oshanna, I feel like crying when you scribble on my papers. Please leave my work alone."
Not: "What are you doing, you little creep! Stop messing with my stuff!"

"Genessa, I get mad when you don't do the dishes, please try to help."
Not: "You lazy slob. You never help."

Family Meetings

Family harmony can and does contribute to individual well-being. I would even say our health *depends* on family harmony. The study of how to live in a family is one that we learn indirectly. Like the Women's Movement, in which women became aware of their roles in society and learned how to gain respect and prestige in a "man's" world, we now find more and more people wanting to learn how to live and function as families in a "man's" world. Most major cities now have family centers that offer classes in family and parenting skills.

Family meetings can also help the family function more smoothly. My own family life is somewhat erratic, (an understatement!) and so are our family meetings, but we have had a few now and then.

How to Have a Family Meeting

Most of the time family meetings are initiated by moms whose interest is twofold: they want more help with chores and they want to work on improving family relations. Sunday afternoons or evenings may be the most agreeable time for meetings. Below is a simple format for a 15 to 30 minute meeting:

OPENING

One way to open a family meeting is by holding hands. By doing so, you will automatically be in a circle. You might want to have a special prayer for the family. Family members can take turns saying a prayer or everyone may want to contribute to it.

Our children give us the opportunity to become the parents we always wish we had.

—Nancy Samalin

APPRECIATIONS AND SHARING

One at a time, go around the circle. Have each family member acknowledge the other members for something special he or she does or has done. Share your lives with each other (*"What did you feel best about doing this week, or what made you feel good this week?"*)

CHORES

Make a list of chores and decide who does what for the week. This is what a chore list from our house might include:

Daily chores: sweep floors, cook breakfast, wash and put away breakfast dishes, wash, dry, fold, and put away laundry, make lunches, cook dinner, set and clear table, wipe counters and stove, wash and put away dinner dishes, feed dog and cats, water garden (spring & summertime only).

1 to 3 times a week: grocery shop, put away groceries, wash kitchen floor, empty and recycle trash, empty compost, vacuum rooms, clean bathroom, feed hamsters and parakeets, check or clean cages, water houseplants, bring in wood (wintertime).

Monthly or so: dust, wash windows, clean cars, clean refrigerator.

Even a three-year-old can put the forks on the table or put away laundry. (Our Joshie puts the forks in our pockets!) True, it is more work to help a three-year-old do a job, but in the end, it will pay off.

Try not to have expectations about how the children do their jobs. They will rarely do them exactly the way we would. If this is a problem, try doing the jobs together.

FEELINGS

Now is the time to talk about ongoing problems or current issues. Remember to talk about *your* feelings and not to attack the other person. (Say, "When you leave your clothes on the floor, I feel like shoving them under the bed." *Not*: "You're such a slob, why can't you pick up your clothes?") Talk about one issue at a time. Work on compromises and make consensus decisions. Parents need to make some family decisions autocratically, but try to make most decisions democratically. After all, where and when are kids going to learn how democracy works if the family operates as a fascist dictatorship—in school?

VALUES

Consult the values list found on pages 227–228. Choose one value a week for discussion. One at a time, have each family member discuss this value. (If you don't have time during family meetings, you could do this at dinnertime or while driving in the car.) Let's say you choose the value of courage:

1. *Identification:* What does courage mean to you?
2. *Examples:* Give examples of how you know when you or someone else being courageous.
3. *Events:* Identify a courageous act, event, or person that you think of as being courageous.

GUIDANCE

The best guidance alternative to blowing up at people because they're not meeting your expectations is to:

1. **Describe** what you see. For example, if your child is creating artwork on the walls with crayons, you might say, *"I see marks on the wall."*
2. State your **feelings**. Don't attack the child. Instead, you might try, *"When I see drawing on the wall, I feel very upset."* Or, *"It's too cold. I don't want to get wet."* Not: *"You brat! You're a bad boy for drawing on the wall."* Or, *"Stop spraying me with water you idiot!"*

A man hath no better thing under the sun, than to eat, and to drink, and to be merry.

—Ecclesiastes 8:15

Simple. Difficult to remember, yet guaranteed to reduce stress and promote harmonious relationships. If the situation needs further clarification you may try this:

1. Guide them to desired behavior: give him some paper to draw on. Explain that people make pictures on paper, not (necessarily) on walls, or show her how to water the flower bed.
2. If the inappropriate behavior continues, remove your child from the situation. Do this without overreacting and with a gentle but firm manner. (Note: This is *not* isolation time for the child; the parent should go with the child.)
3. After your child has been removed from the situation and has calmed down, explain the situation to her in simple language. You might say instead, *"We only write on the walls to record our height."* Or, *"People don't like to get wet unless they're in their bathing suits or they're playing a game."*

For more details on this subject, read *How to Talk so Kids Will Listen & Listen so Kids Will Talk* by Adele Faber and Elaine Mazlish, Avon Books, New York, 1980.

HUMAN FAMILY GUIDELINES

- ✦ respect and sensitivity to others
- ✦ courtesy and good manners
- ✦ make and enjoy friendships
- ✦ empathy toward others
- ✦ good communication skills (listening and speaking)
- ✦ leadership qualities

✦ cooperation/compromise ability
✦ "go with the flow" attitude

THE SEVEN HEAVENLY VIRTUES

1. Peace	(opposite is)	Anger
2. Moderation		Gluttony
3. Service		Sloth
4. Generosity		Greed
5. Contentment		Envy
6. Love		Lechery
7. Modesty		Vanity

LEAD OR GOLD?

A person who is judged:	**can also be:**
learning disabled	learning different
hyperactive	a kinesthetic learner
dyslexic	a spatial learner
aggressive	assertive
plodding	thorough
lazy	relaxed
immature	late bloomer
phobic	cautious
scattered	divergent
daydreaming	imaginative
irritable	sensitive
perserverant	persistent

A professional is one who gives more than she gets.

—Anonymous

Local Homeschooling Perspective

We belong to a county-wide local homeschooling support group *(Sonoma County Homeschooler's Association)* that offers weekly park days. We can also get together for folk dances, gardening classes, craft workshops, camp-outs, holiday gatherings, field trips all over the area, support group meetings, and much more. Our biggest challenge in the group seems to be geography, since we live in a 120-or-so mile circle of each other. Thus, our perspective is one more of a network than a community, but we appreciate each other and now have over 130 families in our membership. Our biggest gathering at any one time may include 30 families.

Our local school's ISP (Independent Study Program), *Harmony Homeschooling*, offers activities three or four times a month. Over the years, we have offered chorus and music classes, dance classes, clay workshops, drama classes, science labs, story writing workshops, library programs, project sharing days, multicultural fairs, career workshops, mural painting, clay workshops, and many other events. We can also participate in public roller-skating sessions especially for homeschoolers (during school hours, of course!), ice skating lessons, and other kinds of "adventure" programs especially for homeschoolers. My children have also attended classes through after-school programs and the local YMCA.

Acculturation is learning to do gracefully that which you don't want to do.

—A.E. Godkin, 1895

Friendship Games

Questions

Ask your child the following questions. Older children may write their answers.

I am happiest when…

People think I am…

I think I am…

What I wish for the most is…

I get angry when…

I don't like it when people…

I am good at…

I'm getting better at…

When you're in a family, you help out, and that's just the way it is.

—Anna Kealoha

Name Bingo

This is a good game to play when a group first gets together. It works for groups that have from 9 to 40 members.

Each person writes his or her name on a **small piece of paper**. These are put into a **box**. Then, each person gets a regular-sized **paper** and folds it into 9, 16, or 25 squares, depending on the number of players. It is not necessary to have a square for each person. Then, each player gets the others to write their names in one of the squares. When all the squares are filled, the game begins. Using **beans, paper clips,** or **small pieces of construction paper**, the players cover up names on their boards as the leader picks names from the box and says them out loud. First person to complete a row horizontally, vertically, or diagonally is the winner, but you may play until everyone has his board covered.

❧ HUMAN HISTORY ☙

History Overview

> *Human history becomes more and more a race between education and catastrophe.*
>
> —*H.G. Wells*

The immense saga of humans on the earth is a fascinating study. Unfortunately most history textbooks are dull and dry. In addition, the focus of these texts is primarily on wars and governmental squabbles. The *real* progress of each era—its philosophers, inventors, artists, and scientists—is relegated to a small section of the total picture. Instead, dates of historical battles, birthdates of presidents, and other trivia are emphasized as necessary information for us to acquire in order to attain cultural literacy.

History should emphasize the study of great thinkers, major religions, and the philosophical tenets of each era instead of wars and catastrophic events. We also need to study history to gain an appreciation of our multicultural world.

Too often, historical accounts will be colored by the perceptions of the writer. We must examine documents for prejudice and bias. We must ask ourselves: "How do I know this is true?" This can be done through a search of the writer's background.

There is an ongoing debate about whether history makes people or people make history. Some believe that certain social and economic situations color human behavior, while others believe that history is a gradual unfolding of a divine plan. Both are probably true. It's also probably true that a few great people have changed the course of history.

For integrating music into history, check out the book *History of the U.S. in Song and Story* by John Anthony Armstrong, Carbondale Il, 1983.

Living History

Living history makes history come alive. Immerse yourself in history by visiting living history fairs and centers, and local historical spots that hold Living History days. For more information contact the *Society for Creative Anacronism*, P.O. Box 743, Milpitas, CA 95035.

I sold craft items at the local renaissance faire for many years. We loved the Faire because it gave us the sense of going back in time. Sometimes at night (after all the customers went home) you really felt as if you had stepped into a time warp. During the day, our children enjoyed Shakespearean plays and colorful parades. Indeed, my oldest daughter, at age eight, was quoting lines from Shakespeare and has developed a keen interest in this wonderful writer as a result of this experience.

Field Trip Ideas
(learn more than just history!)

- Natural Sites (ocean, mountains, estuaries, caves, etc.)
- Bird Watching
- Zoos
- Aquariums
- Farms
- Dairies

- ✦ Aviaries
- ✦ Historical Sites
- ✦ Museums
- ✦ Concerts
- ✦ Airports
- ✦ Construction sites
- ✦ Courthouses
- ✦ Hospitals
- ✦ County Fairs
- ✦ Prisons
- ✦ Offices
- ✦ Printing Presses
- ✦ Bakeries
- ✦ Artists' Studios
- ✦ TV or Radio Stations

Historical Films and Biographies

Emerson said that all of history may be resolved by the biographies of a few great men. Hollywood loves a juicy life-story and will often distort the facts to weave a more compelling tale. Like it or not, most of our kids love to watch TV and movies. Instead of a chicken in every pot, we now all have a VHS in every house. Use the medium well. The following partial list of biographical and historical films is taken (in part) from the *Living History Sourcebook* by Jay Anderson, 1985. (Although I personally don't care for the events based on wars.)Unfortunately, this book is out of print, but I was able to get a copy from the library. Mr. Anderson has listings for Living History museums, events, books, articles, magazines, organizations, suppliers, sketchbooks, films, and simulation games.

HISTORICAL FILMS

Gone with the Wind (Civil War)

Dr. Zhivago (Russia)

Lion in Winter (English history)

Last of the Mohicans (European colonization of America)

The Wobblies (Labor movement)

Time Bandits, 1981. (Comedy; time travel film covers Napoleon, Robin Hood, Agamemnon)

Time after Time, 1980. (Time travel film covers Windsor, 1893, San Francisco, 1979)

Westworld, 1973. (Time travel film covers Roman, medieval, and Western world)

Quest for Fire, 1981. (Stone age)

The War Lord, 1965. (Pre-1066 Norman)

The Seventh Seal, 1975. (14th-century Sweden, the crusades)

Kagemusha, 1980. (16th-century Japan, feudal times)

The Seventh Samurai, 1954. (16th-century Japan)

The Three Musketeers, 1975. (1620's France)

The Silent Enemy, 1930. (Objibwa Native Americans, a silent film)

Tom Jones, 1963. (1740's England)

The Devil's Discipline, 1959. (1777 England)

The Duellists, 1977. (Napoleonic period, based on Joseph Conrad's short story "The Duel")

Jeremiah Johnson, 1972. (American buckskinners)

Man of Aran, 1934. (Folklife of the Aran Islands in Ireland)

The Emigrants, 1970 and *The New Land,* 1972. (19th-century Swedish life in America)

The Red Badge of Courage, 1951. (Civil War)

Stagecoach, 1939. (Arizona, 1885)

Cheyenne Autumn, 1964. (1878, Cheyenne sent to reservations)

Buffalo Bill and the Indians, 1976. (1885 American West)

Hester Street, 1974. (1896 New York City Jewish Russian immigrants)

Zulu, 1964. (Battle of Rorke's Drift between the Zulus and the British, 1879)

Breaker Morant, 1980. (Boer War, Australia, 1901)

McCabe and Mrs. Miller, 1971. (1902 American northwest)

Heartland, 1979. (1910 Wyoming pioneer life)

Days of Heaven, 1978. (Texas, 1916)

Potemkin, 1925. (Silent film, Russia, 1905, Russo-Japan War)

All Quiet on the Western Front, 1930. (World War I)

La Grande Illusion, 1937. (French POW's, World War I)

Zelig, 1983. (1920-1930 America, not particularly historical, but the setting is very authentic. A Woody Allen film.)

The Grapes of Wrath, 1940. (Ozarks, Dust Bowl, 1930's)

Das Boot, 1981. (German U-boat, World War I)

Twelve O'clock High, 1949. (World War II, England)

A Walk in the Sun, 1946. (World War II, Italy)

Battleground, 1949. (Battle of the Bulge, 1944)

BIOGRAPHICAL FILMS

Amadeus (Mozart)

Reds (John Reed)

Gandhi (India's independence from England)

Cleopatra (Egypt)

Becket, 1964. (King Henry II & Thomas Becket, England)

Henry V, 1944. (1415 invasion of France)

Barry Lyndon, 1975. (Irish knave during the Seven Years War, 1756-1763)

HISTORICAL NOVELS AND PICTURE BOOKS

One of the best and most absorbing ways to study history is to read historical novels and picture books; the next best thing to living history. Watching a movie and then reading the book involves higher thinking skills of comparison and evaluation. It is usually better to read the book first, because we create our own pictures when we read, and viewing a film first will cloud our mind's eye with the film's images. The following is a partial list of historical fiction books.

Those who give up essential freedoms for temporary safety deserve neither liberty nor safety.

—Benjamin Franklin

Advice to Persons About to Write History— Don't.

—Lord Acton

NATIVE AMERICAN

The Ceremony of Innocence by Jamake Highwater, 1985.

Education of Little Tree by Forrest Carter, 1976. (Based on life of author as a Cherokee boy in the 1930's.)

The Sign of the Beaver by Elizabeth Speare, 1983. (A young white boy living alone is helped by an Indian boy, 8 & up.)

Where the Buffaloes Begin by Stephen Gammell, 1981.

Wait for Me, Watch for Me, Eula Bee by Patricia Beatty, 1978. (Texas, 1860, 10 & up.)

Only Earth and Sky Last Forever by Nathaniel Benchley, 1972. (Based on true account of Crazy Horse, 10 & up.)

Pocahontas and the Strangers by Clyde Bulla, 1971. (8 & up.)

Bread-and-Butter Indian by Anne Colver, 1964. (A young girl is captured by Indians & her Indian friend helps her escape, 6 & up.)

The Legend of Bluebonnet: An Old Tale of Texas by Tomie DePaola, 1983. (All ages.)

The Star Maiden: An Ojibway Tale by Barbara Esbenson, 1988. (6 & up.)

The Girl Who Loved Wild Horses by Paul Goble, 1978. (All ages.)

Her Seven Brothers by Paul Goble, 1988. (Legend of the Big Dipper, 8 & up.)

Bright Fawn and Me by Hay Leech, 1979. (Cheyenne family at an intertribal fair, late 1800's, 6 & up.)

Little Wolf by Nola Lagner, 1965. (Little Wolf becomes a healer because he does not want to hurt animals, 6 & up.)

Tomahawks and Trombones by Barbara Mitchell, 1982. (True account of the Delawares, who were frightened by trombones, 6 & up.)

Sing Down the Moon by Scott O'Dell, 1970. (Injustices of the uprooted Navajos, 8 & up.)

Island of the Blue Dolphin by Scott O'Dell, 1960. (True story of the last woman left on an island near Santa Barbara, 7 & up. Newberry medal winner.)

Streams to the River, River to the Sea: A Novel of Sacagawea by Scott O'Dell, 1986. (10 & up.)

Groundhog's Horse by Joyce Rockwood, 1978. (The rescue of a stolen horse, 9 & up.)

To Spoil the Sun by Joyce Rockwood, 1976. (Problems brought upon Indians by whites, 10 & up.)

The Eye in the Forest by Mary Steele, 1975. (One Native American captured by another tribe, pre-white invasion, 9 & up.)

The Sunflower Garden by Janice Udry, 1969. (Girl saves her brother from a snakebite, 7 & up.)

In the Shadow of the Wind by Luke Wallin, 1969. (Young Indian girl and white man reconcile their affections, 10 & up.)

Waterless Mountain by Laura Armer, 1931. (Navajo boy's training in the ancient religion of his tribe, 8 & up.)

...And Now Miguel by Jean Charlot, 1953. (True story of a young sheepherder in Taos, New Mexico who wants to join the men, 10 & up.)

14TH CENTURY EUROPE

Captives of Time by Malcolm Bosse, 1987.

VICTORIAN ENGLAND

The Empty Sleeve by Leon Garfield, 1988.
The Ruby in the Smoke by Philip Pullman, 1987.
Shadow in the North by Philip Pullman, (sequel).
Great Expectations, David Copperfield, Tale of Two Cities by
Charles Dickens.

U.S. 1600's

The Serpent Never Sleeps by Scott O'Dell, (Jamestown, 1609.)
John Billington, Friend of Squanto by Clyde Bulla, 1956. (Journey
on the Mayflower, 7 & up.)
A Lion to Guard Us by Michele Chessare, 1981. (Journey of three
English children to America, 8 & up.)
A Story of Early Plymouth by Patricia Clapp, 1968. (Young
colonist's diary, 10 & up.)
This Dear-Bought Land by Jean Latham 1957. (Settlement of
Jamestown, 10 & up.)
The Witch of Blackbird Pond by Elizabeth Speare, 1972. (New
England, 10 & up.)
The Legend of New Amsterdam by Peter Spier, 1979. (5 & up.)

U.S. 1700's

Another Shore by Nancy Bond, 1988. (French settlement—Nova Scotia, 1744.)
When Daylight Comes by Ellen Howard, 1985. (U.S. Virgin Islands, 1733.)
1787 by Joan Anderson, 1988. (Constitutional Convention.)
The Fighting Ground by Avi, 1984. (Revolutionary War, 10 & up.)
Captain Grey by Avi, 1982. (Revolutionary War, 9 & up.)
Jade, by Sally Watson, 1969. (Jade is caught trying to free a shipload of slaves and is
saved by a pirate, 9 & up.)
Jump Ship to Freedom by James Collier, 1981. (Post-Revolutionary War, slavery and
freedom, 9 & up.)
Who is Carrie? by James Collier, 1984. (Post-Revolutionary War, sequel to *Jump
Ship to Freedom,* 9 & up.)
My Brother Sam is Dead by James Collier, 1974. (Revolutionary War, futility of war,
1974.)
War Comes to Willy Freeman by James Collier, 1983. (Revolutionary War- girl's
search for her mother, who is a prisoner of the Redcoats, 9 & up.)
The Winter Hero by James Collier, 1978. (Post-Revolutionary War farmer's revolt, 9
& up.)
Early Thunder by Jean Fritz, 1967. (Based on true story of confrontation between
British troops and townspeople of Salem, 9 & up.)

Johnny Tremain by Ester Forbes (A young man's Revolutionary War experiences, Newberry winner, 10 & up.)

Six Silver Spoons by Janette Lowry, 1971. (Two children carrying silver spoons made by Paul Revere are helped by a British soldier, 6 & up.)

Sarah Bishop by Scott O'Dell, 1980. (A young girl escapes from the British, 10 & up.)

The Boston Coffee Party by Doreen Rappaport. (Boston women's revolt, 6 & up, beginning readers)

Winter Patriot by Benjamin Schneider, 1967. (Revolutionary War, 10 & up.)

U.S. 1800's

The Man Who Was Poe by Avi, 1989. (Life of Edgar Allan Poe.)

Carlotta by Scott O'Dell, 1977. (Young girl in battle in the 1840's, 9 & up.)

A Family Apart by Joan L. Nixon, 1987. (1850's.)

The Bone Wars by Kathryn Lasky, 1988. (Montana, 1874-1878.)

The Long Way Westward by Joan Sandin, 1981. (Swedish immigrants, 1868, 6 & up.)

Voices After Midnight by Richard Peck, 1989. (1888, New York City.)

Chang's Paper Pony by Eleanor Coerr, 1988. (Gold Rush.)

FRONTIER LIFE

Joshua's Westward Journal by Joan Anderson, 1987. (A family moves west, photographed at the Living History Farm in Iowa, 6 & up.)

Brothers of the Heart by Joan W. Blos, 1985. (Frontier life.)

West Against the Wind by Liza K. Murrow, 1987. (Frontier life.)

Sarah, Plain and Tall Patricia MacLachlan, 1985. (Frontier life, 7 & up.)

The Josephina Quilt Story by Eleanor Coerr. (A girl saves her family from robbers on a journey out west, all ages.)

Bread-and-Butter Journey by Anne Colver. (Based on the history of the author's family journey to western Pennsylvania, 8 & up.)

The Golden Venture by Jane Flory, 1967. (Gold Rush, 9 & up.)

Stout-Hearted Seven by Neta Frazier, 1973. (Based on a true story of seven adopted children whose family is attacked by some Indians, 10 & up.)

The Cabin Faced West by Jean Fritz. (Cabin life in Pennsylvania, based on the life of the author's great-grandmother, 8 & up.)

Log Cabin in the Woods by Joanne Henry. (A true story of a 12-year-old growing up in Indiana, all ages.)

Trail of the Apple Blossoms by Irene Hunt, 1968. (A family meets Johnny Appleseed, 8 & up.)

Jim Bridger: The Story of a Mountain Man by David Kherdian. (An explorer falls in love with an Indian girl and discovers the Great Salt Lake, 9 & up.)

What experience and history teach is this—that people and governments never have learned anything from history, or acted on principles deduced from it.

—Georg Hegel

Wheels West by Evelyn Sible, 1969. (Based on the life of Tabitha Brown, a pioneer girl who travels to Oregon, 10 & up.)

The White Stallion by Elizabeth Shub, 1982. (Based on a true account of a young girl who is carried away by an old mare from a wagon train. The mare tried to join a herd of wild horses, 6 & up.)

Carolina's Courage by Elizabeth Yates, 1964. (Journey of a little girl from New Hampshire to the West, 8 & up.)

Riding the Pony Express by Clyde Bull, 1948. (7 & up.)

The Snowbird by Patricia Calver, 1980. (Life with a horse in the Dakota Territory, 10 & up.)

Caddie Woodlawn by Carol Brink, 1935. (Wisconsin frontier through the eyes of an 11-year-old girl, 9 & up.)

A Prairie Boy's Summer by William Kurelek, 1975. (A prairie boy's summer chores, 7 & up.)

Little House in the Big Woods by Laura Ingalls Wilder, 1953. (Beginning of a series of eight books based on life of a pioneer girl. Classic series, loved by many, all ages.)

CIVIL WAR

The Last Silk Dress by Ann Rinaldi, 1988. (Civil War.)

The Deserter: A Spy Story of the Civil War by Peter Burchard. (English—part factual story of Levi Blair, 8 & up.)

The Tamarack Tree by Patricia Clapp (13-year-old British orphan's viewpoint on the siege of Vicksburg, 10 & up.)

Red Badge of Courage by Stephen Crane. (The horror of war as seen through the eyes of a young farm boy who enlists in the army, 10 & up.)

Anthony Burns: The Defeat and Triumph of a Fugitive Slave by Virginia Hamilton. (Anthony escapes, is captured, tried and returned to slavery, 11 & up.)

The Adventure of Charlie and His Wheat-Straw Hat: A Memorat by Bernice Hiser, 1989. (Based on a true incident of a young boy defending his home while his father is in the army, all ages.)

Across Five Aprils by Irene Hunt. (Young boy takes over farm work while men fight the war. Historical details make it a good study of the Civil War, 10 & up.)

Rifles for Watie by Harold Keith. (Cherokee Watie gets Confederate rifles, and another soldier must spy on the Rebels, 10 & up.)

Tad Lincoln's Story by F. N. Monjo. (Fictionalized account of the Battle of Gettysburg through young Lincoln's eyes, 8 & up.)

The Vicksburg Veteran by F.N. Monjo. (View of Gettysburg through son of U.S. Grant, 6 & up.)

> *Real solemn history, I cannot be interested in. The quarrels of popes and kings, with wars and pestilences in every page; the men so good for nothing, and hardly any women at all.*
>
> *—Jane Austen*

POST-CIVIL WAR

Beloved by Toni Morrison, 1987. (Post-Civil War.)

Trouble at the Mines by Doreen Tappaport. (Based on the true story of the 1898 miners' strike in Pennsylvania, 7 & up.)

Anna, Grandpa, and the Big Storm by Carla Stevens. (The New York City blizzard of 1888, 7 & up.)

U.S. 1900's

Rachel and Obadiah by Brinton Turkle. (Life on Nantucket Island, all ages.)

Queenie Peavy by Robert Burch, 1966. (A 13-year-old in the 1930's, 9 & up.)

Stories from the Blue Road by Emily Crofford, 1982. (Arkansas family during the Depression, 8 & up.)

Where the Red Ferns Grow by Wilson Rawls, 1961. (An Ozark boy earns money to buy coon dogs; a touching story, 10 & up.)

Roll of Thunder, Hear My Cry by Mildred Taylor, 1976. (A 9-year-old black girl in the Great Depression, a powerful book, 10 & up.)

A Boy and a Pig, but Mostly Horses by Sherman Kent, 1974. (Three boys on a Nevada ranch in the 1920's, 9 & up.)

Dragonwings by Laurence Yep, 1964. (Life of a Chinese community in San Francisco, early 1900's, 10 & up.)

Geography Games

GEOGRAPHY TREASURE HUNT

Spread out a map on the floor. Announce the name of a place you have found on the map. Everyone else tries to find it. You may wish to give hints by using the coordinates.

WORLD CITIES

Divide into two teams, leaving one person as referee. The referee chooses a major city then specifies a direction, such as: *"Cities East of London."* The first player on each team writes down a town or city east of London, such as *Vienna*, and the next player writes down one east of Vienna, such as *Budapest*. First team done scores ten points, then each team scores one point for a correct answer and loses one point for an incorrect one.

History Resource Guide

A great resource for a framework in history can be found through the California State Department of Education (PO Box 271, Sacramento, CA 95802-0271). Request the *History-Social Science Framework for California Public Schools* for $7.75.

It can be adapted for use in any state, (especially if your children are interested in California history), but I'm sure that most other states have similar guidelines. Write to your State Department of Education.

If...history...teaches us anything, it is that Man, in his quest for knowledge and progress, is determined and cannot be deterred.

—John F. Kennedy

Although you might wish to follow your own timetable in history, I find the state guides useful as a framework. When I wrote them for permission to use their material, they were very helpful, albeit slow, in sending me information. They sent a 128-page book titled *Literature for History-Social Science* (K-8), with a myriad of book selections at each grade level. For example, the kindergarten literature list contains about seventy-five titles of books listed under the following categories: Learning to Work Together; Working Together; Exploring; Creating; Communicating; and Reaching Out to Times Past. They also sent me *The Changing History-Social Science Curriculum—A Booklet for Parents*. The booklet includes a nice Literature List for Parents and Children (K-12), which contains an abbreviated list of the books from the *Literature for History-Social Science* book.

The history of the world is but the biography of great men.

—Thomas Carlyle

Children's concept of space, time and place is still rather vague, and history is divided into units for the sake of educators, not necessarily for the sake of the learners. Don't be afraid to talk about China or the Aztecs with kids just because it isn't part of that year's curriculum. I personally use an eclectic approach to history and like to introduce children to the global community at early ages.

It's interesting that the study of history and acquiring social skills are so intertwined. We learn from the past, yet we most of all learn to relate with others through our families, and it is our family heritage (and our environment) from which we hopefully learn how to be decent human beings.

I shall quote the introduction from the introductory pamphlet to the History-Social Science Framework for California Public Schools:

The children of California will spend their adult lives in the twenty-first century. As educators we have the responsibility of preparing these children for the challenges of living in a fast-changing society. Their lives, like ours, will be affected by domestic and international politics, economic flux, technological developments, demographic shifts, and the stress of social change...

As educators in the field of history-social science,

We want our students to perceive the complexity of social, economic, and political problems.

We want them to know their rights and responsibilities as American citizens.

We want them to understand the meaning of the Constitution as a social contract that defines our democratic government and guarantees our individual rights...

We want them to take an active role as citizens and to know how to work for change in a democratic society...

We want them to develop a keen sense of ethics and citizenship. And...

We want them to care deeply about the quality of life in their community, their nation, and their world.

The California framework, adopted in 1987, presents "a history-based curriculum that integrates geography, the humanities, and other social sciences at every level of instruction. The goals of this framework fall into three broad categories:

✦ **Knowledge and Cultural Understanding**
incorporating learnings from history, ethics, culture, economics, geography, and sociopolitical areas.

✦ **Democratic Understanding and Civic Values**
incorporating an understanding of our national identity, constitutional heritage, civic values, rights and responsibilities.

+ **Skills Attainment and Social Participation**
  including basic study, critical thinking, and participation skills that are essential for effective citizenship.

The following pages present an overview of how California educators approach the study of history at each grade level. For a more detailed account of what to study, write to your State Department of Education and ask to purchase a copy of your state's History-Social Science Framework and Literature for History-Social Science book. In California, you can even purchase a teacher's guide for each grade level. I had originally intended to print suggested readings, but it's hard to condense the 128-page literature book guide into three pages. However, I have listed a few teaching suggestions here and there which may interest you.

KINDERGARTEN (AGES 4-6)

Learning and Working, Now and Long Ago

+ Learning to Work Together (sharing, acquiring values of deliberation and individual responsibility) Teaching Suggestions: Children playing together—store, blocks, dress-up, mini cars...
+ Working Together: Exploring, Creating, and Communicating (learning self-worth)
+ Reaching Out to Times Past (beginning to learn about the past)

GRADE ONE (AGES 5-7)

A Child's Place in Space and Time (Family, Neighborhood)

+ Developing Social Skills and Responsibilities
+ Expanding Children's Geographic and Economic Worlds (neighborhood, town)
  Teaching Suggestions: Build a diorama (3-D map) of the child's immediate geographic region. This teaches development of observational skills, concepts of geographic scale, distance, and relative location. Suggested materials: small building blocks or milk cartons. Photos of buildings may be taped to the front of the models. Model vehicles may be added as well as stop signs, cross walks, mailboxes, signals, and street signs.
+ Developing Awareness of **Cultural Diversity, Now and Long Ago**

Human history is in essence a history of ideas.

—H.G. Wells

GRADE TWO (AGES 6-8)

Groups: Workers, Ancestors, and Other Cultures

+ People Who Supply Our Needs (basic economic understanding of farmers, farm workers, processors and distributors, consumers and producers, and their interdependence)
  Teaching Suggestions: Visit a regional central market, make more community dioramas, do comparative studies of history: how people of the past ground grains and baked bread, cook and bake ethnic foods.

✦ Our Parents, Grandparents, and Ancestors from Long Ago
Teaching Suggestions: Construct a family history (use a tape recorder, then transcribe the tapes). Children can ask grandparents or parents questions like: Where did the family come from? Do photos or letters from that time still exist? Who was in the family then? When did the family come here? How long did the trip take? Were there any adventures? You may also ask questions about religious practices, stories, games, festivals, childhood jobs, dress, manners, and morals.

✦ People From Many Cultures, Now and Long Ago: Native Americans

✦ Non-Native Americans
Teaching Suggestions: Read beginning biographies on the lives of famous scientists and inventors such as George Washington Carver, Marie Curie, Louis Pasteur, Thomas Edison, and other artists, authors, musicians, and athletes from the past.

GRADE THREE (AGES 7-9)

Members of the Community, Cities, Pioneers

✦ Our Local History: Discovering Our Past and Our Traditions
Teaching Suggestions: Take field trips to places of historical or cultural significance. Augment with videotapes, slides, and photographs of the local area. Use geographical terminology such as mountains, valleys, hills, coastal areas, oceans, lakes, and deserts. Study local indigenous peoples: tribal identity, social organization and customs, location of villages, methods used to get food, clothing, tools, utensils, art, and folklore. Visit museums that specialize in Native American artifacts. Do role plays of immigrants today and long ago, study historical pictures from local newspapers or historical societies.

✦ Our Nation's History: Meeting People, Ordinary and Extraordinary, through Biography, Story, Folktale, and Legend.

GRADE FOUR (AGES 8-10)

Regions: Local State History and Government

✦ The Physical Setting
Teaching Suggestions: Locate your state on the map, study it in relationship to the surrounding area. (Note: The rest of the points deal directly with California history. If you live in another state, you will need to find other sources to learn about your local history.)

✦ Pre-Colombian Settlements and People

✦ Exploration and Colonial History

✦ Missions, Ranchos, and the Mexican War for Independence
Teaching Suggestions: Sing songs of the era, take field trips to missions or Early California homes, dramatize a rodeo or fiesta.

✦ Gold Rush, Statehood, and the Westward Movement

✦ The Period of Rapid Population Growth, Large-Scale Agriculture, and Linkage to the Rest of the United States

✦ Modern California: Immigration, Technology, and Cities

GRADE FIVE (AGES 9-11)

Nation: United States History and Geography

- ✦ The Land and People Before Columbus
- ✦ Age of Exploration
- ✦ Settling the Colonies
- ✦ Settling the Trans-Appalachian West
- ✦ The War for Independence
- ✦ Life in the Young Republic
- ✦ The New Nation's Westward Movement
- ✦ Linking Past to Present: The American People, Then and Now

GRADE SIX (AGE 10-12)

World History and Geography/Ancient Civilizations (Ancient World to 500 AD)

- ✦ Early Humankind and the Development of Human Societies
- ✦ The Beginnings of Civilization in the Near East and Africa: Mesopotamia, Egypt, and Cush
- ✦ The Foundation of Western Ideas: The Ancient Hebrews and Greeks
- ✦ West Meets East: The Early Civilizations of India and China
- ✦ East Meets West: Rome

GRADE SEVEN (AGE 11-13)

World History and Geography/ Medieval and Early Modern Times (500-1789 AD)

- ✦ Connecting with Past Learnings: Uncovering the Remote Past
- ✦ Connecting with Past Learnings: The Fall of Rome
- ✦ Growth of Islam
- ✦ African States in the Middle Ages and Early Modern Times
- ✦ Civilizations of the Americas
- ✦ China
- ✦ Japan
- ✦ Medieval Societies: Europe and Japan
- ✦ Europe During the Renaissance, the Reformation, and the Scientific Revolution
- ✦ Early Modern Europe: The Age of Exploration to the Enlightenment

Man's history is waiting in patience for the triumph of the insulted man.

—Rabindranath Tagore

GRADE EIGHT (AGE 12-14)

United States History and Geography

- ✦ Connecting with Past Learnings: Our Colonial Heritage
- ✦ Connecting with Past Learnings: A New Nation
- ✦ The Constitution of the United States
- ✦ Launching the Ship of State

+ The Divergent Paths of the American People 1800-1850:
  The West
  The Northeast
  The South
+ Toward a More Perfect Union: 1850-1879
+ The Rise of Industrial America: 1877-1914

GRADE NINE (AGE 13-15)

Elective Courses in History

+ Our State in the Twentieth Century
+ Physical Geography
+ World Regional Geography
+ The Humanities
+ Comparative World Religions
+ Area Studies: Cultures
+ Anthropology
+ Psychology
+ Sociology
+ Women in Our History
+ Ethnic Studies
+ Law-Related Education

GRADE TEN (AGE 14-16)

World History, Culture, and Geography/The Modern World (1789-Present)

+ Unresolved Problems of the Modern World
+ The Rise of Democratic Ideas
+ The Industrial Revolution
+ The Rise of Imperialism and Colonialism: A Case Study of India
+ World War I and Its Consequences
+ Totalitarianism in the Modern World: Nazi Germany and Stalinist Russia
+ World War II: Its Causes and Consequences
+ Nationalism in the Contemporary World: The Soviet Union and China
+ The Middle East: Israel and Syria
+ Sub-Saharan Africa: Ghana and South Africa
+ Latin America: Mexico and Brazil

GRADE ELEVEN (AGE 15-17)

United States History, Culture, and Geography/
Continuity and Change in the 20th Century

+ Connecting with Past Learnings: The Nation's Beginnings
+ Connecting with Past Learnings: The United States to 1900
+ The Progressive Era

- ✦ The Jazz Age
- ✦ The Great Depression
- ✦ World War II
- ✦ The Cold War
- ✦ Hemispheric Relationships in the Postwar Era
- ✦ The Civil Rights Movement in the Postwar Era
- ✦ American Society in the Postwar Era
- ✦ The United States in Recent Times

GRADE TWELVE (AGE 16-18)

Government and Economics

Principles of American Democracy:
- ✦ The Constitution and the Bill of Rights
- ✦ The Courts and the Governmental Process
- ✦ Our Government Today: The Legislative and Executive Branches
- ✦ Federalism: State and Local Government
- ✦ Comparative Governments, with Emphasis on Communism in the World
- ✦ Contemporary Issues in the World Today

Economics:
- ✦ Fundamental Economic Concepts
- ✦ Comparative Economic Systems
- ✦ Microeconomics
- ✦ Macroeconomics
- ✦ International Economic Concepts

Let us...cherish, therefore, the means of knowledge. Let us dare to read, think, speak, and write... Let every sluice of knowledge be opened and set a-flowing.

—John Adams

Inner World

SPIRIT

Our friend Rick teaches classes on Judaism. Besides teaching the kids about the history and culture of the Jewish people, what his class is really about is values and morals that are found in all major religions. Kids love Rick because he knows how to talk about "heavy" things without boring them and spices up his classes with music, fun, and games.

Once, he had a graduation ceremony for our kids at the beach. As we sat in a circle around a fire, he told us the following story: When his step-son Jacob was two years old, they went into a toy store together. Like a normal two-year-old, Jacob was being a brat and making a fuss, begging his Daddy for "stuff." When Rick took his young son outside to remind him he can't have everything he wants, an old man, who had been watching the commotion, offered these wise words: *"Son, when you are my age you'll be willing to pay any amount of money to return to this moment."*

Just one astute opinion by an elder, yet this nameless, faceless, elderly gentleman has no idea that his simple observation has created such a ripple. Not only did Rick remember his words, but his wife, students, and their parents that night on the beach were also reminded of what a precious gift our children bring to us each moment.

Now, if you readers are moved to share this story with friends, you will be passing the story on as fourth-hand information! The ripple becomes a wave.

Besides being a good maxim for all parents to remember, it also serves to remind us that whatever we say and do is always important. We have *no idea* where our influence, good *and* bad will stop.... So be Good, for Goodness Sake. Jacob is now seventeen and Rick already knows the man is right: babies *are* special creatures. One's and two's *are* the most challenging, time-consuming ages, yet toddlers have a delightful unique angel-like essence. Tuning into a child's essence can bring you closer to the Great Mystery.

Some call knowledge of the spirit the sixth sense. We can't taste, touch, hear, or feel it, but almost everyone agrees it is there, except the public schools. The separation of the spirit from education is like trying to separate the river from the ocean. A child educated without spiritual and moral training will not be much of an asset to society.

No matter what spiritual methodology you choose to follow, it is beneficial only if it helps you become a better person. Study each religion for its moral and ethical teachings; how we can live in a righteous manner for the good of all humanity. The study of each religion's position on creation and the afterlife is awesome and fascinating, but in truth, the most important aspect of religion is the teaching of values.

Find a sense of awe and wonder in the arms of Mother Nature. Spend as much time as possible outside in natural settings. A sense of simplicity, humbleness, surrender, and gratitude are values that communion with nature will instill in us.

Spiritual awakening can take many forms, come at any time, and to any person. Sometimes it happens to people and they don't even know it. Almost anything we do with intensity and pure motives can help us "wake up" from mundane physical reality. My personal favorites for awakening the inner spirit include playing with kids, playing and listening to music, immersion in nature (especially the ocean), yoga, meditating, loving, and being loved.

Babies as Teachers: Mystical Parenting

To become immortal have a child, plant a tree, write a book.

—Proverb

It is interesting that most spiritual teachers were childless or, like the Buddha, abandoned their own families to become enlightened! Householders, it is taught, are supposed to wait and study spiritual matters after their children are grown and gone.

In most religions, the path to enlightenment or heaven requires service and surrender. We struggle to surrender ourselves, even if metaphorically, in devotion to our chosen God. We serve others in the name of our deity. Through this love and devotion, a curious thing happens: we discover great peace of mind and serene satisfaction.

Babies and children also need this kind of total devotion and surrender. They will literally wither and die without it. When we truly surrender to children's needs and free ourselves from impatience, the experience can be just as enlightening as any religious experience. These moments are windows into the spontaneous, creative realm of unconditional love. Jesus isolated himself in the desert for forty days, and Buddha sat beneath the Bodhi tree: *they* didn't change diapers or rock babies to sleep. Compared to parents, their path to enlightenment was easy. Forty days of surrender? How about ten or twenty *years*?

However, as all parents know there are times, usually daily, when we feel resentful of our babies and children's constant needs. We feel depleted and empty, unable to give any more. Yet we will be asked repeatedly to surrender to the needs of our children before we take time to meet our own needs. Thus, if we remember that surrendering to our children is symbolic of surrendering to our chosen god-head, our children become our greatest teachers. *It is essential to cherish children.*

When we pass on, we will have to ask ourselves one and only one important question: "How well did we serve the children?" And now, *I* must go to my young son who asks, "Mommy, are you done with your work now? Will you give me some attention?"

"To raise an infant, to look after it, to educate it, and to give oneself to its service is as much and as good as the work of an adept, because an adept forgets himself in meditation, and a mother forgets herself by giving her life to the child."

—Sufi Hazrat Inayat Khan

Home As Temple

Make your home a place of worship. Let the children know that devotion is not just something to practice in a special place like temple or church. Set aside a special corner for meditation or prayer. A small table can hold devotional objects. Remember to have something to please all the senses: candles, pictures, figurines, rocks, shells, and flowers to please the eyes, incense and flowers for the nose, songs, chants, bells, and drums to please the ears, and food and drink for taste.

Try to spend a few minutes here on a daily basis. Do it if it pleases you, not as a chore. You may wish to meditate, chant, sing, or pray. When my oldest daughter was small, she and I would do yoga together. Then, after we had stretched our bodies, I would sit cross-legged, and she would sit in my lap. Our house was small, so we had no altar to sit in front of. Instead, we looked out a large window into our yard that was filled with beautiful plants and trees. We'd close our eyes and give thanks for our abundance: family and friends, a beautiful place to live, or a special event in our lives.

❦ MEDITATION ❦

Perhaps meditation evolved when the ancients gazed at clouds or stared into a fire or candle flame. Even today, doing this gives us the feeling of being peaceful and relaxed. Meditation is a form of prayer. The goal in meditation and prayer is to get to the place where you are doing it all the time, not just ten minutes a day or just at church or temple. Meditation can give you extra energy and better powers of concentration, thus it can help you become a better learner. It can help you sleep longer and more deeply. Your awareness of yourself and your environment may increase. Meditation can also improve confidence and self-esteem.

Physiological changes of meditation include: a drop in heart rate, breathing rate, and blood pressure, your body uses less oxygen, and your brain makes more *alpha* waves, which is a sign of deep relaxation, (the opposite of the fight-or-flight response).

There are as many ways to meditate as there are people. Some people like to find a quiet place with no distraction, others meditate in their cars, or among a crowd.

TIPS FOR MEDITATION

(Thanks to my yoga teacher Al Graham for this format.❤)

> **Basic Instructions**: To begin, start by wiggling into a comfortable position (either laying down or sitting in a chair or on the floor). Whatever position you assume, be sure to keep your spine as straight as possible: tuck your tummy in and tighten your muscles in your bottom. Then slowly, beginning at your toes, tighten the muscles gradually coming up the body, to the calves, the buttocks, the back, the shoulders, arms, and head. Gradually begin to relax everything, everywhere. As you relax your body, become aware of your breathing. Breathe in slowly, inhaling love, peace, and relaxation. Breathe out frustration, unhappiness, and tension. Continue this slow, deep breathing for at least twelve breaths. Try to be aware of every sound and sensation around you such as: cars, human voices, the wind, the weight of your clothing on your skin, and the air around you.
>
> The key to meditation is to become so aware that your awareness encompasses every sound, smell, and feeling within you and around you, that you rise above your normal consciousness, what Al calls *Conscious Wholeself Awareness*.

For the Very Young: (Time: 45-60 seconds) First, have kids close their eyes and pretend they are in dream time. Then "go within," make a picture (visualize) a loved one, and send that person love and light.

For Older Kids: (Begin each meditation with the general rules found on the previous page.) Suggest special affirmations to repeat. ("Every day in every way, I am getting better and better.") Children might also like to visualize a light in the middle of their foreheads, and send out "positive vibrations" for world peace.

Air Meditation: (Associations: the East, birth, beginnings, spring, the eagle.) Close your eyes and feel the air all around you. Feel it on your face, your arms, and everywhere. Feel it come into your body through your nose and go deep into your lungs. Sense that the air is breathing *you* in and out. Listen to the sounds that travel through the air. Pretend you can fly, and go anywhere you want: to the mountains, the oceans, to the sun and the stars. Pretend you are a cloud floating gently in the sky. Go fly a kite.

Fire Meditation: (Associations: the South, youth, sun, light, summer, the lion.) Light a candle or sit in front of a fire and concentrate on the flame(s). Next, close your eyes and find the reflection of the candle or fire inside yourself: see the yellow outer flame, the blue inner flame, and finally the white inside the blue. Feel the warmth of this fire spreading through your body. Think of *yellow* as the part of the flame that burns away your desires, the *blue* as peace and love, and finally the *white* as the Spirit all around us.

Water Meditation: (Associations: the West, adulthood, ocean, fall, the bear.) Imagine you are a wave in a sparkling blue ocean. Now, feel yourself merge with the ocean, just as the wave merges. Feel the power of the wave as it lifts itself up and crashes on the shore, only to merge again into the great ocean. Hear the sound of the ocean inside your head. Let the peaceful waves rock you.

Earth Meditation: (Associations: the North, elders, wisdom, winter, the buffalo.) Imagine you are the earth. Your body is the rivers, oceans, and mountains as well as the rocks, animals, and people. Feel your roots that go deep into the earth. Climb the highest mountain and feel how close you are to the heavens. Think of the earth as a great school for all the beings to learn about the Great Spirit.

Forest Guided Visualization: Close your eyes and imagine the following scene: You and your loved ones are walking through a forest. There is a small brook next to the trail. It's a warm, sunny day, and you feel the comfortable warmth of the sun on your skin. The woods are very peaceful and the sun sparkles on the leaves and on the water in the brook. You feel a fresh gentle breeze blowing on your skin, and the air is filled with the rich earthy scent of the dirt, trees, plants, and flowers.

> *It is not easy to find happiness in ourselves, and it is not possible to find it elsewhere.*
>
> —*Agnes Repplier*

> *What if we picked the wrong religion? Every week we're just making God madder and madder.*
>
> —*Homer Simpson*

You come to a warm hot springs and you decide to get in. As you relax, the brook is singing to you as it bounces and sparkles over the gem-like rocks. The birds are singing a joyful chorus all around you. You float on your back in the warm water and look at the cobalt blue sky above you. A fluffy cloud amuses you by making magical shapes in the sky. You feel very, very peaceful and relaxed. There is no place to go, nothing to do, but to sit and enjoy yourself. You can stay as long as you like, and when you are ready to come back, you quietly return on the same path you came on.

Healing Meditation: Imagine a powerful crystal blue star high above your head. As you watch, the star bursts and thousands of tiny twinkling stars rain down around you. Each of these stars contains powerful healing energy. When you breathe, you breathe these stars into your body, and as you breathe out, the tiny stars circulate all through your body, just like your blood. As they move through your body, you feel all warm and tingly, the way you do when someone rubs your back. The stars move all over: from your lungs, into your heart, from your heart to stomach, shoulders, arms, and hands. They flow into your legs and down to the tip of your toes.

Spiritual Teachers

In my mind, each of the great spiritual teachers has something of value to teach us. I present the information below as *my* interpretation of what the masters have to teach us. Personal beliefs are just that: very personal. No disrespect or offense is intended to anyone who may interpret these teachings in a different way. I have great respect for anyone whose religion makes them a better person. As you read the stories of the great teachers, you will discover many parallels in their lives.

We are all connected, we just need to interconnect: We are all interconnected, we just need to connect.

—Moira and Steve Snyder

KRISHNA

Krishna was born in India about 3,000 BC. He spent his childhood singing and dancing with the *Gopis* (milkmaids). He was a cheerful lad, full of joy and happiness. As he grew and discovered other people who were unhappy, he spent many years trying to discover why. Finally, in a forest hermitage, he met a great *Rishi* (spiritual teacher) who explained to him that all life is one. He said that the reason people are unhappy is because they do not realize this oneness in their hearts. The Rishi told Krishna, "Your *dharma* (mission) is to bring this knowledge to people by making your own life an example." Many people followed him on his joyful path.

The teachings of Krishna were recorded in the *Bhagavad Gita*, by his disciple Arjuna. Krishna said, *"When we surrender all desires that come to the heart and by the grace of God find the joy of God, then our souls have indeed found peace."* Krishna is usually pictured dancing or playing his flute.

LAO-TZU

Lao-Tzu was a Chinese philosopher, born in 604 BC. He founded the religion of Taoism, and wrote a book called *Tao Te Ching—the Book of the Right Way* to help people understand the simplicity, naturalness, and spontaneity in all the essentials of life.

BUDDHA

In 563 BC, Siddhartha Gautama Buddha was born as a prince in India. He lived a luxurious life and was carefully guarded from observing sickness, old people, and death. When he was thirty, he left the cloistered palace and became aware of human suffering. He also met a holy man who seemed calm and peaceful amid this suffering. He then decided to leave his family and life of luxury to seek out the meaning of life.

At first, he almost starved himself to death, but then realized that a "middle path" was better; not having too much or too little. He vowed to sit beneath a Bodhi tree and meditate until he became enlightened. (This is much like the trip of Jesus to the desert.) In seven days, he received a great awakening and became the Buddha, which means the enlightened one. He spent the rest of his life helping others understand and teaching them the Four Noble Truths and the Noble Eight-Fold Path. The Four Noble Truths are:

1. Life is full of suffering.
2. Suffering is caused by self-desire and self-will.
3. Overcoming self-desire and self-will ends suffering.
4. Nirvana (freedom from suffering and self-desire) is found by following the Eight-Fold Path:

Noble Eight-Fold Path

1. Right understanding
2. Right thought
3. Right speech
4. Right action
5. Right living
6. Right effort
7. Right remembrance
8. Right meditation

CONFUCIUS

Confucius was a contemporary of Buddha. He was an advisor to the governors and the emperor of China. He gave people simple rules of human kindness to follow. He gave special emphasis to family love and loyalty. He also collected the stories and wise sayings of old China. The *I Ching*, book of changes, is one of these books.

MOSES

Moses, along with Abraham, (who is considered the Father of Judaism) is one of the great prophets of the Jews. He was born in Egypt, where his people were held as slaves by the Egyptians. When Pharaoh ordered all the Hebrew babies to be killed, his mother hid him in some rushes on the Nile river where he was found and raised by Pharaoh's daughter. As he grew up, God talked to him. Moses knew it was his destiny to lead his people out of Egypt and into the Promised Land. When the Hebrew slaves finally escaped, they spent a long time wandering through the wilderness. During this time, God called Moses to the top of Mount Sinai to receive the Ten Commandments. When he came down, he found the people worshipping a golden calf. He was so upset, he broke the tablet containing the

The soul takes nothing to the other world but its education and culture and these are of the greatest service or of the greatest injury to the dead man.

—Plato

Spirit is the real and eternal; matter is the unreal and temporal.

—Mary Baker Eddy

commandments. Later, he went to the mountain again. After forty days and nights, he received new tablets. According to tradition, just before he died, when he was 250 years old, he finally reached the Promised Land.

JESUS

About 2,000 years ago, Jesus was born in a stable in Bethlehem to Jewish parents. As a young man, Jesus went out into the desert for forty days, and was tempted by the Devil. After forty days, he became enlightened. When he came back, he began preaching and chose twelve disciples to help him.

Jesus could apparently heal people by placing his hands on them. He made enemies of the priests in the temples, and they sought to have him destroyed. He was crucified on a cross by the Romans. Even then, he said, "Father, forgive them; for they know not what they do." When he was laid in a tomb, his body vanished, and he appeared in the flesh to his disciples. To Christians, it means that the death of the body is not the end of life. Jesus taught people about love. According to one interpretation of the scriptures, he taught that the "Kingdom of God" is here within us, right now, not a place we go when we die.

Dr. Martin Luther King, Jr. said, *"To really carry out the precepts of Jesus would be the most revolutionary and dangerous thing in the world."* As his wife Coretta Scott King says, *"What could be more truly revolutionary than to embrace his (Jesus's) commitment to love our enemies, to forgive them, to share our wealth with the poor, and to refuse to practice violence?"*

MOHAMMED

Mohammed was born in Mecca (now Saudi Arabia) in 570 AD. He is the founder of Islam. Both his parents died when he was young, and he was brought up by his merchant uncle. He grew up around people who believed in many gods and in making animal sacrifices. He also knew both Jews and Christians. He began to believe that there was one God of everyone. One day, as he meditated in a cave, he heard a voice saying, "You are the Messenger of Allah (God)." He continued to receive messages from the angel Gabriel. His friends wrote these messages down and put them in a book, which is called the *Koran*. Islam means inner peace.

Spirit in Other Cultures

THE ANCIENTS

Our ancestors were awed at the forces of nature. Sun and stars, darkness, wind, rain, fires, and oceans were sources of mystery to them. To them, nature was uncertain: sometimes helpful, other times hostile, always powerful and beyond human control. For the most part it still is! Therefore, natural objects were treated as powers in themselves. They believed the elements were controlled by deities that revealed themselves through these natural powers. Some even believed in one great higher spiritual force that controlled the whole universe. Much of their rituals were based on appeasing these natural forces to win favor and protection. This awe and mystery of life continues even today in all religions; mystery combined with ecstasy. In spring, summer, fall, and winter, festivals and revelry are observed by all peoples of all religions.

NATIVE AMERICANS

There are over 500 tribes of Native Americans in this country. While each tribe has its own customs, values, and heritage, some beliefs are shared in common with all tribes, and are values that all people, no matter what their religion will find useful.

+ **Everything is Spirit:** The essence of this belief is that life is awesome and embodies a 'spirit of wonder and mystery.'

+ **We Are All Related:** Everything is connected at the heart, and we need to respect all life, not just our own. The earth does not belong to us, and we have a sacred obligation to care for her.

+ **Sharing:** Peace, in the Native American tradition, is not just the absence of conflict, it is a positive force. In the Iroquois tradition, it is symbolized by a great white pine tree, joining earth and sky, reaching to the four quarters and offering shelter.

+ **Soul-Searching:** A long-standing tradition in this culture is the vision quest. Its basic form is going off by oneself into the wilderness, fasting, and seeking to find your life mission. Jesus and Buddha had their form of vision quests, and any serious student of the spirit would be wise to follow this tradition. Once, as a college student, I fasted and went into the woods for two days by myself. Although I experienced no earth-shaking revelations, by intense observation of the lifeforces surrounding me, I came to see the wisdom in the trees, clouds, and birds.

❧ VALUES ❧

Teach values by setting the example. Point out to children when they are exemplifying the virtues that you wish to instill. Discuss values in family meetings. Values can be developed in three areas:

+ related to the **person:** assertiveness, character, cleanliness, confidence, courage, creativity, determination, enthusiasm, excellence, flexibility, gentleness, humility, idealism, moderation, physical fitness, joyfulness, self-esteem, and self-discipline.

+ related to **others:** caring, compassion, consideration, courtesy, empathy, flexibility, forgiveness, friendliness, generosity, helpfulness, honesty, loving kindness, loyalty, patience, peacefulness, reliability, respectfulness, responsibility, tolerance, and trust.

Which is nearer to infinity, the long time or the short time? The long time is not nearer to infinity, neither is the short time near. Love is closest to infinity.

—Anonymous

Peace comes within the souls of men when they realize their oneness with the universe and all its powers, and realize that the center is really everywhere. It is within each of us.

—Black Elk

✦ related to the **spirit:** faithfulness, mercifulness, prayerfulness, holiness, spirituality.

Knowledge of the Divine must come from within: no one can teach this. Being spiritual involves surrender and quietness, so that we are open to the inner spirit, the "guardian angel" who serves as an inner voice and guides us to do the right thing. When my son Josh was a four-year-old, he claimed his guardian angel's name was Garfield.

❧ GRACE ❧

Saying grace is a simple ritual that reminds us of our dependence and interconnectedness with the earth and the people who toil to bring us our food. You can say grace individually, together, or silently. Our family likes to hold hands when we say grace, especially the baby! Usually, we all contribute something that we are thankful for in our grace such as food, family, love, shelter, good weather, or health. We try to stick to being thankful and not get into supplication. Sometimes we get a bit silly, but even if *I* mind, the Great Spirit probably doesn't. Below are some traditional graces you might enjoy using.

> For food and drink and happy days
> Accept our gratitude and praise.

> In serving others, Lord, may we
> Repay in part our debt to Thee.

> Oh Lord bring all the ingredients of our lives
> together
> And make us into the miracles You want us to be.

> For each new morning with its light
> For rest and shelter of the night
> For health and food, for love and friends
> for everything Thy goodness sends.
>
> *—Ralph Waldo Emerson*

> God in me and God in you
> There lies all the good we do.

> We thank you, Lord, that this is so
> We thank you that we live and grow.

> Thank you for those who help
> to grow and cook our food.

> Make us able
> For all that's on the table.

Why, who makes much of miracles? To me every hour of the light and dark is a miracle, every cubic inch of space is a miracle.

—Walt Whitman

With hearts as well as lips, dear Lord
We thank you for the food
For countless blessings too,
We offer gratitude.

For what we are about to receive
Let us truly be grateful.

Earth who gives to us this food,
Sun who makes it ripe and good,
Dear Earth, dear Sun, by you we live
Our loving thanks to you we give.

—*Christian Morgenstern*

Imagination is more important than information.

—Robert Fulghum

We give thanks for our food, and remember those who are hungry,
We give thanks for our health, and remember those who are ill,
We give thanks for our family, and remember those who are alone.

❦ THINKING, IMAGINATION, AND CREATIVITY ❦

I think I know how to think because I think I have thought about thinking before. I think. Thinkers value creative thinking and novel ideas. I think "they" say that thinking is a skill that, like all other skills takes practice to develop.

Imagination tries to create something new out of what we have already learned. Imagination is regarded as a serious and deeply creative faculty of our minds. Play is a fertile arena for imagination.

One attribute of imagination that is extremely important is called *empathy*. Let's say I'm watching a bird, and I admire her and actually imagine myself flying too: I self-project myself into the bird. This is empathy, and the degree that we have it is the degree that we live life fully. To enjoy any art or literature, we must have empathy: *to actually put ourselves in another's place.* If you can project yourself into the personality of another person, to feel how she feels, not just feel *for* her (which is sympathy), but put yourself in her place, then you have achieved empathy.

Creativity is producing the ideas of our imagination, whether through music, art, dance, or prose. Salvador Dali, the great surrealist painter, found the key to his inner life with a spoon. He would lie down holding a spoon, and just as he drifted off to sleep, the spoon would slip from his fingers and hit a plate he had placed on the floor. He would immediately awaken and begin to sketch the images that came bubbling up from his dream state.

Again and again, step by step, intuition opens the doors that lead to man's design.

—R. Buckminster Fuller

229

THINKING GAMES

- How many ways can you think of to use a toothbrush? (back scratcher for a hamster, mini-windshield wipers for a doll car, flag…)
- How many foods can you think of that are green? Make a green dinner.
- Look at your foot and explain why a footprint is like a map.
- Why is a baby like a flower?
- What if… (there were no music, your nose were on your belly button…)
- Tell the story of *Little Red Riding Hood* from the wolf's point of view.

ROADBLOCK/DETOUR GAME

Ask your child how he would deal with some of the hypothetical situations listed below. Then *you* make up a crazy answer (roadblock) why it wouldn't work. Your child is then forced to make a detour. Switch places and have him think up roadblocks for you. You might want to turn these ideas into a story.

- What would you do if you lost your voice?
- What would you do if I got lost in a store?
- What would you do if you lost all your clothes?
- What would you do if a baby showed up on your doorstep?
- What would you do if you were home alone and the lights went off?
- What would you do if you were running water in the sink and the faucet wouldn't turn off?

BRAINSTORMING

It's interesting that most of our mental pictures of creativity have to do with electricity (the light bulb lighting up) or, as in the image of brainstorming, frenetic, turbulent activity. Creative thinking involves movement. Brainstorming involves:

- Originality: creating unusual or different ideas.
- Fluency: generating many ideas.
- Flexibility: accepting possibly more than one solution.
- Elaboration: taking ideas to the max.

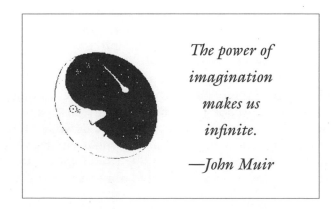

The power of imagination makes us infinite.

—*John Muir*

 Projects

Don't call them assignments or reports. This is a semantical point, but to me, a project just *sounds* more fun than assignment or report!

Autobiography

Autobiography is a classic way to begin a new school year. It can be a fun project for children (people!) of all ages to work on. *Auto* means self, *bio* means life, and *graphy* means writing. Autobiographical writing helps promote a positive self-image, and may provide insights into a person's behavior. Below are ideas for inclusion in an autobiography. Remember that it's all right and even more fun to do projects cooperatively. Parents can do the writing while younger kids dictate to them, or the parent can design a fill-in-the-blank book for the child to use. Pictures may be included in your book.

- ✦ **Chronology:** Write or draw pictures about one important event in your life for each year you've been alive.
- ✦ **Birth:** This may include place, time, day of week, date, year, weight, height, and earliest memory.
- ✦ **Family Tree:** This can be a beautiful art project, including photos of family members such as brothers, sisters, aunts, uncles, cousins, etc. You can make a list of what the family does together, their ages, occupations, or interests.

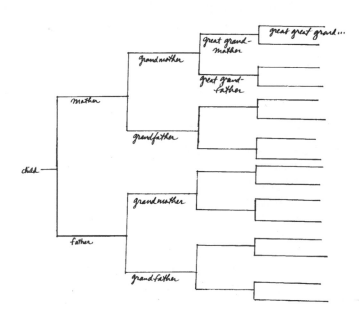

The next thing most like living one's life over again seems to be a recollection of that life, and to make that recollection as durable as possible by putting it down in writing.

—Benjamin Franklin

We must always be ready to give up pet projects when they do not catch the interest and enthusiasm of the children, and to let them take the projects off in directions that we perhaps had not expected.

—John Holt

- ✦ **Address and Phone Number:** Good information for youngsters to know.
- ✦ **Neighborhood:** Make a street map of your neighborhood. Build models of your house and other landmarks to put on the map.
- ✦ **Friends:** List oldest friend, youngest, tallest, shortest, funniest, best friend...
- ✦ **Homeschooling:** Grade level (even homeschoolers don't seem to get away from this configuration), community teacher's or tutor's name(s), favorite subjects, an opinion of self as scholar.
- ✦ **Favorites and Such:** *(This is another good drawing project, especially for younger children.)* Animals, pets, songs, TV programs, sports, toys, colors, foods that you love/hate, favorite books, holidays.
- ✦ **Body:** Draw a picture of yourself that includes eye color, hair, fingerprint, and mouth print. You can also include length of handspan, height, foot length, waist circumference, heartbeat per minute (use a stethoscope) when sitting, running, and jumping. *(The last ideas are great for incorporating math into the project.)* Include a recent photo.
- ✦ **Feet:** Trace feet on a paper and list or write a poem of things your feet would like to do.
- ✦ **Hands:** Trace hands on paper and make a list or write a poem of things your hands would like to do.
- ✦ **Health:** Write or draw about the time when you were most ill; what hurt the most; things you do to keep healthy; what diseases, if any, you have had.
- ✦ **Money:** Write about the most money you ever spent and on what, how much you have saved, how much allowance you get, and what you would do with a million dollars.
- ✦ **Travel:** Write, list, or draw pictures of places you have been or places you'd like to go.
- ✦ **Dreams:** Write, list, or draw pictures of things you'd like to do someday, what you want to be in the future, what things are most important to you in life, and/or things about you that you'd like to change. Write or draw a picture about a memorable dream.
- ✦ **Zodiac:** Look up your birth sign, flower, and gem. Draw a picture or write about it.
- ✦ **Treasures:** Write or draw about some object you valued as a child, answering some of the following questions:
  - ✦ Describe it. ✦ Does it have a name? ✦ Why/how was the name chosen? ✦ Was it something you wanted? ✦ How does it make you feel? ✦ Do you use it now? ✦ Where do you keep it? ✦ Has it changed over the years? ✦ What do you especially like about it? ✦ Is there an incident in your life that includes your treasure?
- ✦ **Famous Last Words:** What saying would you like people to remember you by? Write your epitaph.

OTHER IDEAS

✦ **Chronological year-to-year autobiography:** Parents can fill in the beginning years. Try to remember one special event. Get out the photo albums.

✦ **Outstanding moments:** Try to remember outstanding feelings or emotions such as happiness, fright, excitement, or humor.

✦ **Detective Questions:**

Who am I?

Where do I live?

What will I do with my life?

When will I do what I plan?

Why will I do what I set out to do?

How will I do what I plan?

Utopia

Utopia, or Ideal City, is a great integrative project for children of all ages. It can become increasingly complex as the child grows older. You may cover one or many areas according to personal interests.

The project may include dioramas (3-D display), writing, pictures, maps, or drawings. You may add sample swatches of clothing, a display of food, or examples of art or music. Address any of the following areas:

Those of us who are involved in alternative education do not think of what we do as experimental. We think of it as reasonable, practical, logical ... and obvious.

—Jerry Mintz

Land

climate/weather

environment

geographical size/area

farming/food supply

Home

family

houses/shelters

clothes

animals, pets

People

name of city/country

transportation

stores

population

language

historical reference or significance

relationship with other cities/
countries

reason society is famous or
well known

School/Work/Government

schooling

libraries

jobs

factories

money/economy/banks

garbage/recycling

laws

government

crime/punishment

Beliefs

religion

values

moral/ethical systems

Leisure Time

music

art

drama

dance

sports

entertainment

Inventions

Tools and machines help us do things faster and easier (usually). Where would we be without scissors, water faucets, or CD's? What invention would improve your life, or make a task go faster? Think about:

✦ function

✦ size, dimensions

✦ materials needed

✦ color

✦ price

✦ useful to whom?

ISP's

Wear your learning, like your watch, in a private pocket: and do not pull it out and strike it, merely to show that you have one.

—Earl of Chesterfield

ISP's (Independent Study Projects) is the new jargon for what most of us remember as reports. It is a perfect project for homeschoolers because it is self-directed. The new twist in ISP's is that these reports can be on anything that interests your child and can take any form that is mutually agreed upon. There are many ways to research a subject. Projects may include any of the following strategies:

HOW TO BEGIN:

Webbing is like a paper brainstorm. Write your central idea in the middle of a paper, then list all possible directions and activities that you can include in your topic. Webs are usually better to do with another person, to generate more ideas.

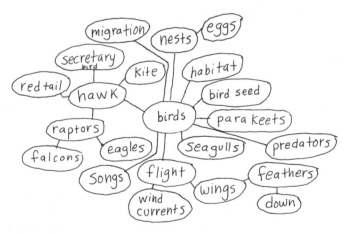

✦ **Interview** people that are knowledgeable about your subject.

✦ **Survey** people's opinions, feelings, or reactions to a fact or idea about your study.

✦ **Library Research*** of your subject. (Use the card catalogue or computer.)

✦ **Phone Book** might have resource people or businesses to visit or phone numbers listed in the yellow pages. Consult business and government listings to get more information about your subject.

✦ **Films** may be available through the county office of education or video stores.

- **Letters** may be sent to request information about your study.
- **Pictures and Charts** can be used.

*One way to facilitate research is to copy facts on a sheet of paper that has been divided into eight squares. One fact or idea goes in each square. After this, cut out the squares and arrange them from most important facts to the least important.

Other Unusual Ideas

- Make a **dictionary** of important words relating to your study.
- Write a **play** to dramatize an aspect of your study.
- Make a **diorama** (3-D display) about some aspect of your subject.
- Create your own **holiday**. What is the name of it, what do you do to celebrate, what foods do you eat?
- Are you interested in **photography?** Start shooting! See if you can tour a real darkroom, or make your own camera. Research the life and works of a famous photographer. Develop your own film.
- Like to **garden?** Visit the garden shop. Learn about the life cycle of plants. Dig in the dirt. Do scientific experiments with plants. Visit nurseries. Make daily observations in your garden. Build a birdhouse. Research drought-resistant plants.
- Do you write **poetry?** Make and illustrate your own poetry book. Visit a real live poet and interview him or her. Get a list of poetry books from the library. If your library has a computer, it will probably spit out any information you want.
- Have an **ISP Day**, and invite other learners to share their ISP's with each other. Get a microphone and let them give an oral presentation about their project to the group.

The very spring and root of honesty and virtue lie in education.

—Plutarch (46-120 BC)

Independent Study Project Ideas

English: Compositions; why do we use punctuation and grammar?; history of the English language

Math: Essential math skills; research on a famous mathematician's life; why is math the "second language" of the world?; how to teach a specific math concept

Physical Science: Robotics, solar heating systems; lasers; nuclear energy; how does sound affect different things?; people in the field; specific types of pollution; science careers

Earth and Life Science: The universe: stars, planets, and moon, water pollution, rocks, erosion, fossils, weather (track the weather for a month and trace a weather front), volcanoes, ozone layer, air and air power, ocean, layers of the earth, earthquakes, aurora borealis, time zones, eclipse, space travel, astronauts, NASA space program

Biology: Food (how it affects us, how it gives us energy), cells, how living things are classified, viruses, plants, animals, adaptation of living organisms, history of the microscope, genetics...

Human Body: circulatory system, digestive system, respiratory system, nervous system, vision, hearing, reproductive system, exercise and sports, diet, drugs...

Careers: research on individual jobs, how to find a job, interviewing prospective employers...

Health: individuals in the health field, research on a specific disease, research on alternative healing methods, new innovations in health, organ transplants...

History and Culture: people, places, events, or things that have affected world history, read historical novel, interview a person who has lived through an historical event, study another culture, U.S. history, historically accurate journal writing...

Civics: any person, place, event or thing and its effect on the government, history of elections (current or past), research on candidate, American Constitution, Bill of Rights, current events...

Economics: compare and contrast two economic systems, advertisement (create your own), product development (invent one), research an economic agency...

Music: write a song, research a composer or musical group, make a chronological list of a composer or a group's music, history of a specific musical era (famous musicians of the era), research an instrument, research a culture's music...

Art: study color, reseach a famous artist, history of pottery or other artistic discipline, reproduction of famous artwork with accompanying research...

Sports: research a famous sports personality, research history of a specific sport...

FRAMEWORK

1. **Introduction:** (1 page) Statement of what your project is all about and why you chose it.
2. **Body:** (3 to 10 pages) Include graphs, documents, or pictures.
3. **Conclusion:** (1 to2 pages) Personalized account of your research, importance of experience, how it related to your daily life, why we use this process or why the person or event is significant?

For the things we have to learn before we can
do them, we learn by doing them.

—Aristotle

Family History: Interview Questions

1. Where were you born?
2. What year were you born in?
3. Tell me about your schooling.
4. What are the names of your parents?
5. Tell me something about your father.
6. Tell me something about your mother.
7. Tell me about something special that happened when you were around my age.
8. What kinds of things do you do for fun (hobbies)?
9. Tell me about your work.
10. Tell me about your goals.

Education is not a product, it's a process.

—Anna Kealoha

Family Folklore

(Thanks to Sybil Rotnicki for these ideas.)

The family story belongs to the oldest body of literature known. In ancient times, all knowledge was passed on orally. Folklore is an ever-growing and changing group of stories that we first hear from our parents, which are told to teach, amuse, and entertain. Things to write or talk about (hey, why not make a movie?) with other family members may include:

Family Traditions: Seasonal rituals, special foods, special stories, and non-holiday traditions.

Old Photographs: Old photos tend to document special joyous events: holidays, birthdays, and vacations. Objects found in pictures can give visual clues as to the architecture, household furnishings, clothes, and cars of different eras.

Heritage: What does your last name mean? Do you have things that have been passed down over generations? What family sayings or nicknames are there? Do you have family recipes? What stories do the elders still tell about "the old days?"

Photojournals: Create a family photojournal to document a particular person or special event.

Community Folktales: Any haunted houses or graveyards in your neighborhood? Any remarkable students or illustrious teachers in your community?

Family Portrait: Base your written portrait on an old photograph, and (depending on what is known about the person) decide whether the portrait will be fact or fiction.

Background Information:

(Begin with:) Once upon a time...

- ✦ Who is this girl?
- ✦ How old is she?
- ✦ Where does she live?
- ✦ What is her home like?
- ✦ Who are her brothers and sisters, their names and ages?
- ✦ Who are her parents, what jobs do they do?
- ✦ What does her family do together?
- ✦ Does she have any pets? Name, breed?

Story Event:

One day...

✦ What adventure happens to the girl and her pet?

✦ Where does it happen?

✦ What are they doing?

✦ What does the girl do? The pet?

✦ How do others respond?

✦ What is the outcome?

Rainbow Mind "Test"

Do you like to:

✦ Write, joke, tell stories or spin tall tales? Do you have a good memory for names, places, dates, or trivia? Do you like to read? Is spelling easy for you? Do you enjoy tongue twisters and nonsense rhymes? Do you like doing crossword puzzles or playing Scrabble? ...You are strong in the world of ***letters***.

✦ Use computers? Solve number problems in your head? Ponder questions such as *Where does the universe end? What happens when we die? When did time begin?* Play chess, checkers or other strategy games? Think things out logically and clearly? Devise experiments to test things you don't understand? Spend time working on logic puzzles such as Rubik's cube?...You are strong in ***numbers***.

✦ Daydream? Read maps, charts, and diagrams? Draw accurate representations of people or things? Engage in art activities? Describe visual detail? Go to the movies, look at slides or pictures? Like jigsaw puzzles or mazes?...You are strong in ***art*** and the world of colors.

We do not inherit the world from our parents, we borrow it from our children.

—Mahatma Gandhi

✦ Sing, play musical instruments? Listen to records, tapes and CD's? Listen to the radio when you're working? Dance and go to music shows? Write music? Sing in the shower?...You are strong in ***music*** and the world of sound.

✦ Hike and backpack? Grow flowers? Go on mushroom walks? Go bird watching? Go rock climbing? Watch sunrises and sunsets? Stargaze? Garden or farm? Go to the ocean or mountains? Read *National Geographic* or *Scientific American*? Live in the country?...You are strong in the ***nature*** world.

✦ Wiggle around, fidget, or "drum" when you sit in a chair? Go swimming, biking, hiking, skateboarding, or running? Enjoy competitive games? Like to touch people when you talk to them? Like crafts such as woodworking, sewing, or carving? Like scarey rides?...You are strong in the ***body world***.

✦ Be with your friends? Belong to groups or clubs? Get involved in group activities? Act as family mediator? Enjoy playing games with your friends?...You enjoy the human family, ***outer world*** qualities.

✦ Empathize with other people's feelings? Feel strong and independent? Have definite opinions? Live in an inner world? Feel a deep sense of self-confidence? Dress uniquely? Work well by yourself?...You are strong in the ***inner world***.

Evaluations

Believe me when I say this: I hate evaluations, I even hate grade level labels. Well, maybe not hate them, but as with most systems of classification, I find there is no room for the exceptions. We all know that people have varying levels of skills, and that no one is strictly a "fourth-grader."

Therefore, I have developed an evaluation in what could be considered a generic education in Letters and Numbers. I developed them to use with my kindergarten to eighth-grade students to keep the bureaucrats happy. I like these evaluations because I can list what the kids can do, not what they can't do, although this may be evident in the unchecked boxes.

What evaluations might give you is a sense of where your kids might possibly be coming from, and whence they might be going. In truth, the person best qualified to evaluate are the students themselves, *not* the teacher, *not* the parent.

We also give self-evaluations to our students that look something like this:

Language Arts: Please tell how you feel about:

Reading_____

Writing_____

Listening_____

Speaking_____

Thinking_____

In Language Arts I am good at:_____

I could improve:_____

How I feel about **Math**_____

I am good at_____

I could improve_____

How I feel about **Science**_____

I am good at_____

I could improve_____

How I feel about **Social Science**_____

I am good at_____

I could improve_____

How I feel about **Physical Education**_____

I am good at_____

I could improve_____

How I feel about **Fine Arts**_____

I am good at_____

I could improve_____

How I feel about **Family and Friends**_____

I am good at_____

I could improve_____

What's even better than evaluations are **portfolios**. Let people (*not* the state) keep a portfolio of the work that pleases them the most. Simple. When you want to find out about a person, just have them show you his or her portfolio.

Math Evaluation

> *Learning is more efficient if guided by a process structure (e.g. learning plan) than by a content structure (e.g. course outline).*
>
> *—Malcolm Knowles*

NUMBERS

☐ works with Cuisenaire rods

☐ works with other manipulatives:_____

☐ beginning additions operations

☐ addition with carrying

☐ addition with regrouping

☐ beginning subtraction

☐ subtraction with regrouping

☐ place value to_____

☐ knows multiplication tables: _____

☐ beginning division

☐ advanced (2- or 3-digit) division

☐ fractions

☐ decimals

☐ Roman numerals

☐ calculates money problems

☐ awareness of expanded notation (134=100+30+4)

☐ awareness of odd and even numbers

MEASUREMENT

☐ knows time vocabulary (hour, minute, second)

☐ knows money vocabulary

☐ knows measuring vocabulary

☐ can figure area calculations

☐ can figure perimeter calculations

☐ can figure volume calculations

☐ displays estimation skills

☐ awareness of Metric system

☐ awareness of temperature (Celsius/Farenheit)

☐ measures with a ruler

GEOMETRY

- ☐ identifies basic geometric shapes (triangle, circle, square)
- ☐ awareness of other geometric shapes_____
- ☐ parallel lines
- ☐ perpendicular lines
- ☐ symmetry
- ☐ angles
- ☐ protractor use

PATTERNS AND FUNCTIONS

- ☐ awareness of pattern sequences
- ☐ displays logical reasoning
- ☐ can round off numbers
- ☐ awareness of ordered pairs; coordinate plane
- ☐ use of scientific notation
- ☐ awareness of mean or average

STATISTICS AND PROBABILITY

- ☐ collects and sorts data
- ☐ records data
- ☐ interprets data
- ☐ identifies and constructs bar graph
- ☐ line graphs
- ☐ pie graphs
- ☐ draws conclusions
- ☐ can use tally marks
- ☐ displays prediction skills

LOGIC

- ☐ can classify with manipulatives (<, >, =)
- ☐ logic vocabulary: if/then statements
- ☐ simple deductive reasoning
- ☐ concepts: before/between/after/next

ALGEBRA

- ☐ reads number sentences (3 + 4 = 7)
- ☐ knows commutative property of addition
- ☐ knows commutative property of multiplication
- ☐ works with integers
- ☐ knows simple algebraic sentences (3 x ? = 12)
- ☐ can use formula: A = L x W

COMMENTS:

Do not confine your children to your own learning, for they were born in another time.

—Hebrew Proverb

Reading

BEGINNING READERS

- ☐ Can draw an identifiable person
- ☐ Voluntarily looks at books
- ☐ Uses stories for dramatic play
- ☐ Understands some environmental print
- ☐ Identifies uppercase letters
- ☐ Identifies lowercase letters
- ☐ Can complete a 15-20 piece jigsaw puzzle
- ☐ Can locate individual letters
- ☐ Identifies words that begin with the same letter (graphophonic system)

DEVELOPING READERS

- ☐ Reads some independently
- ☐ Reads with fluency
- ☐ Identifies rhyming words
- ☐ Retells stories (semantic cue system)
- ☐ Comments on character traits (semantic cue system)
- ☐ Has store of basic sight words

Reading strategies include:
- ☐ decoding
- ☐ contextual clues
- ☐ word meaning

INDEPENDENT READERS

- ☐ Reads silently
- ☐ Makes word predictions (decoding)
- ☐ Displays literal comprehension
- ☐ Interpretive comprehension
- ☐ Critical comprehension
- ☐ Can alphabetize
- ☐ Uses table of contents
- ☐ Uses index

READING ATTITUDES AND BOOK AWARENESS

- ☐ Selects own reading material
- ☐ Borrows books from the library
- ☐ Has own library card
- ☐ Reads for pleasure

- ☐ Reads for information
- ☐ Owns books
- ☐ Fiction/nonfiction awareness
- ☐ Poetry awareness
- ☐ Uses dictionaries
- ☐ Character awareness
- ☐ Compares and contrasts characters from different books

Favorite authors:

_____

_____

_____

Favorite books: _____

_____

_____

READING MATERIALS

- ☐ Picture books
- ☐ Pattern books
- ☐ Easy readers
- ☐ Short novel
- ☐ Poetry
- ☐ Nonfiction
- ☐ Student written
- ☐ Magazines
- ☐ Reference
- ☐ Comic books
- ☐ Newspapers

Other:

_____

_____

Reading Texts:

_____

_____

_____

Topics of interest:_____

_____

_____

_____

Learning by self-directed inquiry is a perpetually self-empowering activity.

—Charles D. Hayes

Writing

BEGINNING WRITERS

- ☐ Prints letters only
- ☐ Prints meaningful groups of words
- ☐ Writes simple sentences
- ☐ Dictates original stories
- ☐ Uses spaces between words
- ☐ Uses invented spellings for unknown words
- ☐ Prints (☐ most ☐ all) uppercase letters

> *...Childhood should be given its full measure of life's draught, for which it has an endless thirst.*
>
> —*Rabindranath Tagore*

DEVELOPING WRITERS

- ☐ Writes one or more sentences
- ☐ Writes a short paragraph
- ☐ Indents for paragraphs
- ☐ Writes own ideas and experiences
- ☐ Writes letters
- ☐ Writes lists, signs, etc.
- ☐ Shares writing with others
- ☐ Asks how to spell words
- ☐ Uses personal spelling dictionary
- ☐ Prints (☐ most ☐ all) lowercase letters
- ☐ Uses capitals appropriately
- ☐ Writes legibly
- ☐ Uses periods
- ☐ Uses commas

INDEPENDENT WRITERS

- ☐ Writes willingly
- ☐ Writes sequenced stories
- ☐ Writes about personal experience
- ☐ Uses dictionary to check spelling
- ☐ Uses cursive handwriting
- ☐ Capitalizes properly
- ☐ Uses punctuation marks (such as quotation marks, exclamation points) when needed
- ☐ Communicates ideas clearly
- ☐ Knows and uses abbreviations
- ☐ Knows some prefixes and suffixes
- ☐ Knows some synonyms
- ☐ Knows some antonyms
- ☐ Knows some homonyms
- ☐ Understands alliteration

- ☐ Understands similes and metaphors
- ☐ Understands personification
- ☐ Can divide words into syllables
- ☐ Revises and edits work
- ☐ Has writing displayed or published

Listening and Speaking

LISTENING

- ☐ Listens to someone reading
- ☐ Listens while others speak
- ☐ Follows through with oral instructions
- ☐ Listens with respect
- ☐ Listens to media (T.V., tapes)
- ☐ Listens in small groups
- ☐ Listens in large groups
- ☐ Can take notes on a speech
- ☐ Can summarize a speech
- ☐ Can evaluate a speech

SPEAKING

- ☐ Communicates ideas clearly
- ☐ Communicates ideas fluently
- ☐ Interacts in discussion
- ☐ Uses language correctly
- ☐ Relates personal experiences
- ☐ Collaborates with others
- ☐ Asks questions
- ☐ Volunteers/shares information
- ☐ Displays empathy towards others
- ☐ Can explain a process (logical reasoning)
- ☐ Displays imaginative qualities
- ☐ Can follow directions
- ☐ Has given 2 to 5 minute informational speech
- ☐ Has given 2 to 5 minute demonstrational speech
- ☐ Has given 3 to 5 minutes persuasive speech
- ☐ Exhibits literal comprehension (facts, details)
- ☐ Exhibits interpretive comprehension (main point, predictions)
- ☐ Exhibits critical comprehension (judges merits or style, reality or fantasy)

In order to reap the full possibilities of youth we must not tie them too rigidly to the theories of an older generation. Their value lies in being a voice, not an echo.

—Willet L. Hurdin

COMMENTS:

Ultimate Aptitude Test

INSTRUCTIONS: Read each question carefully. Answer all questions. Time limit: four hours. Begin immediately.

1. **History:** Describe the history of the papacy, from its origins to the present, concentrating especially, but not exclusively on its social, political, economic, religious, and philosophical impact on Europe, Asia, America, and Africa. Be brief, concise, and specific.

2. **Medicine:** You have been provided with a razor blade, a piece of gauze, and a bottle of Scotch. Remove your appendix. Do not suture until your work has been inspected. You have 15 minutes.

3. **Public Speaking:** 25,000 crazed aborigines are storming your house. Calm them. You may use any ancient language except Latin or Greek.

4. **Biology:** Create life. Estimate the difference in subsequent human culture if this form had developed 500 million years earlier, with special attention to its probable effect on the English parliamentary system. Prove your thesis.

5. **Music:** Write a piano concerto. Orchestrate and perform it with flute and drum. You will find a piano under your seat.

6. **Psychology:** Based on your knowledge of their works, evaluate the emotional stability, degree of adjustment, and repressed frustrations of each of the following: Alexander of Aphrodisias, Ramses II, Gregory of Nicea, and Hammurabi. Support your thesis with quotations from each man's work, making appropriate references. It is not necessary to translate.

7. **Sociology:** Estimate the sociological problems that might accompany the end of the world. Construct an experiment to test your theory.

8. **Engineering:** The disassembled parts of a high-powered rifle have been placed on your desk. You will find an instruction manual printed in Swahili. In three minutes, a hungry Bengal tiger will be admitted to the room. Take whatever action you feel is appropriate. Be prepared to justify your decision.

9. **Economics:** Develop a realistic plan for refining the national debt. Trace the effects of your plan on the following areas: Cubism, the Donatist controversy, and the wave theory of light. Outline a method for preventing these effects. Criticize this method from all possible points of view. Point out the deficiencies in your point of view, as demonstrated by your answer to the last question.

10. **Political Science:** There is a red telephone on the desk beside you. Start World War Three. Report at length on its socio-political effects, if any.

11. **Epistemology:** Take a stand for or against truth. Prove the validity of your position.

12. **Physics:** Explain the nature of matter.

13. **Philosophy:** Sketch the development of human thought. Estimate its significance. Compare the development of any other kind of thought.

14. **General Knowledge:** Describe in detail. Be objective and specific.

College Prep

High school kids (9th-12th grade) need to be aware that most colleges require certain courses for admission. They seem to like to see kids tackle tough subjects. They look for people who display leadership ability and are involved in activities such as community service, art, music, journalism, science clubs, or student counsel. It looks better to admissions officials if you delve deeply into one or two things rather than lightly into many.

Grammar/Composition: Four years.

English/Literature: Three years, at least one year of American Literature.

Math: Three years, including Algebra I & II and Geometry.

History: Three years, including World History, American History, and Civics.

Science: Two years, including General Science and Biology or Chemistry.

Computer Science: Many colleges require freshmen to be computer literate.

Foreign Language: Two years.

Essay Questions from Colleges

Bowdoin College: Greatest challenge you ever met, book you have found most thought-provoking, teacher who has had most significant impact on you.

Cal Tech: What will your letter home say ten years from now? How will college change your life? How fun fits in, and why did you pick Cal Tech?

Colorado College: Discuss a piece of art or literature. What non-essentials would you have on a desert island?

Pomona College: Your choice of the most important scientific development or alternative outcome of an historical event.

Dartmouth: State a question you would ask an applicant and then answer it.

Cornell: Answer a difficult question. Discuss a valued cause or idea.

Drew: Write page 89 of your autobiography.

Occidental: What invention would you create?

Smith: Discuss a world issue of significance. Discuss three items you couldn't live without, or the answer to shrinking earthly resources.

Vassar: Create an encyclopedia entry. Design and discuss a course.

Williams: Describe an experience that defines a value for you.

DePauw: What is one thing every person should experience?

Connecticut: Please discuss your contacts with economic, cultural, or racial diversity.

GENERAL ESSAY QUESTIONS

1. Tell something about yourself that cannot be learned from your application.
2. Discuss some factor that has contributed significantly to your growth.
3. Discuss your uniqueness as a person.
4. Express your unique opinions or feelings in a creative way by discussing a particular topic.

TIPS FOR ESSAY WRITING

1. Be yourself: be authentic, use quotes minimally, and don't plagiarize. Be funny and maybe even clever.
2. If you cannot exemplify or explain your opinion, don't offer it.
3. Be humble. If you have received special awards, you might say, "I was thrilled to receive special recognition for…."
4. Take time to learn about the colleges you are applying to. If you can't visit them, study their literature. It makes a good impression on admissions officers to know that you took the time to learn about their institutions.
5. Use a word processor to write your essay.
6. Read it out loud to check for diction and flow.
7. Make sure your name is on each page, and that each page is numbered.
8. Rewrite the question on your paper, then answer it.

Homeschool College

There are three alternative ways to approach college. One is to do correspondence college, another is to get credit for life experience after you've "graduated" from high school and have done other stuff. The last way is to continue doing what you've been doing: home college.

The following books may help you on your way:

Bear's Guide to Earning Non-Traditional College Degrees by John Bear, Ph.D. Ten Speed Press, Box 7123 Berkeley, CA. 94707.

College Admissions: A Guide for Homeschoolers by Judy Gelner, Poppyseed Press, PO Box 85, Sedalia, CO 80135.

Peterson's Guides P.O. Box 2123, Princeton, NJ 08543. Free catalog of secondary schools, colleges, universities, camps, private schools, and career education courses.

Barron's Student's Concise Encyclopedia—A Complete Reference Guide for Home and School 1,200 pages.

Education

We are in Pain to make them Scholars, but not *Men!* To talk, rather than to know, which is true *Canting.*

The first Thing obvious to Children is what is *sensible;* and that we make no Part of their Rudiments.

We press their Memory too soon, and puzzle, strain and load them with Words and Rules; to know *Grammer* and *Rhetorick,* and a strange Tongue or two, that it is ten to one may never be useful to them: Leaving their natural *Genius* to *Mechanical* and *Physical,* or natural Knowledge uncultivated and neglected; which would be of exceeding Use and Pleasure to them through the whole Course of their Life.

To be sure, Languages are not to be despised or neglected. But Things are still to be preferred.

Children had rather be making of *Tools* and *Instruments* of *Play; Shaping, Drawing, Framing,* and *Building,* &c. than getting some Rules of Propriety of Speech by Heart: And those also would follow with more Judgment, and less Trouble and Time.

It were Happy if we studied Nature more in natural Things: and acted according to Nature; whose Rules are *few, plain and most reasonable.*

Let us begin where she begins, go her Pace, and close always where she ends, and we cannot miss of being good Naturalists.

The Creation would not be longer a Riddle to us: The *Heavens, Earth,* and *Waters,* with their respective, various and numerous Inhabitants: Their Productions, Natures, Seasons, Sympathies and Antipathies; their Use, Benefit and Pleasure, would be better understood by us: and *eternal Wisdom, Power, Majesty* and *Goodness,* very conspicuous to us, thro' those sensible and passing Forms: the World wearing the mark of its *Maker,* whose Stamp is everywhere *visible,* and the *Characters* very *legible* to the Children of Wisdom.

For how could Man find the Confidence to abuse it, while they should see the great Creator stare them in the Face, in all and every Part thereof?

Their Ignorance makes them insensible, and that Insensibility hardy in misusing this noble Creation, that has the Stamp and Voice of a Deity every where, and in every Thing to the Observing.

It is pity therefore that Books have not been composed for *Youth,* by some curious and careful *Naturalists,* and also *Mechanicks,* in the *Latin* Tongue, to be used in Schools, that they might learn Things with Words: Things *Obvious* and *familiar* to them, and which would make the Tongue easier to be obtained by them.

Many able *Gardiners* and *Husbandmen* are yet Ignorant of the *Reason* of their Calling; as most *Artificers* are of the Reason of their own Rules that govern their excellent Workmanship. But a Naturalist and Mechanick of this sort, is *Master* of the Reason of both, and might be of the Practice too, if his Industry kept pace with his Speculation; which were very commendable; and without which he cannot be said to be a complete *Naturalist* or *Mechanick.*

Finally, if Man be the *Index* or *Epitomy* of the World, as *Philosophers* tell us, we have only to read our *selves* to be learned in it. But because there is nothing we less regard than the *Characters* of the Power that made us, which are so clearly written upon us and the World he has given us, and can best tell us what we are and should be, we are even Strangers to our own *Genius:* The *Glass* in which we should see that true instructing and agreeable Variety, which is to be observed in Nature, to the Admiration of that Wisdom and Adoration of that Power which made us all.

—William Penn
Fruits of Solitude, May 1693

Tons of Ways to Say "Very Good"

That's right!
You've got it made!
You are very good at that.
That's much better.
You're doing a good job.

THAT'S IT!

Eureka!
You're getting better every day!

YES!

I *knew* you could do it.
Now you've figured it out.
Not bad!
You are learning fast.
You make it look easy.
That's the right way to do it.
You did it that time.

WOW!!

That's the way!

SENSATIONAL!

That's the way to do it!
That's better.

MAGNIFICENT!

MARAVILLOSO!

MAGNIFICAT!

That's the best you've ever done.
I'm happy to see you working so hard.
Keep working on it; you're good.

FINE!

Now *that's* what I call a job!
You're doing beautifully.
Keep it up!
You've got it down.

TREMENDOUS!

Good for you!
Couldn't 've done it better m'self.
I'm very proud of you.
I think you've got it.
That's really great.
You're right!
Way 'ta go.

That's it!
Congratulations.
Much better!

MARVELOUS!

Keep up the good work!

BEAUTIFUL!

That's *good*!
That's coming along nicely.
Good work!
That's a terrific job.
Wow! That's great!
Now you've got it!

GREAT!

Good for you!
Hallelujah!
I'm impressed.
Nice going.
You haven't missed a thing.
Such nice work!
Nothing can stop you now!

EXCELLENT!

That's the best ever!

SUPER!

Nice work!
You did it well.
Right on!

FANTASTIC!

Perfect.
I like that.

TERRIFIC!

You did a lot of work today.
That's coming along nicely.
You're doing fine!
You outdid yourself!

SUPERB!

Good going!

WONDERFUL!

You really did a good job.

EXCELLENT!

You did good.

To the Children

To the children of the gardens
to the children of all nations
to the children of the earth
to the children of seekers, ex-slaves, and immigrants
to the children of the native born
to the children of workers
to the children of cleaners and cooks
to the children of farmers and peasants
to the children of soldiers
to the children of broken homes
to the children of the night who continue to roam
to the children of street walkers
to the children of the morning star
to the children of the dawn
to the children of dancers, singers, and saxophonists
to the children of poets and storytellers
to the children of public servants
to the children of the four corners
to the children of all directions
to the children of the canyons
to the children of the shores
to the children of the alleyways
to the children left to cry
to the children who will have the courage when the time comes
to the children of mystics
to the children of single mothers
to the children of the underground railroad
to the children of freedom marchers
to the children of the naked, nameless, and homeless
to the children of meditators and yogis
to the children of exiles
to the children of assassinated prophets
to the children of living minstrels
to the children of the choir
to the children of whirling dervishes
to You, dearest one.
You brought me across the waters to these glorious shores
may I return a million times more to be in your Presence.

—Joshua Halpern, 1986

❧ RESOURCES ❧

**Alliance for Parental Involvement
in Education**
PO Box 59
East Chatham, NY 12060

Animal Town
PO Box 2002
Santa Barbara, CA 93120

Cooperative games.

Ampersand Press
PO Box 1205
Point Reyes, CA 94956

Scientific games.

Aristoplay, Ltd.
PO Box 7028
Ann Arbor, MI 48107

Cooperative games.

Bluestocking Press
PO Box 1014
Placerville, CA 95667-1014

*Wonderful books to inspire independent
thinking, emphasizing history and
economics.*

Center for Teaching and Learning
Box 8158 University Station
Grand Forks, ND 58202

*College committed to individualized
instruction, holistic education, and
interdisciplinary perspectives. Publications
include* Insights into Open Education
and Teaching and Learning: The Journal
of Natural Inquiry and Pathways.

Chinaberry Book Service
2780 Via Orange Way
Spring Valley, CA 91978

**Consortium for Whole Brain
Learning**
3348 47th Ave. S
Minneapolis, MN 55406

*Publishes quarterly newsletter that focuses
on current research in education and
offers ideas and suggestions for parents,
teachers, and students.*

Dover Publications
31 E. 2nd Street
Mineola, NY 11501

Books and clip art.

EDC Publishing/Usborne Books
PO Box 470663
Tulsa, OK 74147

*Colorful, descriptive books from England on
just about everything.*

Home Education Press
PO Box 1083-F
Tonasket, WA 98855

*Bi-monthly magazine, published since 1983.
Books from introductory booklets to compre-
hensive books and guides.*

**Homeschool Association of California
(HAC)**
PO Box 231236
Sacramento, CA 95823-0403

*Supports and promotes homeschooling by
providing information, monitoring
legislation, and cultivating connections
among homeschoolers and the society at
large. HSC welcomes anyone interested in
homeschooling.*

Home School Supply House
PO Box 157
Fountain Green, UT 84632-0157

General supplies.

**Holt Associates/
  Growing Without Schooling**
2269 Massachusetts Ave.
Cambridge, MA 02140

*Recognized as the leader in child-led,
home-centered education. Operates
John Holt's Book and Music Store and
publishes bimonthly* GWS (Growing
Without Schooling) *which contains first-
hand accounts of people involved in
homeschooling.*

**National Coalition of Alternative
  Community Schools**
58 Schoolhouse Rd.
Summertown, TN 38483

*Emphasizes equal participation for
educational decisions by parents, teachers,
and learners. Quarterly newsletter, bi-
annual journal,* Skole, *and the* National
Directory of Alternative Schools.

National Homeschool Association
Box 290
Hartland, MI 48353-0290

*Quarterly newsletter, student exchanges,
apprenticeship mentor programs, annual
camp-out, network services, family travel
programs, current information on state
laws and rulings, a resources referral
service, information on supportive colleges
and universities, a parent's union, and
more!*

National Homeschool Service
PO Box 167
Rodeo, NM 88056

New Horizons for Learning
4694 Sunnside N.
Seattle, WA 98103

Tiger Lily Books
PO Box 111
Piercy, CA 95587

*(For additional resources, please refer to
specific section, i.e., music, science...)*

*It is, in fact, nothing short of a miracle that the modern methods of
instruction have not yet entirely strangled the holy curiosity of inquiry;
for this delicate little plant, aside from stimulation, stands mainly in
need of freedom; without this it goes to wrack and ruin without fail. It
is a very grave mistake to think that the enjoyment of seeing and
searching can be promoted by means of coercion and a sense of duty.*

—*Albert Einstein*

Children's Magazines

Art & Man
730 Broadway
New York, NY 10003

Enter *(computers)*
1 Lincoln Plaza
New York, NY 10023

Penny Power *(consumer information)*
PO Box 1906
Marion, OH 43302

Sesame Street
Box 2896
Boulder, CO 80322

Children's Digest *(health)*
PO Box 567
Indianapolis, IN 46206

Cricket *(literature, general interest)*
PO Box 2670
Boulder, CO 80322

Ebony Jr.
820 South Michigan Ave.
Chicago, IL 60650

Cobblestones *(history)*
PO Box 959
Farmingdale, NY 11737

Highlights for Children *(general)*
2300 West 5th Ave.
Columbus, OH 43216

National Geographic World
17th & M Streets NW
Washington, DC 20036

On Key *(music)*
JDL Publications
PO Box 1213
Montclair, NJ 07042

Electric Company
(reading & writing)
Box 2896
Boulder, CO 80322

Boy's Life *(recreation)*
1325 Walnut Hill Lane
Irving, TX 75062

Odyssey *(science)*
59 Front Street
East Toronto, Ontario
Canada M5E1B3

3-2-1-Contact *(science)*
Box 2896
Boulder, CO 80322

Ranger Rick's Nature Magazine
1412 16th Street NW
Washington, DC 20036

Stone Soup *(writing)*
PO Box 83
Santa Cruz, CA 95063

Ladybug *(3-6 literature)*
PO Box 2670
Boulder, CO 80322

❧ BIBLIOGRAPHY ❧

Anderson, Jay. *The Living History Sourcebook*. American Association for State and Local History, Nashville, TN, 1985.

Armstrong, Thomas. *In Their Own Way*. JP Tarcher, Los Angeles, CA, 1987.

Ashton-Warner, Sylvia. *Teacher*. Bantam Books, New York, NY, 1971.

Asimov, Isaac. *Realm of Numbers*. Houghton Mifflin Company, Boston, MA, 1959.

Bartlett, John. *Familiar Quotations*. Little, Brown & Co., Boston, MA, 1980. (15th edition)

Bos, Bev. *Don't Move the Muffin Tins*. Turn the Page Press, Roseville, CA, 1978.

Bos, Bev. *Before the Basics*. Turn the Page Press, Roseville, CA, 1983.

Brooks, Mona. *Drawing with Children*. St. Martin's Press, New York, NY, 1988.

Burns, Marilyn. *The I Hate Mathematics Book*. Little, Brown & Co., Boston, MA, 1975.

Cardoza, Peter. *The Whole Kids' Do-It-Yourself Scrapbook*. Bantam Books Canada, Inc., Toronto, 1979.

Carmichael, Viola. *Science Experiences for Young Children*. R & E Research Associates, Inc, 1982.

Carson, Anne, ed. *Spiritual Parenting in the New Age*. The Crossing Press, Freedom, CA, 1989.

Chakravarty, Amiya, ed. *A Tagore Reader*. Beacon Press, Boston, MA, 1961.

Challand, Helen. *Activities in the Earth Sciences*. Children's Press, Chicago, IL, 1982.

Cheyney, Arnold B. *The Writing Corner*. Goodyear Publishing Company, Inc., Santa Monica, CA, 1979.

Colfax, David and Micki. *Homeschooling for Excellence*. Mountain House Press, Philo, CA, 1988.

Dean, John. *Games Make Spelling Fun*. Fearon Publishers, Inc., Belmont, CA, 1973.

Dent, Jenny. *Great Teachers*. The White Eagle Publishing Trust, England, 1982.

Edwards, Betty. *Drawing on the Right Side of the Brain*. Tarcher Press, Los Angeles, CA, 1989.

Faber, Adele and Elaine Mazlish. *How to Talk So Kids Will Listen & Listen So Kids Will Talk*. Avon Books, New York, NY, 1980.

Facklam, Margery and Margaret Thomas. *The Kid's World Almanac of Amazing Facts about Numbers, Math and Money.* Pharos Books, New York, NY, 1992.

Foster, Leslie. *Mathematics Encyclopedia.* Rand McNally, New York, NY, 1985.

Frank, Marjorie. *If You're Trying to Teach Kids How to Write, You've Gotta Have This Book!* Incentive Publications, Inc., Nashville, TN, 1979.

Gardner, Martin. *Mathematical Puzzles & Diversions.* Simon and Schuster, Inc. New York, NY, 1960.

Garfield, Laeh Maggie. *Sound Medicine: Healing with Music, Voice & Song.* Celestial Arts, Berkeley, CA, 1987.

Gatto, John Taylor. *Dumbing Us Down.* New Society Publishers, Philadelphia, PA, 1992.

Gentry, Richard. *Spel...is a Four Letter Word.* Heinmann Ed. Books, Inc. Portsmouth, NH, 1987.

Gross, Ronald. *Peak Learning.* St. Martin's Press, New York, NY, 1991.

Halpern, Joshua, and Sedonia Cahill. *Ceremonial Circle.* HarperCollins Publishers, San Francisco, CA, 1992.

Halpern, Joshua. *Children of the Dawn: Visions of the New Family..* Only With Love Publications, Bodega, CA, 1986.

Hegener, Mark and Helen. *Alternatives in Education.* Home Education Press, Tonasket, WA, 1987.

Herman, Marina, et al. *Teaching Kinds to Love the Earth.* Pfiefer-Hamilton Publishers, Duluth, MN, 1991.

Hodgins, Audrey. *Ideas for Teachers from Teachers: Elementary Language Arts.* National Council of Teachers of English, USA, 1983.

Holt, John. *Learning All the Time.* Addison-Wesley Publishing Co. Inc., New York, NY, 1989.

Holt, John. *Teach Your Own.* Delacorte Press, New York, NY, 1981.

Holt, John. *What Do I Do on Monday?* John Holt Associates, Boston, MA, 1994.

Hurwitz, Abraham. *Number Games to Improve Your Child's Arithmetic.* Funk & Wagnalls, New York, NY, 1975.

Kaseman, Larry and Susan. *Taking Charge Through Homeschooling.* Koshkonong Press, 1990.

Kaye, Peggy. *Games for Learning.* HarperCollins Canada Ltd., 1991.

Kaye, Peggy. *Games for Math*. Pantheon Books, New York, NY, 1987.

Kaye, Peggy. *Games for Reading*. Pantheon Books, New York, NY, 1984.

Kerr, Jean, Virginia Stenmark, and Ruth Cossey. *Family Math*. Lawrence Hall of Science, Berkeley, CA, 1986.

Knowles, Malcolm. *Self-Directed Learning*. Follett Publishing Company, Chicago, IL, 1985.

Koehler, Nan. *Artemis Speaks: VBAC stories and natural childbirth information*. Artemis Press, Sebastopol, CA.

Kohl, Herb. *Mathematical Puzzlements*. Schocken Books, New York, NY, 1987.

Kohl, Herb. *A Book of Puzzlements*. Schocken Books, New York, NY, 1981.

Lee, Winifred Trask. *A Forest of Pencils*. Bobbs Merril Co., New York, NY, 1973.

Leistico, Agnes. *I Learn Better By Teaching Myself*. Home Education Press, 1990.

Liedloff, Jean. *The Continuum Concept*. Alfred A. Knopf, New York, NY, 1977.

Lim, Robin. *After the Baby's Birth …A Woman's Way to Wellness*. Celestial Arts, Berkeley, CA, 1991.

Llewellyn, Grace. *The Teenage Liberation Handbook*. Lowry House, Eugene, OR, 1991.

Marzollo, Jean. *The New Kindergarten*. Harper & Row Publishers, New York, NY, 1987.

Montessori, Maria. *The Child in the Family*. Avon Books, New York, NY, 1956.

Moore, Raymond and Dorothy. *Homestyle Teaching*. Word Book, Waco, TX, 1984.

Neill, A.S. *Summerhill—A Radical Approach to Child Rearing*. Hart Publishing, New York, NY, 1960.

Newman, Dana. *The New Teacher's Almanack*. The Center for Applied Research in Education, West Nyack, New York, 1980.

Parker, Don H. *Schooling for Individual Excellence*. Dynamic Publishers, Carmel, CA, 1989.

Pedersen, Anne and Peggy O'Mara, ed. *Schooling at Home*. John Muir Publishing, Santa Fe, NM, 1990.

Postman, Neil and Charles Weingartner. *Teaching as a Subversive Activity*. Delta Book, New York, NY, 1969.

Ravielli, Anthony. *An Adventure in Geometry*. Viking Press, New York, NY, 1957.

Reed, Donn. *The Home School Source Book*. Brook Farm Books, Bridgewater, MA, 1991.

Root, Betty. *Help Your Child Learn to Read*. Usborne Publishing, 1988.

Rucker, Rudy. *Mind Tools*. Houghton Mifflin Company, Boston, MA, 1987.

Solomon, Charles. *Mathematics*. Grosset & Dunlap, New York, NY, 1971.

Stoddard, Lynn. *The Three Dimensions of Human Greatness*. Holistic Education Review, Spring 1990.

Strazicich, Mirko, Ed. *History-Social Science Framework*. California State Department of Education, Sacramento, CA, 1988.

Van Cleave, Janice. *Math for Every Kid*. John Wiley & Son, New York, NY, 1991.

Wade, Theodore E. *The Home School Manual*. Gazelle Publications, 1991.

Warren, Jean. *Open-ended Art Activities for Young Children*. Warren Publishing Inc., Auburn, CA, 1985.

Williams, Robin. *The Little Mac Book*. Peachpit Press, Berkeley, CA, 1991.

Williams, Robin. *The Mac Is Not a Typewriter*. Performance Enhancement Products, Santa Rosa, CA, 1989.

Williams, Robin. *Pagemaker 4, an Easy Desk Reference*. Peachpit Press, Berkeley, CA, 1991.

My Song

This song of mine will wind its music around you, my child,

like the fond arms of love.

This song of mine will touch your forehead

like a kiss of blessing.

When you are alone it will sit by your side

and whisper in your ear,

when you are in the crowd

it will fence you about with aloofness.

My song will be like a pair of wings to your dreams,

it will transport your heart

to the verge of the unknown.

It will be like the faithful star overhead

when dark night is over your road.

My song will sit in the pupils of your eyes,

and will carry your sight into the heart of things

And when my voice is silent in death,

my song will speak in your living heart.

—*Rabindranath Tagore*

INDEX

Symbols

A

B

❂ Songs of the Earth—Music of the World

A veritable treasury of chants, rounds, graces, birthing songs, and circle songs from all over the world. —Ladyslipper Review

The introduction includes an explanation on the physical, historical, and spiritual aspects of music. The book is chock-full of inspiring music-related quotes by poets, musicians and philosophers. An extensive section on music theory includes various modal scales, melodic notations, and basic harmonic chords for piano and guitar.

❂ Songs of the Earth—a Musical Sampling (cassette tape)

This devoted group of musicians connects us with the sacred through deeply rooted primal drumming and soaring angelic chorals. One experiences the unity of humanity listening to the spiritual music of several traditions including African, Buddhist, Christian, Hindu, Islamic, Jewish, Native American, and Neoteric. …Suitable as well for ritual, meditation and making pancakes. One of the best circle song albums we've heard. —Heartsong Review

❂ Pleasure Point—Passionate Songs of Mystic Night Wanderings

Sensual, lofty, erotic poems inspired by the great Persian and Indian mystics such as Tagore, Mirabai, Kabir, and Rumi, gleened from two decades of journal keeping.

❂ The Beetle Bug Band Sings Letter Loving Songs
(cassette tape and songbook)

Hilarious, whacky, alliterative songs about letters. Will appeal to both kids and their grownups. Helps youngsters learn to read in a spontaneous fashion. The songbook is charmingly and deftly illustrated by the author's daughter. For ordering information please write to:

Flaggenbagg Productions
13140 Frati Lane
Sebastopol, CA 95472

Rosaleen Talisman

Intertwining hearts whose points create a center star.

Hearts promote a sense of inner peace.

Ensures strong relationships and encourages spiritual growth.

Found on the south cross at Clonmacnoise, a spiritual center of Ireland.

Also found in the Book of Kells.